For the Strategic Future of Our Nation

I0449014

The New Deal

An

Election 2008 Primer

by Orion Karl Daley

Dedication

This book is dedicated to my wife and family, where without their help, it would not have been possible.

Contents

For the Strategic Future of Our Nation

Introduction

In 2004, 21% of the voter population elected the Bush administration. Kerry had another 20%, and 60% did not vote. For 2008, 70% of the voter population is already looking for real solutions from presidential candidates.

Since the Bush administration, many of the nuts and bolts that held our government, economy and foreign policy together have come loose. Our voter population has been subjected to its ripple affect and is looking forward to strategic leadership of our nation.

The broken system consists of many parts. The Iraq War, its costs and impact on our daily lives are in the fore front. But then there is our lack of competent foreign policy with Iran, the Middle East and North Korea and in conducting free trade.

Globally, the balance of power is shifting. The West is loosing its position of influence due to economic over extension. Asia is gaining economic and political presence by being our lenders, and Islamic nations are stepping into the nuclear age.

The equity in our local economy is over inflated with a dollar that is boat anchored to foreign debt. The actual money is for the few. Personal empowerment for employment, good health care and sustainable education systems have dried with the absence of commerce in our communities.

Our social welfare entitlements have been regarded arrogantly by the Bush administration that also put our *Bill of Rights* on hold until further notice.

Bush is responsible for the day to day management of a government that has about 65% dysfunctional overhead and additional tax payer costs in trying to get its branches and departments in order.

There has been extensive constitutional confrontation, or infighting between the branches of government. This is expensive and is an unneeded luxury for tax payers. In not using the time to do the work for and of the people places the strategic direction of our nation in question.

For the Strategic Future of Our Nation

We are sliding into a third world economy of what was once known as a super power. The immigration issue has been carefully crafted and tossed at us for distraction. Our environment and energy policies are fuzzy gestures and we are told to lower our expectations.

The New Deal as an Election 2008 primer provides strategic solutions for the future of our nation. This is with our health, safety and welfare in mind. Its basic message is *Leave No American Behind* .

It consists of groups of plans to make our government more cost effective in doing the work of the people, to stimulate the economy, promote community commerce and return personal empowerment.

The New Deal proposes a means for a stable and solvent economy, cost effective government, fair immigration policy and a secure nation.

Environment and energy reform are addressed for how they are to improve our living standards; and lower our costs in transportation and in infrastructure. A nationalized health care plan and others for veteran's rights, Social Security stabilization, Education and housing for all are provided.

Guidelines for the plans are based on 5 principles. They are transparent and accountable government for serving the people, The Dignity of Human rights in how we are to regard each other, Balanced Trade with our foreign counterparts, Economic Solvency to insure our National Security, and in conducting workable foreign policy.

These principles are to assure the framework of the United States Constitution and the Bill of Rights from compromise. This stabilizes the common ground for our nation which has been up to now becoming a n*o man's land.*

We can lay firm foundations for plans that have to do with economic program development and for social welfare by putting this as the first priority of government. We can see a timely return on the investments in our nation.

There is no reason to lower our expectations of, nor accept baseless promises from election 2008 presidential candidates. Sound bites will not stabilize the future of our nation and the voter population is more than a consumer.

The New Deal, an Election 2008 Primer

The politician's focus is based on consumerism where statesmen serve tax payers. All who are willing to step up to the plate have the time available to instead of being part of the problem by complaining about it, to build their vision for our nation as not consumers, but 'we the people' who are the tax payers.

Any candidate should be scrutinized for who they say they are, and what they plan to do for our nation. If it can't put on paper then its worth should be in question.

The New Deal, I offer as my qualifications and experience for Presidential Office in 2008.

I ask you to scrutinize the New Deal. It is meant to be realistic plans with workable solutions that make sense for our nation. From this standpoint, it provides standards to serve as an Election 2008 Primer for setting expectations for a platform that is worth voting for.

Chapter 1

Principles for 2008

In December 2004, I concluded that between the *spin, smoke and mirrors* of the Republicans, and the *cry of injustice* from the Democrats, that they only serve to promote each other; but fall far short in serving the people.

The Balanced Party is based on five basic principles that I found lacking in the other major political parties:

- **Transparent and Accountable Government** to serve the people

- **The Dignity of Human Rights** in our mutual regard

- **Balanced Trade** with foreign imports

- **Economic Solvency** for our National Security

- **Workable Foreign Policy** that demonstrates a standard for mutual respect

Being the underpinnings in the *New Deal,* the principles are to efficiently and effectively empower the framework of the United States Constitution and The Bill of Rights for managing the United States of America while providing the gravity needed to unite peoples of different political parties and faiths.

"But every difference of opinion is not a difference of principle" - Thomas Jefferson

The common ground is the reliance on government for its top down accountability in doing the work of and for the people; the regard for their unquestionable balanced rights; a solvent and manageable economic environment that serves the people; and foreign policy that reflects these as standards in how we regard and set our expectations of others. The Government of the United States of America is to set the example that will inspire *peace* and *dignity* for all throughout the world.

This chapter describes these principles which are the standards for the plans in the *New Deal* for 2008.

The New Deal, an Election 2008 Primer

1.1 Transparency and Accountability

I view that *power* is something we can only manage. It is not something that in of itself can be controlled.

> On Dec. 18, 2000 President-elect George Bush, in an interview on CNN, said that he had told the four congressional leaders *"that there were going to be some times where we don't agree with each other. But that's OK. If this were a dictatorship, it'd be a heck of a lot easier, just so long as I'm the dictator."*

The *management of power* in government can only be accomplished through transparency and accountability.

Power that is not managed becomes unfettered and ungoverned power.

> *"Historically, dictators have been parasites at the cost of their nation and in their reach into the world" - okd*

Accountability is first stewarded in government and then in the people it represents. John F. Kennedy told the nation "Ask not what your country can do for you, ask what you can do for your country".

I see that this goes first for the representatives of the people, if it is to be expected of them. As a standard, any future leadership whose platform is based on the Balanced Party understands the purpose is to serve the people through accountability.

I also see that it is the over all leadership in government that must steward accountability in order to steward the accountability, and therefore, the leadership in others of any representation and/or following.

To establish a transparent and accountable administration that works with the House and the Senate, then they are obliged to do the same.

I believe through this , efficiency and cost effective government can be achieved. This is where policy and legislative action can take on measurable significance for the benefit of the people.

By improving the efficiency and effectiveness of the different branches of government, in working together sets the standards in how departments in government bodies are to operate, work together and communicate cost effectively in getting the peoples work done.

For the Strategic Future of Our Nation

This in turn sets standards for our economy and in the businesses that make up the producers, and for the people who are the consumers.

The country is its people, and the people are the country. Our country is made up of many walks of life, being the origins of immigrants from all over the globe.

Consequently, we the people are all races and the colors, creeds, religions, beliefs, thoughts and points of views and opinions. Our representatives in government are the same as its people. The people are the underpinnings of the United States of America, and this must represent government.

United we stand, divided we fall intends a democracy that derives a united position based on the unified direction or representation of the people of this country. *Divided we fall* consequently means that if our system is broken, in its disunity, we as Americans have allowed our elected representatives to put our country at risk; and further have not set examples and standards for expectations for our personal empowerment.

Being unified, America is strong, but divided, our country becomes weak. Unification is similar to a team where all the people from all walks of life in this country make it up. Dogmatism, Fascism, or any 'Isms', or encouraging the 'Will' of the most powerful onto the many can only polarize us into groups. This polarization ultimately can break our system of productive representation in our country as this in of itself can steward the roots of tyranny and terror.

> *"Those who desire to give up freedom in order to gain security will not have, nor do they deserve, either one." Ben Franklin*

Being united is not one particular direction over another, as much as it is the derived direction that the two houses of Congress, and the President of the United States come to agreement on behalf of the people that voted them into office. Elected representatives are to represent the needs foremost of the people. When this becomes a *broken process*, it is time to further seek our unification through balance as opposed to compounding our discontinuity. We have to be able to ask our representatives what they can do for us, and be able to galvanize this as a message across our nation.

Democracy and its representation are key to achieving this strength through unity. The Balanced Party is founded on the belief that representation, whether Republican, Democrat, Libertarian, Green, Nadar like, Independent, Red, Blue, or otherwise from groups that make up views and represent the needs of the people all share a solid common ground in it through transparent and accountable representation.

The New Deal, an Election 2008 Primer

1.2 The Dignity of Human Rights

The *'Bill of Rights'* is intended for every American. It is viewed to serve as the foundation for the recognition of basic human rights. The expression for the need in regarding human rights in the United States of America also has in its history, the Freedom from Slavery and Civil Rights. The need for Human Rights has further evolved into fundamental labor and discrimination laws, and in our society today, the need for such things as consumer protection.

As this need continues to evolve, in parallel, there is a perpetual attempt to whittle away at the aspects of human rights in one form or another. Simple examples are *binding arbitration agreements* that you unwittingly have to accept as an after the fact item from your employers and creditors. Then there was the *Patriot Act* that shoe horned exceptions to your basic Bill of Rights. It consists of 'new and improved' non-debatable legislation that is supposedly intended to be on behalf of the American citizen's security.

For me, the human rights message is *live and let live* where it is not at the cost of others same rights in a civilized society governed by laws.

Our individual rights as Americans come with the inherent responsibility of these rights; and in the respect of our fellow Americans. This is regardless if it is to do with the 'Right to Dissent', the 'Right of Expression', or to just the right to be safe from exploitation.

Saying that we are all equal in the eyes of the law, for me represents basic dignity that we are to respect others with, and in turn should expect for ourselves.

The respect for our individual rights intends all individuals, where our founding fathers had the wisdom for the need of these rights at no compromise by late hour midnight amendments by any political party in the houses of congress and the executive branch.

The Declaration of Rights, and related laws should not be something that can be signed away, or lost, nor compromised by any legal agreement. It is arrogant in regard, otherwise.

The maintenance and respect for individual rights as Americans must be achieved through competent representation in the Executive, Legislative, and Judiciary branches of Federal and State Government. This is to be with respect to the Bill of Rights, and the rights and laws that have evolved since in its spirit.

For the Strategic Future of Our Nation

As government representatives, and for every American citizen, to have our rights and personal views respected, we must respect the rights and views of others, or in effect, cannot really say that we should expect others to respect ours. This also is a fundamental tolerance needed in our communities for our social evolution as a 21st century nation.

The respect of views and opinions is the basic core of our Republic; that is, unless we are willing to accept *Democratic Imperialism* for common value systems and underlying agendas that are dictated by those that we have elected in good faith to represent us.

In true Democracy, given that one's values possess no mal intent toward, or the exploitation of others, one's values should be respected as intended in Amendment 1 of the US Constitution.

Moral values as an example cannot be owned by one political following over another or defined by some majority over some minority's views; but have to be viewed as the expression of 'the basic maintenance of human rights' over all. Fundamentally, no one political party in the branches of government has the right to manipulate our Bill of Rights.

I also see that moral values should not be the basis of coercion in influencing other's sense of them; or for the use of compliance of one by another's interest.

When we talk about moral values, simply this has to be more than just a political slogan to attract a following. It must serve the people, as even labor laws, and consumer protection should be viewed from the standpoint of morality.

This is simply being, again, consistent with Amendment 1 of the Constitution.

Fundamentally, moral values have to be considered one's own, and that each of us have to hold ourselves accountable through our personal guidelines in our daily judgments and decisions that we make, and that no government, neither Federal or State, or corporation, special interest or otherwise has the right to dictate or set the terms of compromise nor coercion.

Further that these values being unique within each of us are one's own and are considered separate from legislated laws and do not dictate law. Instead they require law to protect them for all US citizens.

The New Deal, an Election 2008 Primer

1.3 Balanced Trade

Trade can be balanced or imbalanced. Trade regulated by volume, and not by price, enables trade to become economically balanced.

Artificial trade tariffs, which is the most our government has been able to do is like trying to plug a dike.

A tax incentive for not 'outsourcing' is also a long shot when considering that they are overshadowed by manipulating the cost of offshore labor to make up the differences.

The volume of imports is not regulated, and when putting a higher price on foreign TV's , as an example, that are dumped on our shores, just means more compromise of foreign workers rights in order to realize the same profit for the foreign manufacturer.

By limiting import volume into the United States, the price of the import would increase due to level of availability and in order to obtain a reasonable profit margin. This is supply and demand mechanics. By regaining the value in the US dollar through economic reform, local industry can be on par with offshore competitors.

Balanced Trade dampens volume and provides less incentive for moving manufacturing operations offshore. This is while not having to be compromised in back room negotiations on import price with foreign governments based on our debt obligations to them.

When volume is the gating factor, then the volume that is normally coming through our ports would have to go elsewhere to be sold.

For example, if China cannot sell excessive volume to the US, it will have to eventually sell to itself. This would require their standards of wage to increase in order to afford their own TV's and other finished goods.

By losing the offshore incentive, US manufacturers would not need a domestic tax incentive as was promoted by John Kerry in 2004, while also not needing to lose their local workers from our communities.

The same principles of trade volume in manufacturing and textiles can be applied to agriculture, as well as the outsourcing of technology labor.

For the Strategic Future of Our Nation

1.4 Economic Solvency:

Since 2001, the term 'Economic Cycle' has been basically omitted when addressing the economy. The cycle consists of a debt and then an equity stage. They occur together typically in a 12 month period. From 2001 to present, without this cycle the United States has been in deficit spending where debt ceilings have become fatigued.

The United States has been only borrowing to afford its spending. The government has only made minimum investments in infrastructure or other areas of related economy in our communities.

Just between years 2000 to 2001, our country has gone from a projected surplus of $5 trillion to a deficit of over $5 trillion. Gross Federal Debt is projected to climb from the $5.8 trillion in 2001 to $14.9 trillion by 2014. This is conservatively estimated to reach or exceed $46,660 in debt for each American citizen by 2014. This is only a few years away.

The perception of a *good economy* has been for a chosen few. Profits have been predominately in the defense industry, closed door energy policy manipulation, pharmaceuticals and in predatory consumer lending practices such as in unregulated credit card profits.

The fuzzy math of George Bush in claiming that the deficit is coming down as usual is not credible. The only way he can make these claims is by comparing his new deficit projection to its previously inflated estimate such as was for February 2004.

In 2004, the $521 billion deficit projection was never realistic and was clearly inflated fuzzy math so that Bush could claim as usual an improvement later in the year even when there was none.

The debt of the United States in lacking a horizon is owned by foreign interest. This obligation subjects our level of economic security to their agendas.

Increased taxation of average wages does nothing but recreate the equivalent of the Rice Famine of Mao's China. Further compromising wages and increasing ongoing unemployment, regardless if it is not statistically recognized as the *unemployment number*, further disenfranchises the citizens of the United States.

Further, when hearing on the Senate Floor, that d*eficits don't matter* can only encourage the bodies of government and then the people to only focus on the 'here and now'.

The New Deal, an Election 2008 Primer

Extended debt compounds our country's insolvency. As its people, we will be broad sided by this. Eventually it will not just be a trickle down impact on those who become disenfranchised but compromise this country, its solvency, and in turn our national security.

Our nation as a super power in today's world is not one if it becomes a third world economy with foreign owners of our debt. Our nation must be an economic super power in the 21st Century in order to be viewed in today's world as sustainable. As much as economic insolvency ultimately stewards a third world standard for living, the growing homeless of our nation normally do not vote. In putting our nation back to work empowers it to be the Republic of active voters that our founding fathers intended.

By having a more local productive economy, we can in turn more readily address our foreign debt. This enhances our level of *national economic security* . It is in this productivity where the United States can anchor itself against the forces that are encouraging it to become insolvent.

It is in the opportunity of productivity that this country can supply itself, feed itself, provide employment, and improve infrastructure for the standards of living that are inherent in a solvent economy.

Regaining the value of our dollar also provides further incentives to invest in the US for manufacturers and providers. With more money in the Treasury, infrastructure investments also can be enabled. This will lower the cost for the transportation of goods which makes our industries more competitive.

By balancing trade, having transparency and accountability in management, and the true regard of the people, enables the United States to embrace economic solvency in times where the basic foundation of this country is being washed out from under us.

Economic solvency enables the 'Economic Cycle' where investments in our tomorrow can be made.

Energy alternatives and new technologies can be more economically realized with a stable dollar.

New technologies can further steward more competitive *balanced trade* and enhance our positions in foreign policy.

Balanced trade can affect the economies of the world while enabling third world nations to become economically stable nations.

For the Strategic Future of Our Nation

1.5 Conduct Workable Foreign Policy that Demonstrates a Standard for Mutual Respect

War is an extremely profitable item for the few at the cost of the many. Technology Investments into weapons enables jobs; but again, for the few, at the cost of the many who cannot benefit from it.

Insolvent nations are typically more oriented towards war than solvent ones.

By being a solvent nation enables the United States to shape its foreign policy. Technology can be used for building foreign economies where accountability, human rights, balanced trade, and economic solvency are the standards of structure behind it.

In other words, our standards that we set for ourselves are the requirement for compliance by foreign nations in order to benefit from the guidance and foreign aid provided by the United States.

Chapter 2

The New Deal

a summary

"Let us raise a standard to which the wise and the honest can repair. The event is in the hand of God". George Washington

The New Deal is for assuring the strategic future of our nation. It addresses our national security and economy; and the health, safety, and welfare of our people as a nation.

The following describes, in summary form, detailed plans and projects from the many chapters of the book. Its scope and focus is based on what is called 'the Promise'. This is a State of the Union Address in Appendix I.

When our country is looking for the best solutions, I see that any election 2008 candidate should match or exceed what is proposed in providing a fair and square deal that is backed by true commitment in his or her leadership when entrusted and held accountable for, by our nation's people, and with respect to the world around us.

With the current state of our nation, we cannot leave room for assumption, or just 'promises' which add up to only memorable sound bites.

Real solutions that we can count on is the mandate for our strategic future as a nation. In this book, this is called 'trust, but verify' for the solutions proposed in this summary.

In this manner, let the best in leadership win the regard of the people in 2008.

2.1- Summary

Franklin Delano Roosevelt reached out when our nation was in need for a 'New Deal'. He showed that he gave a damn about our people as a nation.

FDR took on the mess that Herbert Hoover had created. This included: caring neither about our veterans nor the people, a debt burdened US dollar, and the over inflated stock market which Hoover allowed to crash. As a result, FDR put America in a direction for her recovery through his *new deal*.

I see that the health, safety and welfare of the people represents the state of the soundness of this nation. For me, it is in the combination of these uniquely distinguishable, inseparable factors that provide the purpose of the Government and nothing further, nor less. It is in the standards of measure for this soundness that the state of its people and thus the Union is served.

I believe that we need another New Deal today. What is needed is reform in our economy, and how government and corporations must also reform in order to recover it. Further, we must demonstrate leadership in the environment with safe and clean, cheap energy. We can then afford assured health care, more employment, a working educational system, and community empowerment to drive representation in Congress for our strategic future.

The New Deal, an Election 2008 Primer

2.2 The Role of the Economy in Our Communities

The role of the economy for our communities is the means of their empowerment. The flow of money and commerce in our communities is essential for our social empowerment. Currently estimated, about $800 billion does not flow in our communities per year and is instead shipped offshore by visiting labor.

Much of our industry has also left to go to foreign countries. This is something that we must recapture in our communities for our fundamental empowerment as individuals.

2.3- A Proactive Plan of Projects

In order to empower our communities, our government must work for us, and our industries must be able to provide the goods and services we need. Our economy must feed local commerce that can then provide both white and blue collar jobs which have been previously lost to foreign cheap labor or outsourced.

The New Deal is based on solutions and plans for the health, safety, and welfare of our nation as its people. The plans are proactive and address shared needs that we all can relate to.

For example, through innovation, energy sources can be of less impact to the environment and can help lower our costs of operation. This lowers the cost of transportation, goods, and industry at a minimum.

Like dominoes, this lowers the cost of infrastructure which enables jobs to be created in our communities.

Strategically, with a reformed government, it can then be cost effective to provide many needed community empowerment programs, and viable guidelines in how our corporations are to behave in conducting free enterprise. It can further establish how the economy is to serve us.

When the government demonstrates leadership in reform, and commits to research and development for our future, and market development for investment and employment, the private sector will follow the lead.

This also holds true when we are seen as consumers by the private sector of assured health care coverage and working educational systems in our communities.

For the Strategic Future of Our Nation

2.4 - Financing Plans and Projects

To create and accomplish milestones for the *New Deal*, many projects can be enumerated from its plans. To pay as you go, most projects and solutions proposed look at Government bonds for funding. These are generally referred to throughout all the plans as 'government investment bonds'. They are to fund *government grant programs* that are more dynamic and go many steps further than existing grant programs.

The Government Investment Bond type is not to be paid back by taxpayers, but, as in the *Economic Reform plan* of Chapter 4, to be exercised in the financial markets. Two main categories of bonds are proposed: the social welfare and program development bonds.

They are to be totally tax exempt, and be available for both public and institutional investment. It is my view that any investment through government bonds in the nation should be tax exempt.

Such bonds are to be purchased by institutional banks on Wall Street for improving their bottom line; and for helping to assure the future of their intellectual capital and of this country.

Additionally, these bonds are to be available to the public at large for tax-exempt investment. Being purchased with pre-tax dollars and income lowers the actual federal taxes that one normally pays.

Funds from bonds are considered for only their specific purpose. In other words, the federal government will not manipulate the funds from specific initiatives for other purposes.

Funding for key research and development is for improving the environment and removing foreign energy dependencies while reducing transportation and infrastructure costs.

Projects are to be funded by Government Bonds for providing the necessary grants. Cheaper clean energy is to provide a collateral benefit for reducing the cost of transportation, goods, and infrastructure.

Funding programs in this manner also provide the impetus for the private sector to make investments. This can be for the cases of research, education, health care, and for other needs. The cost then for community empowerment is no longer an unaffordable luxury but an investment that enables the standards for people to live by as a nation. Working educational systems, real health care, and community empowerment can then be realized.

The New Deal, an Election 2008 Primer

2.5 The Government Reform Act

The sound bite *big government* generally implies a government that is not serving you very well. It is to suggest a government that is inefficient and costly in what it actually accomplishes. It has been exploited in order to defer its leadership responsibility to free enterprise. An example is how health care is regarded.

To serve the people, cost effective operation of our government is only through transparency and accountability.

Only with a more operational government are we able to address other things, such as corporate and economic reform. This provides the incentive for reform in our private sector for reliable investment and therefore, employment of our people.

A government that can serve the people responsibly is a cost effective government. In being in the 'Information Age' , at a minimum, we must address our government's ability to manage information; as at a minimum, this is required to serve us. A cost effective government is one that manages its information properly.

I propose a *Federal Information Plan* for the initial steps of reform that can provide needed transparency in government operations. In this manner, the branches and departments of government can be more accountable. In other words, when the branches of government work more efficiently, more work and service can be accomplished for our nation cost effectively.

The government's management of information is currently seen as dysfunctional. It is estimated that 65% of administrative overhead can be removed in the current costs for running our government.

Our government can provide better services at less cost. In doing so we can afford many needed programs which are currently slashed in its budget. The cost effective government facilitates the means for affording needed programs. Then it can support program development bonds for grant programs to pay for research and development.

Government Reform is elaborated on in Chapter 3. It describes my view of the executive branch in its management practices based on the '*will of the people*', a Congress that represents participatory communities as opposed to special interests, and the expectations of three branches of government in working cooperatively and openly to serve the people.

For the Strategic Future of Our Nation

2.6 The Economic Reform Act

Although some Election 08 candidates speak of an economy that has never before been so good, it actually is quite lopsided. Economists see it heading towards a recession. I consider the idea of a recession as being conservative in assessment when one does not wish to 'yell fire' instead when seeing an over inflated stock market, and a US dollar that has never before known such debt in US history.

In our current direction, we will get off easily if only a recession occurs. We could be instead setting ourselves up for another1929 market crash. Consider also that, the dollar had less debt proportionally than today.

The core of the Economic Reform, described in Chapter 4, consists firstly of the tactical move for enabling an economic cycle of debt and equity, secondly of new trade policies to balance the flow of US dollars, and finally, a strategic plan for economic solvency.

1- Tactical Reform: In addition to harnessing government spending, this is to recoup over $300 billion dollars for the current year by cutting spending entitlements and earmarks and corporate welfare. Then we must tax capital gains, and reverse the tax cuts of the wealthiest 2% of our population. Further we must close the tax gap through proactive remedies. The **tax gap** represents an erroneous and noncollectable amount of personal tax issues. This is to be remedied by *1*- closure by financing with diminished penalty and interest there by obtaining a realistic gap that has a payment schedule; and *2*- filling that gap in the interim by selling debt bonds to the institutional banking Fixed Income markets for financing closure.

2- New Trade Policy: This is to be achieved through what was introduced in Chapter 1 as Balanced Trade. It is intended to recover $800 billion per year back into our communities that was from previous outsourcing. It is to further reduce offshore incentives of US based manufacturing companies. Balanced Trade is to provide fair parity in world trade, re-instill incentives for local manufacturing, limit foreign imports proportionally to exports, to promote more competitive local goods, and for encouraging parity in labor and wage internationally.

3- Economic Solvency: This can be achieved and strategically sustained by evolving to an *investment based economy*. I view that only through economic solvency do we have true 'National Security'. The premise to this is *1*- Wall Street knows that it is better to invest the dollar than to spend it, *2*- to make the US Government the most treasured client on Wall Street, and *3*- to put the world financial markets to work for bettering the US economy. It is intended to pay down interest rates radically and eventually pay off foreign debt.

The New Deal, an Election 2008 Primer

2.7 Corporate Reform Act

Within the domain of Economic Reform, boundaries for what has been self regulating free enterprise are needed. Corporate Reform as discussed in Chapter 4, plays a vital role in the stability of our economy.

Guidelines are to be provided by Congress for fair and ethical performance measures for corporations that wish to operate, and or continue to operate in the United States. In general, Corporate Reform must include but not be limited to:

1. Provide an accurate representation of shareholder value.

2. Instill employee loyalty through benefits and allow fair union representation and compliance with nationally stated affirmative action policies.

3- The removal of binding arbitration agreements with employees and consumers.

4- To be scrutinized closely in the areas of market manipulation and predatory practices.

2.8 Government Bond Funded Grant Programs

With Economic Reform, we are enabled to structure proactive investments in our nation. The 'areas' range in everything from environment reform, renewable energy alternatives, transportation systems, and infrastructure; and commercial and consumer housing lending and improvement, employment opportunities, to sound education systems, universal health care, reassuring and improving Social Security entitlements, and social services.

Every funding initiative is to be based on tax exempt *Government Investment Bonds*. Being tax exempt, and investment based, they are intended to instill a new era of investment in our nations future. Instead of ".com booms", we have opened the same market momentum for needed programs. Like the ".com boom, it is also to provide incentives for entrepreneurs to answer many of our needs and to finance sustainable solutions developed by them.

Each of the noted 'areas' are considered opportunities for economic boom when handled in an ethical and regulated manner. Projects invite venture capital from the private sector when seen as proof of vision. To further enhance free market interest locally, debt financing for bonds, and equity financing of venture capital can be structured further in the institutional markets for our current state of the economy as Equity Linked Notes.

2.9 Environment Program Focus

I see our environment as a matter of economics. In other words, without an environment there is no economy. This relationship, and its significance of impact is discussed the 'Environmental Reform Plan' in Chapter 4. It is summarized here.

Environment as reform is considered applicable to federal, state, and community scope. Managed programs have to be provided for each of these, and how they can also work together.

The focus is to include the clean up of infrastructure, land, water, and air. We can make demonstrative moves in environment reform, as in an every day example, if only to stop littering. This can demonstrate world leadership in Environment. For example, setting a 'no litter' consumer standard sends a message to industry that it cannot lay waste to our environment.

As far as carbon trading loopholes which do nothing more than provide incentives for an industry to charge consumers for polluting, we must eventually exceed the Kyoto standards. This instead provides the incentive for producing cheap and clean energy. Its payback is also for reducing emissions of pollutants, green house gases, and reduction of acid rain.

The impact of our leadership is not measured globally when other nations ignore compliance. But it does matter in terms of providing a clean place to live. As a standard of living, its value is also what others are to eventually envy in our environmental leadership.

Programs are to be emphasized as we must clean up our past abuse of the environment in order to live here longer.

Environmental impact is compromised by the amount of carbon we emit into the air, the water and ground that we pollute, and the lack of replenishment of the resources that we have taken from our land.

Commitments are to be made for proactive pollution prevention and environmental cleanup and recovery. Ordinances that appear to be lopsided at the cost of the environment will be revised by federal statue.

Program deployment will be monitored by Congress and the EPA; and other related Federal industry oriented agencies. Program measurements are to be viewed as key to keeping the promise for clean up and recovery, and will be made public as determined in review by Congress.

The New Deal, an Election 2008 Primer

2.10 Energy Alternatives Program Focus:

Our use and misuse of energy is key to how we impact our environment. We have an additional incentive to become 'energy independent' as it is also a matter of National Security to remove energy dependencies from foreign nations which in themselves can be unstable.

Economically, through safe, cheap and clean energy, we will be making our environment far more cost effective to flourish in. We should demonstratively seek programs that determine the best alternatives for the purposes of producing electricity, and powering our transportation systems, infrastructure and homes. I see that it is essential to help expedite this by using grant programs based on the noted *government program development bonds*.

It serves us well to consider all alternatives as on the table. Not one is to be considered at the exclusion of others. An entrepreneur can even bring a new improvement to an existing energy technology and should have that opportunity.

What we will also find is that we can even combine solutions in some cases which provides benefit over cost, and in other cases opting for one over another. There are pros and cons, and special interests regardless of an energy alternative, and therefore, each must be looked at fairly in terms of grant research programs for eventual free enterprise investment.

Nuclear energy is considered clean, but in having its history of serious problems is frowned upon by those who do not want it in their back yard; but its strategic value then has to be assessed.

Bio fuels are a new frontier that should be developed and calls for more investment. Bio fuels can in some circumstances be more applicable when its cost and efficiency are achieved over and above a nuclear power plant.

Solar, Wind , Hydro-Electric, Geothermal Energy technology is improving, and becoming cheaper by the *watt* to produce. In some cases consumers should also become providers over smart grids as proposed by former Vice President Al Gore. Clean coal too is a new technology which merits accelerated research. Further, pumping obnoxious gases through a nation wide plumbing system could possibly help stimulate oil shale in exhausted oil fields.

Due to innovation, there are newer technologies yet to be really discovered like hydrogen fuel cells that over the next ten years should have cost effective benefits as an alternative fuel for powering vehicles.

For the Strategic Future of Our Nation

2.11 The Transportation Modernization Act

Proposed is a *Transportation Modernization Act.* Its message is to 'Go Electric' where possible and the reduction of carbon based fuel consumption. It is intended to lower the cost in the transportation of goods, raw materials, and services. It is also to address the reduction of cost for commuters.

2.11.1 Electric High Speed Rail:

In Europe they have been demonstrating electro magnetic rail trains that travel upwards of 220 mph's. Can you imagine this as a commuter rail system across the deserts of the United States, or between Los Angeles and San Francisco ? We can spread city suburban communities much further and have less city congestion by improving our transportation systems alone. This also can lower the cost of living requirements, and provide reasonable space for communities to flourish.

In transportation of goods and services, a pure high speed electric rail across our nation serves many benefits. This includes lower cost of transport and delivery, lowered interstate high way congestion of carbon based fueled vehicles, reduction of carbon based fuel consumption and emissions, and less wear and tear on infrastructure while having more rapid and timely delivery.

2.11.2 Modularized Automotive Industry

Europe also has a 45 miles per gallon standard, and they still have nice cars that, unlike ours, do not look like they will shatter upon impact. By setting this mileage cap we have also sent a message to OPEC of less demand and a lowered price per gallon expectation if they want to be a supplier.

Our automotive industry in addition must plan to design in modularization. In other words, why can't cars be built based on version as well as model type?

A version of a vehicle can be in the context of the fuel that is available for use such as in a particular state like ethanol, etc. In other cases, the Hydrogen Fuel Cell can be another version of the same vehicle.

In this manner, the automotive industry is not required to bet their future on one direction or another, and innovation is not boat anchored to a stalemate of least risk / best reward scenarios.

This further gives the automotive industry reason to 'tool up' domestically, and the UAW to answer the call for its labor.

2.12 Community Empowerment Act

As the federal government is to have transparent and accountable practices, and enact this in industry as corporate reform, this should reach into our communities.

2.12.1 The Current State of Many Communities

Communities that are short changed in terms of Homeland Security funding cannot provide safety where it must meet the needs of *first responders*. Today this is only symptomatic of many underlying issues that our communities can have. For the most part this can be answered by structured assistance, and having the resources necessary in our own space to tolerate each other.

Our communities can be multicultural where today tolerance for diversity and even for our neighbors is not common. Language differences have become a contentious issue for politics as opposed to ways to communicate. We are reinforced to lack self esteem and to think about 'beating the system'. We are even taught to regard the aged with little importance.

Our veterans, when they are fortunate enough to return to our communities, in many ways may still be where we sent them. Wounds can be physical but also their spirit can be shattered.

There are family breakdowns where rehabilitation assistance for abuse is needed by many.

The jobless and homeless can be anyone, and in respectful communities can be viewed as an inconvenience. And for most, basic health care is no where to be found.

Without adequate Federal assistance, we are missing many needed safety nets in our communities and in our social welfare policies. When we re-enfranchise the disenfranchised we build stronger communities. By communities providing support services and safety nets, I am interested in pursuing further tax incentives for subsidized assistance to help augment this effort.

What is most important for each and every individual is to be an active part of this great nation. This is with their Constitutional rights well secured, and tolerated by others in how we all wish respect. When we are at a disadvantage, it is the responsibility of our nation as a government, to help us become a part of it once again.

2.12.2 The Need for Federally Subsidized Programs

Federally subsidized programs are needed that enhance the viability of the needs at the local level for community safety.

We must endeavor on an ongoing basis to see that there are no hiatuses in federal government for the delivery of subsidized funds to states, and that funds and related programs are not cut; and where signed into law are not shorted; and where states deem the need for more support, that the federal government hears and responds to the stated needs in a timely manner.

As programs, this is not limited to Homeland Security, but includes comprehensive and affordable national health care, and a Federal based unemployment management system to get people back to work. Further needed is an Education Reform Act that enables 'No Child Left Behind' to become available on a graduated scale of requirements as opposed to an all or nothing merit system. Most of all, a 'No One Left Behind' in our communities should be considered our goal.

Communities have to be empowered to develop the skills and abilities of its local youth such as in after school programs. Tutoring must be available where necessary, and other areas of focus that reinforce the sense of self esteem in the youth where attraction to gangs and frustrated groups of kids become less of an issue.

The reduction of crime itself reduces the cost of enforcement for both community and personal safety. It is my expectation that communities will understand the need for compliance with fair commerce practices within their areas. This will enhance the effectiveness of federally subsidized budgets overall.

It is a collective interest to see involvement from ACLU, NAACP and the AFL-CIO in addition to after school care programs and differing faith based followings in assisting communities in developing such programs.

Chapter 3

On Government Reform

The U.S. Constitution has served as the cornerstone in how our government is structured and in terms of the basic rules for its operation. The addition of the first 10 Amendments accounted for fundamental rights for the nation's people.

For me, it is beyond question that the spirit of the U.S Constitution represents a government whose purpose is to serve the people, and not itself. It is composed of the people. For those that contend this, the simple question is what purpose does the government serve since the Constitution's first 3 words are 'We the People' ?

The Constitution notes a 'Republican Government'. I interpret this to mean a representative government with no reference to a political party. It is to represent the people 's *will* that have elected their leadership and representatives democratically.

Our 3 branches of government as thought out by John Locke, are to provide a balance of power. It is divided into the judicial, legislative and executive branches for a civilized society. In the Constitution, each is described in terms of its balance and separation of power in order to work efficiently, and therefore, cost effectively on behalf of doing the work of and for the people.

When government in its branches demonstrate extensive contention, and when in its operations are not cost effective, nor efficient for serving the people; and when leadership and representatives are subject to other influences, we must look at the need to reform government. This is in order to ensure the framework of the Constitution and Bill of Rights for the strategic future of our nation.

The following addresses government reform. This is from the standpoint of *Constitutional confrontation*, Transparency and Accountability through the F*ederal Information Plan*, the description of the president's job and how to work with Congress through c*ooperative information exchange and sharing*; and a more on line participatory public to drive closer representation in Congress. This also addresses lobbyist reform to r*educe misrepresentation*, and election reform to *remove alternative incentives* for seeking leadership and representatives' roles in government.

For the Strategic Future of Our Nation

3.1 The Cost of Government in doing nothing for the People

The following is an example of how the branches of government in its contention, which is casually referred to as 'politics', does not operate efficiently nor cost effectively on behalf of and for the people. Through the history of the United States, we must question how often this is or not the case. Only then can we start to understand the direct and indirect or collateral costs in the operation of our government. Only then can we reduce this cost for the purposes of nothing more, or less than serving the people, which is its sole purpose. Further, by improving the federal government's use of information, it is estimated that cost can be reduced up to **65%** in operational and administrative overhead, where needed programs for education, and investment in our nation as a people do not have to be compromised in the name of *reducing big government.*

3.1.1 Constitutional Confrontation and Tax Payer Costs

The legitimacy of one branch of government over another should not have to be demonstrated through constitutional confrontation when doing the work of, and for the people. When the branches of government work together in a more transparent and accountable manner, the matters of the people are served cost effectively.

There has been the need of showdowns from Congress in many related discovery processes of the George Bush executive branch. One example is over the firings of eight federal prosecutors by the Bush administration. It has escalated to a showdown between Senator Patrick Leahy who wants testimony under oath by White House staff and the president offering his usual alternative of an informal meet behind closed doors.

I do not question the significance and value in the due diligence of the House Judiciary Subcommittee for its intent and purpose. In general, oversight is a Constitutional duty of the legislative branch. This is noted in the Constitution, Section 8 *Powers of Congress* which states 'To constitute Tribunals inferior to the Supreme Court'. I do view that no matter if we consider it correct that White House representatives such as Karl Rove should be under oath, or that President George Bush prefers non-binding informal conversations, that it should not be necessary for Senator Patrick Leahy to subpoena White House representatives, nor should it be necessary for Bush to try to perpetually exercise *executive privilege*. This ultimately becomes a matter of unnecessary cost and overhead in our government in the exercise of due diligence.

Left with no alternative but to escalate to a potential Supreme Court matter is indicative of further tax dollars for settling differences.

The New Deal, an Election 2008 Primer

When the branches of government do not work together in a transparent and accountable manner in the first place, they are accomplishing no more than tolerating and not working with each other. This is at tax payer expense.

Although constitutional confrontation is healthy for our nation such as in testing 'Free Speech', when used to test the checks and balances between the powers of government, its cost is paid for by the tax payer for accomplishing no more than just putting the branches of government in order.

The question I pose is "what really in fact is *big government* if not the overhead of costs derived from the contention between its branches as opposed to being able to do the business of and for the people?" .

As per the Constitution, the branches of government are to demonstrate a mutual respect, where the branches should be fully cooperative with each other. This is to minimize the time and cost required for any internal issues.

Going a step further, I feel that if the branches were to inform each other of scheduled initiatives, then after the fact cost intensive discoveries can be minimized by Congress, and the executive branch can focus on more critical things for the people.

3.2 - The Federal Information Plan for Cost Effective Government

Plausible Deniability is made obsolete through the proper design of the Federal Information System. All Federal Information Services will be based on an Ubiquitous Service Architecture that will be able to interconnect for the purposes of serving the people.

3.2.1 The Cost Ineffective Government

The Transparent and Accountable Government no matter at what scale is the most effective means of serving the people. The image of what was called *big government* comes from the Ronald Reagan days. A lot of what President Reagan did is admirable, but his move to produce a Hoover 'trickle down economy' favored the belief that free enterprise could regulate itself based on market demand, and therefore, is self regulating. In spirit, this appears efficient, but free enterprise also is responsible for creating its markets, and is effective in creating demand. When dealing with a challenging economy, market demand can be created in terms of dependencies. Immediate examples are predatory lending practices, health care and pharmaceutical drug companies.

His idea was ostensibly to reduce *big government* which in many aspects represents both a cost ineffective convoluted bureaucracy, and an imposition in our daily lives. Reagan thought to improve this part of the image by lowering taxes. This got the approval of many, but it misfired later in George Bush senior's tenure in office with his *read my lips, I will not raise taxes* promise.

For a government that is supposed to serve the people, like any service, it can be easier to provide diminishing returns when led by criminally incompetent management. This is then compounded by the growing complexity of our social structure that is then left to capitalism at its worst to take advantage of.

Since 2000, with the trickle down message, 'let them eat cake', it becomes easier and easier to defer on true regard, and responsibility by those responsible for upholding standards for our nation.

With our cake, we are also told to lower our expectations and standards starting with the Bill of Rights. This requires us to ultimately devalue our own sense of self esteem. In other words, why are we told in media that we must have such a low value of life ? It then becomes even easier then to offer only diminishing returns by our leadership and those who they serve as opposed to the people.

The New Deal, an Election 2008 Primer

Power that is not managed becomes unfettered and ungoverned power.

> "In Democratic Imperialism, what appears as a single elected dictator only represents greater ones" okd

This model can work until it is squeezed to death where it then topples over.

In our history, Herbert Hoover represented this type of criminal incompetence. This was with his lopsided economy that caused the stock market to crash in 1929, and with his absolute disregard for the people. Like the current administration's model, his ran on inefficiency until it broke like Bush's savings and loan deals. But what is at stake now is on a national scale with international repercussions.

3.2.3 The Cost Effective Government

The only means of social welfare in our nation is first through government reform. This will require in its evolution corporate reform where the management of power can only be accomplished through transparency and accountability in government.

As noted, it is the over all leadership in government that must steward accountability in order to steward the leadership in others of any representation.

In leading by example, accountability in government stewards accountability of the people it represents. In other words:

> " Ask what your representatives can do for you, and then ask what you can do in your community to galvanize this as a message across our nation."
> okd

In establishing transparent and accountable branches of government they are obliged to work together.

Hence efficiency and cost effective government are then achieved. Policy and legislative action can then take on measurable significance for the benefit of the people.

For the Strategic Future of Our Nation

3.2.4 Government Efficiency and Effectiveness:

A government that can serve the people responsibly is a cost effective government. Today, being cost effective is to manage its information properly within and between the branches; and in their many departments.

One of the most important parts of our government is in the management of information. This is not intended to suggest abuse, loss of citizens privacy, or that we all have some hidden DNA profile with the government, but that the information systems themselves are fundamentally obsolete and not effective in serving our needs.

Like a used car that keeps breaking, there are salient examples of this inefficiency. To cite a few, there are government departments that have separate computing systems that require manual processes between them; or the loss of a veteran's records by Walter Reed Army hospital; and how FEMA was not able to communicate to 'Homeland Security' adequately about hurricane Katrina rescue needs; and in general, inter-intra communication of information in government departments. The out right lack of accountability from Tom Ridge to Congress about Homeland Security did not help this either.

There has been plausible deniability in government, where *accountability* and *transparency* are considered paramount.

Further examples are the failures of Intelligence that led up to 9/11, Abu Grab prison abuse, and the lack of Armor in Iraq, etc. To put this in further perspective, the question should be posed that could 9/11 have been avoided, or minimized if our government was not compromised by inefficient information management?

Further, could the war in Iraq have been avoided if not postponed while we determined actual evidence of WMD and our priorities?

In all cases it is not a proactive but reactive damage control response that the government is limited to when having dysfunctional information management.

'Waste, fraud and abuse' of taxpayer money is typically an intensive cost based process of after the fact discovery.

Collateral costs to the tax payer such as in oversights like in the Katrina disaster, and any required oversight/discovery and investigative process about the government itself, is considered unneeded costs where through functional information management it can be avoided.

The New Deal, an Election 2008 Primer

Without minimizing the concern of extensive risks in national security, what is prevalent in the few examples given, is the lack of definition, and ubiquitous implementation of information sharing and its 'role based management' in government. Secrecy is thought to be the means to political power but ultimately promotes this discontinuity and cost in government.

Our information age will work against us if not accounting for its escalating scope and complexity of needs. We also have a diminishing bandwidth to determine what is relevant in the burgeoning volume of information in use for managing the government.

Until a cost effective information system plan is in place, government employees are more than just limited in the ability to do their jobs which for its stated purpose is to serve the people.

The government as a result operates at a much higher or inflated cost to the tax payer than is needed.

It is within reason to estimate that **65%** of the cost of administrative over head can be reduced. The government can operate at a cost of only **35%** of what it use to. This is by the improvement of its information management. This is while not having program cuts like for our *first responders* but being able to enhance them.

Without a top down federal information systems plan, there is no way to fix a broken and dysfunctional information system.

The sharing of intelligence, the protection, and privacy of, or the lack of, and the confusion of what information, its quality and accuracy, rights of use, potential misuse, its purpose in serving efficiency, and effectiveness in managing the government and protecting the people all have to be based on a top down Federal Information Plan that the branches of government participate in creating.

For the Strategic Future of Our Nation

3.2.5 Federal Information Plan

In being elected the President of the United States in 2008, my commitment is to help steward Congress in order to address the issues at hand, the functional requirements of government departments, and the criterion of classification, and share-ability. The outcome of this is to be an *Information Bill*. It is to serve as the guideline for the Federal Information Plan. This further is to steward our national IT economy to build what is needed.

All Federal Information Services will be based on a ubiquitous service architecture. This is to be able to interconnect for the purposes of serving the people.

This will additionally allow the ability to reduce perception of a convoluted non connected bureaucracy. It will make branches and departments of government work cost effectively within themselves and with each others. It will further leverage Federal Information services to be provided for public access and use.

The Federal Information Plan must regard needs, rights, security, cost, and effectiveness, and the strategic map for this, and how to properly manage information in the government for all levels, over all. The following is the straw man Pro forma plan for the information hierarchy for shared opinion and refinement by Congress.

A-The Information Hierarchy Top Down View

This is to be designed as on a 'need to know' for active participants, and on a 'should know basis' for oversight. At the executive branch, the *knowing* could be in some instances, as obtaining facts about solders who are the *boots on the ground*, intelligence releases that could have been lost in issue contention, or to verify the completeness of a Presidential Daily Briefing.

This enables the ability to obtain facts when necessary from direct levels of government so as to prevent information sanitizing prior to when arriving in other forms to the president's desk.

> Information Access by Cabinet Level, and other members of the administration is to be defined according to their roles in the same top down manner.

This must be made available from the executive branch for the Houses of Congress, and committee investigations.

The New Deal, an Election 2008 Primer

B-Information Efficiency, Use and Effectiveness

Information sharing is to be considered bi-directional for periodic review of government departments, agencies and services; and from congressional members themselves. It was not until well after 9/11 that Congress had learned of a shadow government in place where they were not included.

The executive branch, congress and the judiciary should all share intended plans and schedules in an open and transparent way. Actions can be accounted for in a proactive manner as opposed to a cost intensive reactive discovery process.

C-The Information Hierarchy Bottom Up

The protection and security of sensitive information must also be maintained such as not to compromise our National Security.

D-Interdepartmental Sharing of Information

This is to be defined by type and purpose of information as agreed upon by the executive branch, congress and judicial system.

E-Intradepartmental Sharing for information

For the purposes of departmental agents accomplishing their work, the hierarchy of information view within unique departments is also for congress to review for clarity and purposes of protection and efficiency.

F-Information Audit and Security

This includes identity and trust management, and the guard against threat and vulnerability. It will be an additional plan that is requested to come from Congress.

In this manner, data of US citizens is protected within the partitions of the Federal Information System Plan as formalized by congress. In a participatory government where the people can voice their opinion, this can be further refined.

Accountability and transparency in government is to be based on the classification of information, and where it can be made available as public to the people, and the private sector based on the absence of sensitive classification, and the 'need to know', and 'should know basis'.

For the Strategic Future of Our Nation

3.3 The President of the United States of America, The Job Description

3.3.1 Preface:

There have been many presidents. Some are remembered for the good they did for the people, and others for what they did not do for the people. Most of all, to be a good president for the people, history affords examples to draw lessons from.

When we do not base our thinking on lessons learned, then what a president has to offer the people is in question. Because of this, much has come undone that great presidents have instituted.

In today's *Campaign '08*, most Republican contenders will try to associate with Ronald Reagan, where Democrats in the 2004 race said that they associated with John F. Kennedy, and William Clinton.

I see it is best to not say how much you are like another, but how to use lessons learned.

Two presidents that have made major contributions to our country are Theodore Roosevelt with his *Square Deal*, and Franklin Delano Roosevelt with his *New Deal*.

The most critical lesson is that they gave a damned about the people. In terms of the Constitution, this is what a president is supposed to be about when swearing the oath:

> "I do solemnly swear that I will faithfully execute the Office of President of the United States, and will to the best of my Ability, preserve, protect and defend the Constitution of the United States".

Today, we have to understand what this means. In particular, does the 'separation of powers' allow presidential signings, and *executive privilege* as being described as *executive branch rights ?*

Since 2001, this has been demonstrated in the complete autonomous actions of George Jr. without concurrence with other branches of government.

Due to the limited job description by the Constitution, the following is what I view as the scope and focus of the role of the president of the United States to serve the people.

3.3.2 Summary

The Constitution's limited description is intentional in purpose for describing the role of the president. This is to avoid not having 'Ad hoc' adaptation of description by a sitting president. It is intended to minimize the interpretation of the role to serving based on *the people's will.*

In the Separation of Powers, the president is responsible for the day to day management in doing the *will of the people*. This *will* is communicated by the legislative branch that represents the people that is within the constraints of settled law of the judicial branch.

In the nation's management, the president is considered responsible for the State of the Union, which includes the strategic path of the nation and its 'National Security'.

As the executive management, the president is also to represent the world icon of diplomacy, and the commander and chief of the armed forces, where the *will of the people,* is to declare war as an act of Congress.

3.3.3 Day to Day management

In doing the will of the people, from time to time (annually) , the president is to provide a 'State of the Union Address' to the nation. To serve our nation this must address its health, safety and welfare, and also in terms of its relation to the world. In Appendix I, The State of the Union Address authored is based on the following:

"The health, safety and welfare of the people represents the state of the soundness of this nation. It is in the combination of these uniquely distinguishable, inseparable factors, that provides the purpose of the Government and nothing further, nor less. It is in the standards of measure for this soundness, that the state of its people, and thus the Union is served. These factors are regarded for their importance at a personal level for each of us, at the community level where we live with others, and in terms of federal government in its responsibility to all of us as a nation."

3.3.4 To Ensure the Strategic Future of the Nation

The president is to shepherd to the people, and the branches of government, what he sees as viable plans when confronted with such factors as government, economic and corporate reform, and/or to demonstrate leadership in the environment with clean, cheap energy. For personal empowerment, this is in how to afford assured health care, more employment, and a working educational system; and how to provide and sustain this in our communities.

For the Strategic Future of Our Nation

3.3.5 To Ensure National Security and Economic Solvency

We must be on the higher ground in our foreign policy. As described in chapter 6, it is considered paramount, that diplomacy should not be an attitude, and defense should not be weak.

3.4 In Relation to the Legislative Branch

The legitimacy of one branch of government over another should not have to be at issue when doing the work of, and for the people. When the branches of government work together in a more transparent and accountable manner, the matters of the people are served.

It is required to have a transparent and accountable executive branch that works with both the House and the Senate. The House and the Senate are obliged to provide the same to the executive branch.

This is how policy and legislative action can take on measurable significance for the benefit of the people.

If there is legislation presented for signing into law, any president should determine that it *reflects the will of the people* being that it made it through the houses of Congress. It is not a matter of reflecting the president's personal beliefs or purposes but can reflect his opinion of the *will* of the people.

Where Veto power has its significance, is *if and only if* legislation appears to have questionable purpose, where it might *not reflect the will of the people*, but other agendas. The Veto in this case serves notice that what is presented has reason to be scrutinized. It is not for the purposes of self serving political capital.

As a matter of procedure, balance is provided to Veto power if both houses of the legislative branch demonstrate being in full agreement of the legislation. So in effect, things get self regulated if the Congress itself is transparent and held accountable to the people.

The true value of political capital is ultimately gained between the branches of government when they work together where no longer is it a matter of tolerance, but becomes a valued and verifiable trust in doing the work for and of the people.

With this efficiency, the government can have an economy for active representation, where the *will of the people* is represented in real time on the floors of Congress.

The New Deal, an Election 2008 Primer

3.5 The Economy of Active Representation

To be heard is true Democracy, to be represented is the truth of Democracy.

3.5.1 Participatory Government

Every 4 years a president is voted into office. For every 6 years it is for a Senator, and 2 for a member of the House of Representatives.

There is a *wisdom* behind this when it comes to the communication between the constituents and their representatives. From the standpoint of a senator from say California before the mid 1900's this would work out quite well. Distance was more of a challenge then. If the representative only spoke with his/her constituents it would be at least every 4, 6 and 2 years respectively.

Today, in addition to such networks as C-SPAN, all Senate members, and House Representatives have web sites. They have web-form email for the constituent to voice input, but do not take polls on House Senate Bills being voted on the floor.

Due to the assumed 1,000's of emails that each receives, based on subject the email can be cherry picked for review by office aids to communicate what is considered relevant to the member of congress.

In observing Congress over the past few years on the floor of the Senate and the House of Representatives, and in their committees, and sub-committees, rarely does one hear that "This is what my constituents want" as opposed to "This is what I feel is best for my constituents."

For the Strategic Future of Our Nation

Since the 20th Century, an entity known as the lobbyist has taken on a major role in decisions, as well as the focus of issues that members of Congress vote on. This is common accepted practice, where prior to the 20th century the practice was considered unethical and punishable by incarceration.

The most prominent lobbying bodies today are munitions and defense; health care policy driven by pharmaceutical and insurance interests; and predatory consumer lending practice policies by unregulated credit card business and banking interests. Consider that even closed door energy policy manipulation by Vice President Cheny was condoned by the Supreme Court.

It takes a lot of money to run for government office, which explains the appeal of the lobbyist. Constituents cannot be expected to pay the bill.

It also can explain why there are so few political parties that have any real viability. This issue is addressed as Election Reform which is discussed later in this chapter.

3.5.2 For Hearing The Constituents Voice

The Constitutional definition of a Republic is:

> "A government in which supreme power is held by the citizens entitled to vote and is exercised by elected officers and representatives governing according to law" .

Technically and ethically, the member of Congress is supposed to represent the *constituents' voice*. This is not to come second to that of the lobbyist. This can be accomplished also in real time, cost affectively thanks to the Web and email.

For representation, the following is what is proposed for hearing the constituent's voice clearly on a timely basis.

1- Leadership offices such as from the Senate and House send out email to registered constituents about a pending bill or house resolution number.

2- Constituents can respond by voting on the issue at the Senate or Representatives website.

3- This leaves little room for lobbyist influence when taking the constituents' real time vote to the floor.

The New Deal, an Election 2008 Primer

A- Email Notifications of Issues:

There is no real reason that for every constituent who provides an email address, that an issue to be discussed or voted on in the houses of Congress cannot be emailed for their awareness. As opposed to already having voted on the issue for various reasons, the constituent can get a heads up by the representative. Currently the members of Congress do post issues on their web sites and as one of the thousands of constituents you can receive email notifications. It is what they choose to send. You can also voice an email opinion for someone to maybe look at.

A1-The *Heads Up Email* : This instills far more interest by the constituent than just giving them the one vote during election time if that's what we really want in our government representation. For the voting record of the representative, this too can be provided via a simple link in the email to the respective *official voting records web page* for both houses.

We could argue that this is not cost effective and that the constituent has put their trust in the representative to have their best interest in mind. I contend that it is far more cost effective to notify constituents prior to voting for the following reasons:

- It reaffirms respect for the constituent in being offered the awareness that they are considered besides just during election times.

- It helps prevent bills and omnibus bills like the Patriot Act from being pushed through Congress in midnight sessions.

- Reinforces the significance, importance and trust of the representative in doing their job on behalf of the constituent.

- Enables the representative to obtain support for an amendment that the representative wishes to make on a bill.

- Offers private sector business opportunities to provide polling campaign technology through GSA contracts.

For the Strategic Future of Our Nation

B-Representative Postings

The Senate and House must be required to post on their websites all related accounting detail. This is to include expenses that are accounted for as expenditures and related balances while in office and to document cross referenced sources of identified funds. This is regardless of being related to operational, subsidized directly or indirectly by tax dollars, and / or campaign based. This is to also account for *soft dollar incentives* such as from any and all lobbyist related activities including paid trips or any kind or otherwise benefits that can be construed as gifts.

- It demonstrates honesty, transparency and accountability.

- It provides constituent awareness of related costs, and budget competence of representatives.

- It exonerates the representative from any concerns of influence peddling by lobbyists.

C-Voter / Constituent Polling

Email campaigns and web technology can easily establish voting on a per issue bases. This can offer significant lead time to know the position that a representative must take for the majority of their constituents.

Benefits are:

- The timely representation and awareness of constituent's interests, needs, and positions.

- It requires clarification of representative if he/her differs from the majority of constituents.

- It can provide public graphical display of constituent votes for both representatives, and constituents.

- It provides active participation of constituents in the government's decisions.

- It is easily implemented with existing technology.

- It encourages debate to be more focused on behalf of constituents.

- It demonstrates clearer representation to the president of Senate and House positions.

3.6- On the Judicial Systems

The US Supreme Court

3.6.1 About a Civilized Society

"MEN being, as has been said, by nature, all free, equal, and independent, no one can be put out of this estate, and subjected to the political power of another, without his own consent. The only way whereby any one divests himself of his natural liberty, and puts on the bonds of civil society, is by agreeing with other men to join and unite into a community for their comfortable, safe, and peaceable living one amongst another, in a secure enjoyment of their properties, and a greater security against any, that are not of it." from John Locke (The Second Treatise of Civil Government, Chapter VIII Section 95)

3.6.2 The Right and the Wrong of Law

My personal view is that laws are supposed to serve the people as opposed to controlling them. Additionally if it is not determined by a collective, that in the wrong way, it is made to serve the few.

This sometimes does not work. One example is prohibition. It was eventually repealed. Noted earlier, we can only manage as we cannot control. As much as this applies to our children, this also applies to our civil society. Hence, if our government is intended to control, then it is useless.

Law makers collectively or individually also do not necessarily have an innate wisdom. Who is to also say that they seek a truth or even understand that it could be something that is only relative, and not necessarily absolute?

3.6.3 On Retribution

The punishment for breaking a law I think should also be reviewed. The law might have validity, yet the punishment might not be legitimate. It could be very little, or arbitrary or overly harsh. As we evolve as a society, laws can only be for serving the people, and that punishments are for the purposes of rehabilitation and community service, as opposed to being used as deterrents, revenge or for manipulation. Consider the following:

> If someone was to hurt my love ones, what law could stop me from responding ? Here I have made my own law in the name of revenge as being only human. This is why laws must be made by a collective like the Congress and measured in their management by the Supreme Court.

> On the flip side, if my child were to do something against the law, I am partly responsible no matter how old my child is. If someone breaks the law we are all partly responsible in our communities.

I am not saying one should have a 'get out of jail free card' when being a convicted felon, but incarceration without anything else does not serve any real good.

3.6.4 The Trickle Down Regard for Law

As laws are to basically serve as a means of maintenance for our society, we also have to look at collateral influences in our social structure. We have to have laws serve us. We have to reestablish our expectations where we are no longer manipulated for other's agendas. In placing a high value for life, and human rights is where this starts. This affects our environment, living and working standards as people.

Our environment can have regard by having the active representation in Congress for it. Where we live can have laws for community standards, available jobs, fair cost for energy and affordable living standards.

Industry must observe corporate reform laws. Our corporations are to no longer see foreign labor where an American can fill the job, nor just see employee and account numbers. Instead they are to see that people have rights, and where 'binding arbitration agreements' are considered as unconstitutional and are fundamentally outlawed. Our corporations are to further know that self regulation has its limits, and that predatory practices and market manipulation is not acceptable.

3.7- Lobbyist Reform

"It is easy to make acquaintances but difficult to shake them off, however irksome and unprofitable they are found after we have committed ourselves to them" - George Washington

Lobbying the U.S Government is supposed to be in compliance with the Lobbying Disclosure Act . Lobbying ostensibly serves a special purpose in terms of need for, or wanting representation with our government.

The lobbying consulting firm "Carmen Lobbying Group" states the business or purpose of their lobbying as follows:

> "We seek to affect policy and educate policy makers with arguments based on provable facts. We regard access as one of many key factors in the complex array of a lobbying campaign. We enjoy the access of experts with a reputation for achieving results. "

As an arbitrary example of one out of thousands of lobbying entities, they represent clients who have a focus in affecting business within the U.S. Government and related policies in defense, education, health care, homeland security, international trade, marketing procurement, postal, transportation, water resources and environment, etc.

For the Strategic Future of Our Nation

In judiciary testimony, Thomas M. Susman, a partner in the law firm of Ropes Gray in Washington, D.C., when representing the American League of Lobbyists, stated his interest in improving the LDA process on behalf of the American people.

> "Recent polls indicate that a majority of Americans do not trust lobbyists. The public often views the lobbyist as an unsavory figure, an "influence peddler" who secures for clients an unfair advantage in the inner-workings of government. The fear stems from the belief that lobbyists make secret deals with legislators to benefit special interests at the expense of the general welfare, or even that unsavory influences (in the forms of bribes, under-the-table deals, or coercion) have been brought to bear upon legislators, or that some groups are well represented in the lobbying process while others go substantially or completely unrepresented."

3.7.1 The Need for Full Public Disclosure of Lobbying Activities

In a similar manner as a tobacco company stewards 'anti-smoking' initiatives, what was omitted is the need for full public disclosure of lobbying activities when proposing revision of the Lobbying Disclosure Act.

The following proposed LDA revisions are for limiting misrepresentation and abuse of influence:

- Transparency in government entity association with lobbyists

- Transparency in lobbyist associations to government entities

- Transparency of lobbyist clients

Because of the Internet, the opportunity avails itself for transparency in disclosure to the public about all relations that are directly or indirectly related between lobbyists and government entities. These entities in scope include all of government.

3.7.2 The Proposed LDA Full Disclosure Public Web Site

The Government can incorporate in the LDA a full disclosure public web site that documents the following information categories for a registered lobbyist where updates should be considered on periodic basis:

- **Clear Identification of Lobbyist:** This is to include individuals, employees, consultants, members, partners , clients of, or otherwise that directly or indirectly represent a lobbyist entity by association are considered here as a lobbyist.

- **Related Lobbying Campaigns:** Enterprises that the lobbyist represents as focus/purpose in the communication, socialization, or otherwise can be construed as a relationship, either casual, or active with a government entity must be considered related to a campaign for/of in the affiliation of a related Bill/Amendment; this is regardless if there is any monitory identification which can be associated, or even 0%.

    - A lobbyist when associated with a government entity is related to all campaigns that are associated to them.

- **Related Government Bills/Amendments:** Based on the government entity that is referenced by Senate / House Committee for the specific Bill/Amendment in question, that the lobbyist entity is associated with, the lobbyist is considered to be associated with the Bill/Amendment in question.

- **Related Government Entity/Contracts:** Contracts that are associated with, or directly aligned with a department within the government entity that is provided as a Bid/No bid contract for services/products provided by a non-government entity, that is based on budgets from a Bill/Amendment, is considered to be associated with the lobbyist entity that is associated with the Bill / Amendment in question.

- **Related Government Entity/Representative**(s): including but not limited to elected official, public assigned position, or government organization are to be clearly indicated that are either associated through 'related lobbying campaigns; Bills/Amendments and committees that are associated with the Bill /Amendment in question; and government entity/contracts that are awarded that the lobbyist entity is associated with.

For the Strategic Future of Our Nation

- **Contributions**: This includes, but is not limited to, monitory gift, travel, promotion, soft dollar, or otherwise that are provided either directly or indirectly to a government entity/representative from a lobbyist, or indirectly from with respect to association via a lobbyist client.

- **Related Client Lists:** Including the direct client, (and/or their intermediary, corporations, firms, partnerships, organizations, , subsidiaries or holding entities) that is represented by the lobbyist entity that is of direct or indirect benefit, or involved in the related government/entity contract must be clearly identified as a client entity of the lobbyist entity.

- **Tax Statements:** Current filings of said lobbyist and client entities must be available by reference within the LDA registration.

- **Sec Filings**: Current filings of said lobbyist and client entities must be available by reference within the LDA registration.

- **Legal / Litigation Cases:** Current filings of said lobbyist and client entities must be available by reference within the LDA registration.

- **All Financial Audits:** Current and previous year audit filings of said lobbyist and client entities must be available by reference within the LDA registration.

M. WUERKER

To get the word out in 2004, the presidential election cost a major fortune. Key to this was advertising on network TV, radio and web. Ad spots could just as easily have gone to a Cialis pill commercial, but is provided by the highest bidder for the time, length and day. Moreover targeted advertising into demographic zones is vitally important. This is in terms of focusing on a particular issue over another. This is also class 101 in consumer advertising.

For the Strategic Future of Our Nation

In addition to direct candidate and party promotions there are the soft dollar groups that add their fill to the airwaves. The most financially endowed gets the airwaves for their candidate. Only 2 political parties are known by most. The two are also the longest established which could speak to the validity of the imbalance, or that they are simply the best financed.

In 2004, over $800 million was spent on 2 candidates' public relations. The purpose was not to offer anything to the people, but to criticize the other candidate. Voter turn out was about 40% where 21% decided what was supposed to be the leadership.

In the case of choosing between the Democrats and Republicans, it comes down to a matter for some as which party they believe is the safest of choices in the midst of smoke and mirrors. This is while not really having an idea of what other parties provide as a platform. For those who sat this one out, had just let someone else decide for them.

Diversity has its merits, and this is one of the key benefits in what can be offered compared to the lack of differences between the Democrats and Republicans.

In fact if all registered parties had significant presence in the election period, constituent awareness could hold into account what the true differences and similarities exist in different parties. This is where the public deserves more fair choices.

Case in point, the Balanced Party is based on 5 fundamental principles that help the stewardship of the United States Constitution and Bill of Rights without compromise for the American people. From this, any policy that emanates from the Balanced Party is guided by these principles. Question is, what do other parties actually offer?

From the standpoint of being grass roots, it would serve the country well if the party promotion machine could be on an equal playing field.

The closest it will come to the leveled field is in how Election Reform itself takes form. There are many ways to do this, and there have been Bills in Congress that are touted to help achieve this, but they are not pro-active.

The New Deal, an Election 2008 Primer

3.8.1 Pro-Active Reform:

Corporate taxes are reduced by write off's called business expenses. This is where the public makes up the differences for what the US Treasury needs for budgets. Since corporations either directly or indirectly shape a government representative's policies, there will always be business expenses.

A different kind of write off can be provided for advertising entities if given as the alternative to profit based advertising of candidates.

Election Reform can really mean something if, for example, 'candidate, and candidate party' promotion is under the domain of '*equal time public service announcements'*. Advertising entities can receive tax credits for this equivalent to the profits they earn for paid advertising.

The alternative is to have a government sponsored channel that anyone can tune into, less the advertising. This should give impetus for commercial channels to follow the lead.

In addition to better representation of candidates, by getting the word out, can provide incentives to the underlying political parties. A better platform for the American people can be presented than just offering a limited 'sound bite' that is thought necessary.

In short, the voter does not have to lower their expectations as there will be far more competition by political parties to win that vote. The advertising industry in providing 'equal air time' for this, then is truly doing a public service while earning tax credits.

3.8.2 Regulation of Soft Dollar Groups

Soft dollar groups have served as an additional means for image shaping of election candidates. These groups can focus an advertisement based on the message that they wish to tailor. Regardless if true or false in content, they are able to reserve as much forward air-time as their budgets allow.

Fair representation of candidates can be compromised at the cost of merit. Politics should not have to be dirty in order to win an election as this does a disservice to our country based on misrepresentation.

I would want to see legislation enacted that regulates soft dollar groups to facts only, and the ability to only purchase equal air-time of opposing ones. To serve their candidate fairly, they are serving the voter with options for a fair choice.

For the Strategic Future of Our Nation

3.9 - The Nation's Safety

3.9.1 Summary

Our nation's safety is dependent on our economic solvency. This solvency is what affords our homeland and national security; and the *Nation's Intelligence System.*

Our safety is first and foremost subject to the *welfare of our nation.* The welfare of the nation is by my definition, the welfare of the people. For me, this is a financial matter.

The level of our nation's *economic solvency* is the foundation for the financial welfare of the people. Consequently, there is no way for us to be assured of our health, safety and welfare unless the nation as a whole is sound financially.

There is no way for the nation to have independence and autonomy, and standards in its foreign policy, if the nation is not fiscally sound.

Our nation cannot afford a real Homeland Security program or a National Defense System that is backed with competent diplomacy, or a National Intelligence System that works, without the nation's fiscal soundness.

The Nation's Safety Program proposed is to provide:

- Transparency and Accountability in our national security programs.

- The Homeland Security budgets that meet the supported expectations of each state.

- The sharing of information between our *first responders* and the Homeland Security Department.

- The furthering of purpose and responsibility of commissions to enhance our position against threats.

- Provide a robust National Security platform that is built with strong defense posture and diplomacy with wisdom.

- The further refinement of our Intelligence Systems through the proposed plans that follow.

The New Deal, an Election 2008 Primer

3.9.2 National Security

In his speech on January 17th, 1961 President Eisenhower stated:

"A vital element in keeping the peace is our military establishment. Our arms must be mighty, ready for instant action. So that no potential aggressor may be tempted his own destruction . . . In the councils of government we must guard against the acquisition of unwarranted influence. Whether sought or unsought, by the military industrial complex. The potential for the disastrous rise of misplaced power exists and persists".

I contend that instead of being well endowed, that our nation's security has been exploited as a climate for fear since 9/11 by the Bush administration.

The Bush administration has been overly secretive and evasive with respect to congressional inquiry. It has further attempted to take the budgetary process, or the 'purse strings' from Congress for managing Homeland Security and our defense systems.

The Bush administration has further created slush funds to spend at will based on the full latitude of its interests. In this, Congress has all but abdicated its responsibility in the budgetary process. This is to the point of being able to fund wars that have not been declared by Congress.

Congress was disabled early on from having oversight on the purpose of Homeland Security budgets or its actual management.

The Defense Department, or what could have been called the *Rumsfeld Empire* at the time, additionally had funds to spend based only on its discretion. Congress, the people's representation, has had no voice here either.

The Defense Department, like Homeland Security has become a free wheeling agency of an incompetent executive branch. The loyalty requirement for people like Tom Ridge and Rumsfeld is to fall on one's sword if needed. This makes these agencies to be strategically ineffective to serve our national security.

For the balance of power, Congress will have to become re-empowered in its budgetary process and oversight role on national security. Further, I propose that the Patriot Act is to be rolled back and reformed by my administration and Congress. If needed, instead a *'National Security Act'* can be the result. What this will also do is insure the Bill of Rights.

For the Strategic Future of Our Nation

3.9.3 The Common Sense of Foreign Policy

Although detailed in Chapter 6, concerns of the impact of foreign policy are summarized here. Foreign policy is seen as not an attitude and defense not being weak.

> In 2003, our foreign policy was 'either you are with us or against us', and 'bring it on !'

> Today, our defense system is over stretched and fatigued.

Such attitudes toward others and miss use of our military cannot be blamed on being a conservative or a liberal. It is a question of the management of the executive branch of government.

We walk with two legs and not one. We should not view diplomacy and defense as being exclusive of the other, but mutually dependent on each other for their effectiveness in serving the other.

> This is to be resolved at the Cabinet level, where the Secretaries of Defense and State work hand and hand together as part of the National Security Council with the president. In this role, these secretaries are to be peers, and not subordinate to the National Security Advisory.

For National Security, the Defense System gives *diplomacy its teeth*, and Diplomacy provides Defense its *faculty of reason*. I view that the two are inseparable when embracing preemptive or unilateral actions.

Combined, our actions towards others have a more formidable and daunting mission purpose. This enables a viable conclusion that is conservative in the use of our military forces, where in foreign policy we can provide an exit strategy such as for Iraq and the rest of the Middle East where our intent as a great nation is beyond reproach and cannot be construed as global manifest destiny.

With creditable reputation, our foreign policy is also affective in helping others find *their exit strategies* such as for nuclear prone nations like Iran and North Korea.

Diplomacy orphaned from defense can only be 'meaningless lip service'. Defense when orphaned from diplomacy can continue in a non focused manner that is subject to tangential agenda's. Calling it for what it is, National Offense is simply the business of war at the cost of squandering American lives as well as the innocent.

The New Deal, an Election 2008 Primer

If the two halves of a brain cannot work together, then the body cannot function properly. If the two vital components of national security do not work together, then it does not serve our nation's safety.

In the 21st century, strategically, we have to have economic solutions for world peace.

This first must be built on mutual respect. It can only come from respecting others as we do ourselves. Our foreign policy must set this expectation as how others are to respect us.

In foreign policy we are to mean what we say; and in our defense system, say what we mean in complete clarity of mission execution.

3.9.4 Military Defense Planning

A strong military is a necessary component in successful foreign policy. Our military has been over stretched and funded by supplemental budgets without constraints for discretion. Strategically, it is impossible to have a mission based military under these conditions.

Over time, Middle East military expenditures will be reduced based on the plans in foreign policy described in chapter 6. This enables our nation to regroup and rebuild our military as necessary. This will require a budget that is managed with close oversight from Congress.

To Rebuild as Necessary calls for budget requests from the Joint Chiefs of Staff and what the Defense Department sees as necessary for a strong military. This is to be weighed by the State Department and White House council for priorities with the Defense Department.

As this is a significant project, it will be managed and submitted to Congress on an *as needed basis*. In this manner, each area for budget requests can be reviewed competently and for allocation in an acceptable time frame.

As supplemental(s), they will be added into the military budget that represents total of planned expenditures. It is to be mutually agreed on by Congress and the Executive Branch. What is to be allocated for the military in order to prevent war, and what is necessary to manage a war is to be accounted for.

3.9.5 Homeland Security:

Those who give up liberty for the sake of security deserve neither liberty nor security.- Ben Franklin

The Dept. of Homeland Security started on unstable ground. It was misrepresented by the executive branch for its purpose; and from the budgetary standpoint was able to avoid oversight by congress.

It now consists of over 170,000 employees of 22 government agencies where even Civil Service laws of been ignored. The purpose stated for clumping together of these agencies as a critical mass was supposed to be so that they can communicate affectively in coordinating our homeland security.

Previously, each agency was subject to congressional oversight, but now they are cloaked in the insulation of the Homeland Security Department. They represent no critical mass of information sharing and interoperability. Homeland Security to present has only demonstrated incompetence.

Through the Patriot Act, Homeland Security has been able to ignore the Freedom of Information Act and is able to avoid disclosure to congress. As opposed to serving for the purposes of security, it is permitted to persecute the American citizen at will which is a threat to the very basis of our 3 branches of government.

In the Federalist Number 76, Alexander Hamilton wrote:

"It will readily be comprehended, that a man who had himself the sole disposition of offices, would be governed much more by his private inclinations and interests, than when he was bound to submit the property of his choice to the discussion and determination of a different independent body, and that body an entire branch of the legislature. The possibility of rejection would be a strong motive to care in proposing."

To serve the people, homeland security should not be a witch hunt on our shores for suspicious foreigners, or for use by political agendas.

It should be competently developed by both the executive branch and congress, and adequately funded as a group of monitored programs. This is to address our needs for homeland security, and the necessary watchdog committees to remain in place such as the 911 Commission.

The New Deal, an Election 2008 Primer

These committees are to review and advise ongoing about the effectiveness and competence of these programs. They are to be aware of, and address tangential issues that could directly or indirectly relate to the quality and usefulness of our homeland security in serving the United States.

- Homeland Security Dept. budgets for first responders are not to be slashed. Instead they are to be reinforced with delivery dates that will meet the expectations of our communities.

- It is further the commitment my administration to steward the proactive participation of commissions in managing, and furthering transparency and accountability and the discovery process for its needs in government, and in the private sector.

- Homeland Security policy will not endorse the incarceration of people without fare representation, and scheduled due process in criminal and civil courts.

  Amendment 6: "In all criminal prosecutions, the accused shall enjoy the right to a speedy and public trial, by an impartial jury of the State and district wherein the crime shall have been committed, which district shall have been previously ascertained by law, and to be informed of the nature and cause of the accusation; to be confronted with the witnesses against him; to have compulsory process for obtaining witnesses in his favor, and to have the Assistance of Counsel for his defense."

- Moreover, Amendment I of the Bill of Rights will remain as it is.

  Amendment 1: "Congress shall make no law respecting an establishment of religion, or prohibiting the free exercise thereof; or abridging the freedom of speech, or of the press; or the right of the people peaceably to assemble, and to petition the Government for a redress of grievances."

For the Strategic Future of Our Nation

3.9.6 The Nation's Intelligence System:

This was key in initial focus of the original 9/11 Commission report. The military must have its real time use of Intelligence, as well as Homeland Security.

A National Intelligence System is proposed. Its purpose is to bridge National and Homeland Security. It will provide reporting of Intelligence events to both the executive staff and to Congress; and the intended oversight commissions.

In this manner, Intelligence will have the rapid delivery that is needed to those *who need to know* with the necessary transparency for those *who should a*lso know of its content and use.

Based on the Federal Information Plan our National Intelligence System is to have parity in its level of integration and the needed flexibility for the dissemination of information.

This will aid all intelligence systems in becoming more intelligent in the first place, and domestically will help overt FEMA – Homeland Security national disasters like in the incompetence demonstrated in New Orleans.

Our NORAD (North American Aerospace Defense Command) does not have to be oblivious to commercial airliners about to hit buildings, as it is alerted by message type and severity that is multi cast to specific listeners. First responders can likewise receive immediate intelligence about a threat.

Chapter 4

Economic Reform Plan

Economic Reform has three dimensions. The first is accounting for our government, financial markets and foreign policy in terms of trade. The second is domestic policies in how we use our environment and lower the cost of operations. The third is strategic industry initiatives such as for revitalizing infrastructure and our transportation systems.

In all cases noted, the state of the nation is considered the state of all its communities. This represents the state of the people. The nation's job force can be affected by any one of the dimensions noted of the economy.

Without government policies on economy that serve the people, a financial market that enable jobs, and the ability to compete with foreign trade, with a high cost of living in fatigued infrastructure and over used transportation systems, the economy ultimately does not serve its communities and therefore, the people of our nation.

To recover the failing economy at its core, our plans must address its fundamental survival, then to stabilize, and then give it a strategic future.

This chapter is divided into the noted dimensions as key areas of remediation. Each area is reviewed for the issues. Proposed solutions are provided that are to work in concert with the other noted dimension.

The first dimension is in the order of economic recovery, balanced trade, economic solvency, and corporate reform. The second is environment and energy reform. The third are summary plans on infrastructure and transportation revitalization. Combined, this is to provide an economy where fair commercial business real estate, and personal residential loans become with in reason.

For the Strategic Future of Our Nation

4.1 The State of the Great Divide in our Economy

Reported on June 1, 2007, the Commerce Department said that the economy less than crawled at a 0.6 percent pace in the opening quarter of 2007. The performance was far less that the weak 1.8 percent that was forecast by some economists. Some even speculate a recession. Consider that being conservative is the safe way to go. Alan Greenspan noted that there was only a 1 out of 3, or 33% chance of a recession. Can we say that it pays not to panic the world, but also pays to be able to cover the 'I warned you' part too !

The current Bush Federal Reserve Chairman, Ben Bernanke, however, has said he doesn't believe the economic expansion, now in its sixth year, is in danger of fizzling out. Neither does the Bush administration. This is while many in Congress, and the George Jr. administration are urging you to privatize your Social Security as the trust fund is due to run out !

1929 Stock Market Crash

We have not had an *economic cycle* which is necessary for an economy's momentum. We have instead, the heaviest debt in our history where markets as fundamentally inflated. This creates the stagnant economy.

Further, just about every thing is a target for being off shored, and the great divide between those *who have* and *those who have not* continues getting wider.

Most importantly, regardless of the fairness question, a lopsided economy represented by an inflated stock market that is actually boat anchored to the depreciating US dollar can even look more alarming than in Hoover's time.

The New Deal, an Election 2008 Primer

If the market collapses, then perhaps the advocates of this lopsided economic model might ask 'who could believe that it could have happened ?'

Like a snake eating its tail, the more the gap widens between 'those who have, and those that do not', the common thread of consumerism that holds it together will eventually snap. Considering that twice in our short history we have had a market crash, this could be inevitable just based on fundamentals. Or at the minimum, we could slide into an awaiting third world economy.

Without *economic security*, we do not have *national security*, and especially when our lenders are economic super powers like China.

Some of the contributing factors that are undermining our economy is the depreciating US dollar and those things that exacerbate it. This includes the wealth spread between the those "*who have* and *those who have not* ", corporate welfare, mergers and acquisitions, predator consumer financial services, CEO and corporate board pay, off shoring of manufacturing and services, and hiring cheap visa based foreigners for temporary local labor needs.

4.1.1 The Depreciating US Dollar

For purchase value in the world economy, the US dollar (USD) has been falling. This is due to being burdened by extensive debt. The level of debt is greater than in Hoover's time which ended in the Stock Market crash.

This debt burden is due to our government's indiscriminate borrowing from China and Japan; and raping existing Treasury Trusts like Social Security and Agriculture. It is sort of reminiscent of George junior's saving and loan banking failure where now he is advocating to defer on Social Security obligations.

From year 2000 to 2001, the country went from a projected surplus of $5 trillion to a deficit of over -$5 trillion. Gross Federal Debt is projected to climb from the $5.8 trillion in 2001 to $14.9 trillion in 2014. This is estimated to reach into $46,660 in debt for each American citizen by 2014. But then we also have to account for the difference in Foreign Currency that this forecast does not. In other words, for those fortunately who are employed, as tax payers can owe much more than currently projected.

When we borrow Japanese Yen, (JPY) , the debt is backed by only who is employed to pay tax. We also have to back the difference in currency value. This debt is not paid back in USD, but in the currency that it was borrowed in. In other words, if we borrow $100 billion from Japan, we could end up paying back $400 billion of original debt plus its interest.

For the Strategic Future of Our Nation

Our estimated debt is subject to market rates which is not accounted for. Our long term debt forecasts look at best case scenarios. The tax payer can expect to owe more than expected. Consider that it's no wonder why the US wants another lender, China, to devalue its currency in terms of what we also owe them.

Our extensive debt is to afford developing *American interests of manifest destiny i*n Iraq through a costly war, and military support in the Middle East and Asia. In the meantime, the Government has also not encouraged US based company investments in our country such as manufacturing infrastructure.

This dependency applies at a minimum to readily replenish the equipment for our own military. Consider the current automotive industry as an example. It use to make our military tanks in WWII. Now to get armored equipment has become a challenging order to fill for needs in Iraq.

Then there are many other areas in our communities of related economy that must be addressed in order to achieve balance.

Since September 12th, 2001 the term *Economic Cycle* has basically been omitted when addressing the economy. In a normal economy the debt and equity stages typically occur as a pair in a 12 month cycle.

Since 2001 there has been no cycle. The United States has been in deficit spending where its ceiling has become fatigued. During this period, V.P. Cheny in the news has promoted the message - d*eficits don't matter*. When hearing on the Senate Floor, that our obligations do not matter can only encourage the bodies of government, and therefore the people, to only focus on the 'here and now'.

The *debt / equity cycle* in fact is like a gyroscope. When it stops spinning for a period of time, it will fall over. This further compounds the insolvency that this country has, where we will be broad sided by it.

As our debt becomes greater to foreign lenders, it is supposed to be paid by taxes from what work force, which is now instead, becoming unemployed..

Misfortune has trickled down on those who become disenfranchised due to a failing economy. It also compromises this country and its solvency; and in turn our national security with respect to foreign lenders.

Increased taxation of average wages does nothing but recreate the equivalent of the Rice Famine of Mao's China. Simply, we can only beat a dead horse till it collapses.

The New Deal, an Election 2008 Primer

4.1.2 Wealth Spread:

The wealth spread is a great divide in this country. In the past 10 years, our economy can be represented as 2% of the population that owns about 50% of our assets or about $10 trillion in private wealth And then there is the rest of us who own 100% of the year 2014, projected $14.9 trillion in debt.

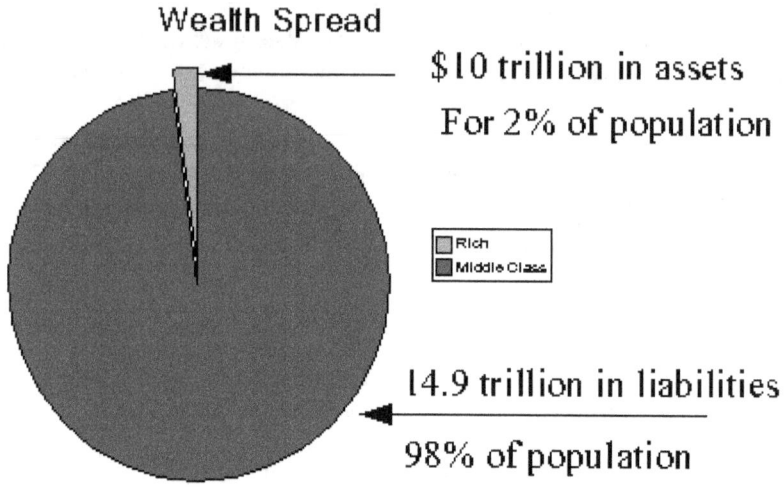

For the moment, the economy seems perfect for the rich. Certain entitlements are awarded to the well off by our government. This includes tax breaks that do not even scratch their investment portfolios. But comparably, this could be worth as much as what the rest of us try to pay in taxes which includes the perceived tax gap.

As the USD depreciates, this special 2% are empowered to hedge their $10 trillion dollars of investments . They can protect themselves while small investors and business can loose their shirts.

An example is in hedging the Foreign Exchange derivative markets. This insulates fortunes by being converted to other currencies that can reside in foreign or offshore accounts. The following example can help explain this dynamic:

> If you bought Japanese Yen (JPY) in 1998 it was 140 JPY to 1 USD. Today, it is 100 JPY to 1 USD. In other words, you would make more than what you invested in less than a few years.

For the Strategic Future of Our Nation

Normally good investments in a stable domestic stock market go at a 6% rate per year. But in the case of needing to jump ship you can sell your USD for a more stable currency.

This makes wealth management relatively immune to the liability side of the falling USD. That is, until a market crash.

Meantime, there is an over inflated market. This over inflation is indicated by a climbing Dow Jones Index, where the NASDAQ 500 Index has declined. The Dow represents corporate wealth, where the NASDAQ index represents the underlying technology sector.

Relatively speaking to the decline in the domestic economy, consider the Dow was at 10,000 , and the NASDAQ was at 4,000 when USD = 140 JPY in 1999. Today, the Dow soars at 13,000 while the NASDAQ holds at 2500 where the USD = 120 JPY. Our Dow proportionally has lost almost a third of its value with respect to the global economy, and our NASDAQ is far worse off.

The burgeoning unemployed and/or bankrupt are considered the consumers of the industries that are traded in the markets either directly or indirectly. In doing the math, if there is no consumer, ultimately the value of the stock must take losses. Because it was over valued in the first place, and the actual USD cash value is less than it should be in the world markets, the value of the stock is actually like vapor. When put to a test of market endurance it will evaporate if it does not have good underlying fundamentals in its equity and debt ratio.

When the value of the USD is boat anchored in debt, this is like an investment being overcome by a whirlpool that will sink it.

The New Deal, an Election 2008 Primer

4.1.3 Corporate Welfare

Corporate welfare that consists of jimmy rigging pork barrel projects in Congress, and obtaining special tax breaks, and wired deals has not really helped the economy. This compromise is similar to the days of feudalism that controlled weak governments.

Examples of corporate welfare is the Government's no bid defense contracts to some of the largest corporations that have based themselves for the time in the US.

In essence, to be eligible for corporate welfare, like in the days of feudalism, you just buy votes in congress that are needed for obtaining your business goals. Some simple examples are:

- In federal government this is seen in the cost plus no bid contracts awarded to the defense, environment, petroleum / energy, agriculture, manufacturing. In the service industries the example is Halliburton. few.

- In the retail industry, Wal-Mart received over $1 billion in public subsidies from state and local governments. Like in feudalism, local merchants paid tax dollars to subsidize their biggest competitor.

Policy and laws in congress, as an example, have justified corporate welfare as in helping 'entrepreneurs', and enabling the Reagan *trickle down economy* model. Like in Hoover's time this was supposed to trickle some drops into our communities in order help business provide jobs. Unfortunately, these 'drops' tend to evaporate in a dry economy.

Comparatively as well, for Reagan, Lockheed was considered what an entrepreneur was as opposed to small business start ups. To present when the term is used on the floor of Congress, it refers to a capacity like Lockheed or Boeing. These corporations do have communities of employees, but the profits do not go to them.

4.1.4 CEO Compensation

Like in feudalism, CEO compensation currently ranges up to $98 million per year such as in the case of United Technologies CEO George David. The average is about $14 million. This is considered reward for raising stock prices and profits by reducing costs. CEO's follow the lead of the US President, who is functionally the **Chief Executive Officer** or CEO of the Nation. Therefore the president must set the example for corporate CEO's.

For the Strategic Future of Our Nation

4.1.5 Mergers and Acquisitions (M&A)

M&A has further pruned the who's who list of the wealthiest. Its repercussions also include adding more of the middle class to the unemployed and/or bankrupt.

When business is supposed to regulate itself, M&A can be used in many ways:

- For building larger banks that can offer both commercial and institutional services. This is where the money flow goes from the profits of predatory lending and consumer banking services as capital into their institutional investment side. Until recently this was not permitted by the government for many purposeful reasons like the WorldComm fiasco. This also prunes labor forces to only what is still needed. During bank mergers and acquisitions, to be cost effective duplicate labor is generally fired to join the unemployed.

- In order to obtain cash for other investments, to liquidate another company's assets if they show little debt and little profit. Our labor forces are again diminished.

- To obtain another companies liabilities, and write this off as your own to protect the profit side of your business. Obviously the existing labor force will join the unemployed.

For portfolio investors, M&A deals can look good. In their wake, M&A can devastate towns that have depended on an industry for employment and capital flow into their communities.

M&A deals today are basically under self regulation except for a little after the fact oversight from Congress.

In 1983 it was considered a good idea to break up AT&T (Ma Bell) which ultimately allowed the Internet to be realized. It is coming time to do this again while also considering other industries.

What is most important is to limit the scope and number of M&A deals that can be clustered ultimately under one corporate roof. And for those that are above this high mark, to deregulate back into the market again as separate companies. The scope of anti trust laws can be extended.

The New Deal, an Election 2008 Primer

4.1.6 Off Shoring

When I was building my ".dot com" startup in 98, countless offers for offshore labor were presented. From the business, and budgets standpoint, using foreign labor could save upwards of 90% of the labor start up costs. So theoretically you can get 10 times the amount of labor for the same US dollars. This always looks good when on paper.

In reality, off shoring of labor puts a company at a much higher risk in quality assurance. You are typically dealing with third party management of the labor, and a foreign labor force that has no affiliations with your interest as a company.

Because of looking good on paper, it is a major move that most companies which can, will do in order to reduce near term costs.

Off shoring or *wage gouging* (nickel and dimming for cheap foreign worker local labor rates) on employment offerings with preferences for visitors with green cards and migrant farm or factory workers has caused an earthquake in our economy. This is in terms of unemployed Americans.

Off shoring ships an estimated $800 billion USD out of our country each year as opposed to having this flow through our communities. In essence, our communities are shorted $800 billion in their empowerment for their quality of life.

For states and local municipalities, this means less tax for infrastructure and transportation systems investments, and less quality service to the people.

> Even Mayor Bloomberg in New York City had to close down many firehouses as a result of our economy. This put many communities at a loss in adequate protection. In New York, Police pay is at an all time low.

Off shoring on its present course ultimately backfires on US industry. When collectively off shoring, they are disenfranchising their potential consumers who are the growing blue and white collar jobless in our nation.

It further compromises wages, and increases ongoing unemployment, regardless if it is not statistically recognized as the 'unemployment number'. Basically it further disenfranchises the citizens of the United States.

For the Strategic Future of Our Nation

4.2 The Economic Reform Plan

The welfare of the Nation is by definition, the welfare of the people. It is a financial matter. The level of *economic solvency* of the nation is the foundation for the financial welfare of the people.

Consequently, there is no way for the people of our nation to be assured of their health, safety and welfare unless, as a whole, it is sound financially.

There is no way to have a safe nation without fiscal soundness. An economy can easily fold in on itself which puts the nation at risk. This can be due to internal issues such as riots and insurrection while also being compromised in foreign policy due to having a lender's burden.

There is no way for our nation to have independence and autonomy, and standards in its foreign policy if it is not fiscally sound. The debt of the United States is lacking a horizon and is owned by foreign interest. This subjects our level of economic security to their agendas.

A *super power* in today's world is not a one if it becomes a third world economy with foreign owners of its debt.

In our communities, you cannot make a fair living, have a vision for your tomorrow, let alone even consider having a job tomorrow without fiscal soundness in the nation. This limits basic personal empowerment.

There is no way to enact and to back all the needed federal programs without fiscal soundness. As consequence, our communities and we suffer; but most importantly, our children do ! There is no way to further business development in this country if there is not fiscal soundness, and there is no way to recover lost jobs without a strong US dollar.

It is not a solution to just tax more, although some should be able to pay more. It is not a solution to just borrow more foreign money and then hope for the best. It is not a solution to attempt to close tax gaps on those who have outstanding taxes, as in this economy, they simply might not have the ability to pay. It is not a solution to further lose the value of the U.S dollar, or to offshore while telling you in the same breadth to go out and get new education and training in order to replace the job that you lost.

Simply, *deficits do matter*, and it is the commitment of my administration to achieve fiscal soundness, and in this way to achieve economic solvency. Our nation must be an economic super power in the 21st century in order to be viewed in today's world as a sustained one.

The New Deal, an Election 2008 Primer

4.2.1 The Economic Reform Act

By having a more local productive economy, we can more readily address our foreign debt. This enhances our level of national economic security. It is in this productivity where the United States can anchor itself against the forces that are encouraging it to become insolvent. It is the opportunity through productivity that this country can supply and feed itself, provide employment, and improve infrastructure for the standards of living that are inherent in a solvent economy. The Economic Reform Act is based firstly on a tactical move for enabling an economic cycle of debt and equity, secondly on new trade policies, and finally, a strategic plan for economic solvency.

We must first stabilize the US dollar, then correct the out flow of our economy, and then provide its strategic future. This requires in addition to a specific Economic Reform Act, that government and corporate reform likewise must be embraced. We then can invest in our country. This is in terms of our environment, renewable energy alternatives, and in lowering the cost of transportation and infrastructure. This empowers our communities to be employed, provide a financial means for our educational systems, and a national health care plan that we can all count on. What's more, we can ensure our Social Security system as an assured annuity in addition to other new investments in our newborns.

4.2.1 A- Tactical Reform: This is to put $1.2 trillion dollars back into our economy. It consists of cutting spending entitlements, earmarks, and corporate welfare. Then we must properly tax capital gains and reverse the tax cuts of the wealthiest 2% of the population. This is estimated to recoup over $300 billion dollars for the current year. Additionally we are to close the tax gap through proactive remedies. In foreign policy, we must close the door to the outflow of about $800 billion annually.

a. **Government Reform:** This must take place in order to stop borrowing and compounding foreign debt. The Government in of itself also has to become cost efficient otherwise it is not empowered to serve us. This is addressed firstly in the means of its information management, and is seen to be able to cut 65% of its overhead as discussed in Chapter 3 for a more efficient and effective system. This is while providing a better service level to the people.

b. **Corporate Reform:** This must take place where it has instead been self regulating in creating consumer demand and dependencies. The scope must include over all business practices such as M&As, and CEO/Board pay. By limiting the scale of M&A we provide a means for more participants in building the economy and benefiting from it. By limiting profit incentives, business can be strategically more stable in its contributions to our economy.

For the Strategic Future of Our Nation

4.2.1 B - New Trade Policy:

Fair trade is to be achieved through what is termed *'Balanced Trade Policy'*
from chapter 1. It is the intended means to provide fair parity in world trade,
re-instill incentives for local manufacturing, limiting foreign imports,
promoting more competitive local goods, and encouraging parity in labor and
wage internationally.

Balanced Trade - %import = %export

By limiting import volume into the United States to our export volume, the
price of the import will increase due to level of availability and in order to
obtain a reasonable profit margin.

It creates a market for local infrastructure development. Balanced Trade
dampens volume and provide less incentive for having manufacturing
operations offshore.

In Balanced Trade, we also do not have to be compromised on import price
with foreign governments based on our debt obligations to them.

When volume is the gating factor, then the volume that is normally coming
through our ports will have to go elsewhere.

By losing the offshore incentive, US manufacturers would not need a
domestic tax incentive, while also not needing to lose their workers.

The same principles for trade volume in manufacturing and textiles, can be
applied to agriculture, as well as the outsourcing of technology labor.

In earning an income, local manufactured goods become more affordable.

The New Deal, an Election 2008 Primer

4.2.1 C - Economic Solvency:

I view that only through economic solvency do we have true *national security*. Economic solvency is a strategic goal when in our current debt obligations. This is by being able to pay down interest rates radically, and eventually pay off US foreign held debt.

For the 21st century, economic solvency can be achieved and sustained strategically by moving toward an investment based economy. The premise to this is that Wall Street knows that it is better to invest the dollar than to spend it; to make the US Government the most treasured and assured client on Wall Street; and put the world financial markets to work for bettering the US economy.

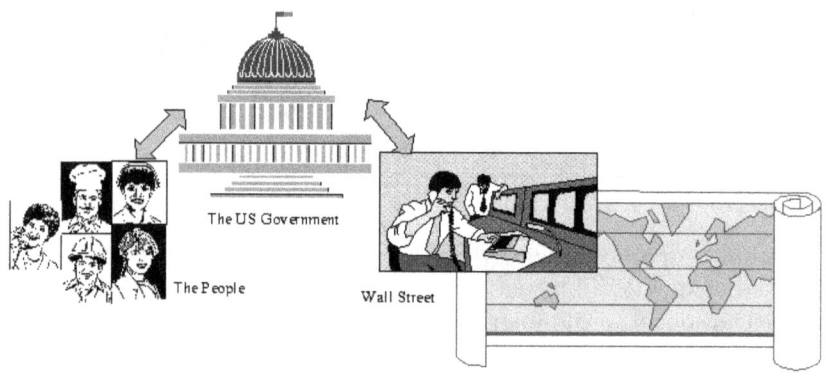

The bottom line is that the US Treasury is to become the most cherished investor as our proxy on Wall Street by institutional banks. This is described later in detail as *The United States Treasury Trust Management System* or USTTMS. The intended collateral affects are:

* Regaining of investor confidence as Wall Street demonstrates performance for the Treasury Dept.

* Obviating the need for more SEC overhead due to compliance incentives on the part of the market makers.

* Institutional and market investment strategies evolve through the liquidity of funds.

* For the *economic gyroscope*, to create momentum in the world economy due to new momentum on Wall Street.

For the Strategic Future of Our Nation

The paradigm for the US Treasury investment on Wall Street consists of three (3) basic components:

1- A Perpetual Investment Engine: It is also referred to here as *'PIE'*. It is to be composed of the institutional banking systems of this world, commercial investment firms and companies. Most of them make significant returns on their investment strategies, regardless of the state of the economy.

2- The Government/People: A client of this *Perpetual Investment Engine.* In other words, let the money managers do what they do best for you, but "under a performance / bid commitment".

For the banks, either make money or pay the equivalent. Simply, if they make money, we make money. This also assures an impetus for a predicted return and the needed market momentum on Wall Street.

The Government is the representative investor of American tax dollars and is actually hands off except for such purposes as investment performance audits by the Treasury Dept. It is not a regulator as much as a preferred client, and being the government has an *assured return.*

Market makers bid to commit the highest return on the use of small allocations on a quarterly basis. The one with the highest bid for return to the Government is awarded the quarterly contract.

If the market maker earns more on the use of the monies that was committed in the bid, then the market maker keeps the difference. If the market maker earns less, then it comes out of the market maker's pocket to make up the difference.

3- The Return On Investment: A reinvestment, and then going to pay for such things as the principal behind the national debt. This is applied to foreign debt interest rates; eventually towards existing debt; and then as a return to what was the 'tax payer', but functionally now is a monthly investor. i.e. 'We the People'.

If the return is not in dollars, then it is in having an empowered and robust federal government that can assist the states financially for needed programs.

As much as we still have needs for carts, we can't outright drop taxes and that is not what is suggested here. What is proposed is investing in our country.

The New Deal, an Election 2008 Primer

When considering the no-win of expected escalating trillions in debt, and then assuming that who ever is left from layoffs per month to pay for it all, we can instead evolve to a more productive investment *based econom*y for the 21st Century by putting Wall Street to work for us.

We are then in the position to fund all federal programs in a similar manner over a period of time.

This is intended to address the funding our environmental , energy, transportation, industry and agricultural reform, and for investments for our health care and educational systems.

For the Strategic Future of Our Nation

4.2.2 The Government Investment Bond

Government Bond Funded Grant Programs are intended to instill a new era of investment in our nation's future. The programs are intended to provide incentives to entrepreneurs in answering many of our needs and to finance sustainable solutions for them.

It is my view that any investment in the nation should be tax exempt or it undermines its very purpose. Government Investment Bonds are to be available to the public at large and to be purchased by institutional banks on Wall Street.

They are for improving the strategic future, physical health and intellectual capital of this country. These bonds are to be used for environment reclamation and recovery, energy research and venture programs, to develop transportation cost reduction, for our health care and educational system, and to close our extensive tax gap.

Each of these areas are considered opportunities for economic boom when handled in an ethical and regulated manner. It also invites venture capital from the private sector when seen as proof of vision.

Normally, the bond issue is to be about 4 times what is needed in liquidity. Here, 25% of the bond will remain liquid in the Treasury for immediate cash flow for the specific purpose or program that it is based on.

Government Investment Bond

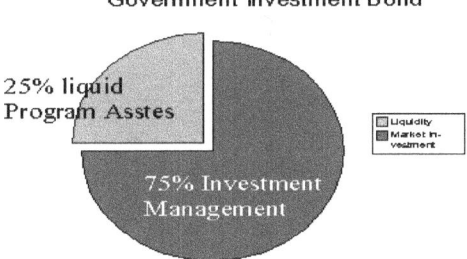

The other 75% is to be applied into the investment economy as described earlier. The ratio of profit vs. debt is adjusted accordingly by being tax exempt. This puts it on par with other current investment vehicles.

Debt financing for bonds, and equity financing of venture capital can be structured further in the institutional markets. In this manner, we can eventually achieve a very efficient economy that can effectively serve us while lowering the cost of taxes. We can then afford what FDR had seen for America as an 'Economic Bill of Rights'.

The New Deal, an Election 2008 Primer

4.2.2.1 Government Investment Bond Types

Due to varying purpose, 2 bond types are proposed to meet the needs of social welfare and program development. They are envisioned to be managed in Treasury investment portfolios based on category.

A- The Social Welfare Bond can be used for the purposes of nationalized health care funding and for education reform projects. Both applications are unique and can be enumerated such as in veteran health care and education benefits.

In general, 25% of the Social Welfare Bond is in liquidity for use, and 75% to be applied into the investment management system.

> In normal bond investment, returns are based on interest rates and are eventually taxed.

> Social Welfare Bond returns are tax exempt, and are based on the performance of the 75% of the bond. It is subject to the performance of the institutional banking systems. This allows returns to exceed the equivalent taxable return.

B- The Program Development Bond shares a similar 25%/75% split for use in managed returns, but allows the *'for use'* part to become eventually an equity stake in the program. This can then become structured like Equity Linked notes.

Program Development Bonds are for funding environment programs and energy research projects where the *for use* part is similar to Angel investments. The larger the portfolio of projects, the greater is the opportunity on returns on investment in these evolving industries. This stewards the venture capital incentive for mature members in the portfolio.

C- Treasury Investment Portfolio

During the *.com boom*, startups were over leveraged, and were not handled in a managed way. What equity they had was on paper only. Most required a greater maturity horizon to pay their debt when it was due.

In the case of the Treasury Investment Portfolio, like a garden, seedlings are managed to eventually grow into strong stocks. Market trading then on well founded IPO's can now be worth while.

For the Strategic Future of Our Nation

4.3 Tax Reform Plan

4.3.1 Our Patriotic Duty:

Second to dying for our country, the most patriotic duty we have is paying taxes. Currently for most workers, two (2) of every 5 days that we work are to support our federal government; where a third day can be considered toward state, city, and sales taxes. For every 40 hours that we get to work, 16 of those hours we are entitled to use to support our families, pay fixed costs, apply to savings, and invest for the long term, or if required, to pay back taxes.

4.3.2 Things to Consider:

The majority of tax payers visiting the IRS are the working poor. The question is, the way Congress was oblivious to the conditions of Walter Reed Army Hospital, are they also aware of the working poor trying to find ways to pay their taxes through a dysfunctional tax collection system?

Are we also aware that the tax breaks for the richest 2% of Americans that have not contributed to bettering the economy for all. For parity, has it also been considered that if this 2% did not have their tax break, that others, such as the working and the working poor could keep more of their hard earned income to better and improve their lives, if not just to stay afloat ?

Further, lets consider if the richest 2% did not have a tax cut, what that could do for our economy even if in fact conditions were not alleviated for others ?

What ever benefit, in all cases, it becomes ever more challenging when the value of the US dollar decreases, and when there is no efficiency or effectiveness in the management of tax collection.

Regardless when some day someone promises you that taxes can be lowered, they can't be without fixing a broken tax system first.

Regardless if we believe that we are over taxed or not, what is wrong is in allowing the reliance on a broken system that is ultimately intended to serve the people.

4.3.3 Efficiency and Effectiveness of Tax Collection

Efficiency and effectiveness of tax collection is in question when considering the huge tax gaps, questionable schedules, cuts, and the overhead of the Internal Revenue Service in of itself in dealing with their responsibilities.

It is my promise to pursue fare and effective tax collection that is cost effective in aiding our economy. To do this, the IRS as a department must be modernized for efficiency of work flow.

What incentive does the IRS employee have for the efficiency and effectiveness in doing their job when the processes in place are not efficient or effective ?

It is easier to opt out in order to get the desk cleared which does a disservice to both the IRS in its stated purpose and to the tax payer who it is ultimately serving.

What return on cost does the IRS provide in having broken processes to manage with ?

Any operation, that is <u>broken in procedures and processes,</u> ultimately wastes their budgets as opposed to effectively using them to serve that operation.

How do you fix broken processes when the Tax system achieves nothing further than painting itself into a corner in compounded complexities ?

<u>Functional Design of anything must be top down</u>, or there are functional bugs that are inherent in the outcome of our expectations.

As part of the Federal Information Plan from chapter 3, The US Treasury will also stand a major overhaul, and the IRS will be modernized.

It is to enable the IRS annual budget to not be wasted on inefficiency, but applied for cost effective results in managing the tax system.

This modernization is to provide the right tools and processes to put in place 'Fair Remedy Case Closure', reducing the tax gap, and to provide more graduated and balanced tax system.

For the Strategic Future of Our Nation

4.3.4 Minimum Tax Reform

We must help the Treasury Department and IRS to stream line costs based on the following:

4.3.4.1 Stabilizing the Falling US Dollar

As the dollar falls to pay our foreign debt, our taxes must go up to attain parity in the differences of currencies.

Through tactical reform, we are able to recoup about $300 billion annually, and through balanced trade regulation about another $800 billion. This allows about $1.2 trillion dollars back into our communities per year that can be circulated to stimulate the economy while not borrowing further.

This strengthens the dollar as it is being circulated in our communities and having its depreciation halted by no longer borrowing.

Our tax dollars no longer will escalate as our spending dollar will no longer depreciate.

Our war expenditures for the Middle East are also about $100 billion per year. In Chapter 6 in Foreign Policy this is obviated.

4.3.4.2 Tax Cuts and Questionable Schedules

This can be like *free falling*, where the experience is similar to the absence of gravity until we hit the solid ground of our debt's impact. The dollars that are saved by the top 2% in drastic cuts ultimately become of less value. Perhaps, those in the top 2% are smart enough to offset such a loss in their investment management, but ultimately they too are subject our nation's level of debt.

Tax schedules and cuts can be graduated for 'All' based on the level of Solvency vs. Debt Burden that the nation has. It is then no longer necessary to say *read my lips*. This allows flexibility for financial planning top down from the Government to the people it serves.

To offset the expectation of the erroneous tax gap collection benefit, there is upwards of $15 billion a year in capital gains that can pay for the operation and use of the IRS itself annually. In having a 12 month lead, and a 12 month budget provides the capability in place $30 billion in the markets annually. This means that on a per month basis of investment return can pay for this department of government. This can also help finance the Tax Gap as described in tax gap financing later.

The New Deal, an Election 2008 Primer

4.3.4.3 IRS Processes that Lead to No Where

Processes that lead to no where or without *fair and remedied schedule of conclusion* does nothing but (a)- cost the IRS's budget, and (b) - compounds the challenge of the tax payer in dealing with their escalating tax burden.

This can even motivate predatory lending practices to exploit the opportunity of the tax payer. This in turn just further burdens the tax payer in paying future taxes. The IRS must serve the people in order to serve the government cost effectively.

Accounting serves value, but its value is truly realized when given forethought and hindsight. Good accounting practices deal with balancing ledgers, where the cost of money itself is accounted for. Interest and penalties serve a purpose in the tax system. But without *scheduled and fair conclusion for remedy*, what was once perhaps $1,000.00 owed can become easily $10,000.00 owed.

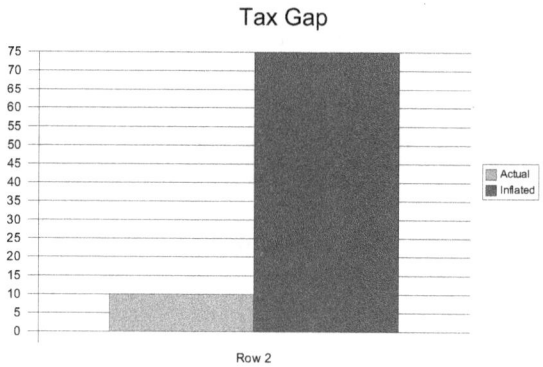

Multiply this by only 40,000 taxpayers and the IRS has an unmanageable level of $400,000,000 of *wishful thinking but unobtainable tax revenue* to *try* to collect. That is instead an actual $40,000,000 with reasonable interest to collect. Interest and fees are unrealistic venues when considering the related labor and processing costs in not collecting what looks good on the books.

For both the IRS, and the tax payer, it would be best to get the tax paid at $1,000.00 than having to deal with irresolvable and unrealistic interests, charges, fees and related costs in the wishful thinking of $10,000 * 40,000 taxpayers.

Both the IRS and the tax payer must work together to seek remedies where the IRS can obtain what is really due in a timely manner without disenfranchising the tax payer from being also future viable tax payer.

For the Strategic Future of Our Nation

Closure is in the IRS structuring the debt early on so that it can be paid through structured loans by the tax payer, and default where there is no possibility in collecting. This reduces the over all collection costs and time frames for closure. It helps provide a more accurate budget needed for the IRS.

It also requires far less levels of IRS management to work with lower sums of money than larger ones.

4.3.4.4 IRS Agents can do their work

IRS Agents can do their work when information is made available to them. Much of the time, information can already be on file, but not accessible to the agent. The agent under such circumstances will put the onus on the tax payer for reproducing this, as well as other laundry list items of information within a period of time that serves the convenience of the agents work load.

Through modernization:

- The agent has the right information access tools. The agent's work load becomes lighter for the same given case load.

- The tax payer has more bandwidth to meet the agent's time frame for the balance of a requested laundry list.

- Case tracking can be established for historical audits on case performance closure, as well as case inheritance.

- Case exceptions and escalation / resolution can be achieved more readily.

- Cost / benefit analysis can be measured on *Fair Remedy Conclusion*.

- Effectiveness of the agent for closures can be immediately scored.

- The tax payer can get on with their life sooner at less impact on livelihood.

The New Deal, an Election 2008 Primer

4.3.4.5 Tax Gap Financing:

The tax gap is to be remedied by:

1- Closure by financing with diminished penalty and interest there by obtaining a realistic gap that has a payment schedule.

2- Filling that gap in the interim by selling debt bonds to the institutional banking Fixed Income markets for financing closure.

To close the gap on a timely basis, I propose using a Social Welfare Bond type. By funding the actual value of the gap, it can be closed with a payment structure that goes towards the bond's payment.

As tax obligations are remedied, they are financed by the Tax Gap Bond. Further, the portion of the bond traded in the markets in return can apply to both investors and reinvested to build further robustness in the bond.

Federal Bonds in general can evolve to this investment model.

4.3.3.6 Municipal Sales Tax Bonds:

I propose that US States and municipalities collect sales tax on an annual basis. These taxes then can become invested in a similar manner as in Federal Investment Management.

Consider that normal sales tax devalues the spending dollar and the proposed builds it. It is a matter of keeping it in circulation, or it's dissipated in use.

In normal sales tax policy, if the original purchasing amount was $100 for example, you would pay about $20 on its use with a purchase value of $80 dollars. When this $80 is used, its purchase value is actually $70. In a logarithmic manner purchase value eventually dissipates to $0, with $0 sales tax dollars to offer.

In the proposed, annually sales tax dollars are collected and invested. As the economy flourishes, the sales tax dollars grow as investments and collection can be adjusted annually. This adjustment is based on the growth of commerce. The original purchasing amount circulates, and builds with new purchasing dollars from economic growth cycles.

This enables local economies to grow, and municipalities to forecast tax needs more accurately. Further, as being accepted in all states, offers parity to local commerce.

For the Strategic Future of Our Nation

4.4 – Corporate Reform Plan

Brooklyn Bridge, New York

The bottom line is the 'Quality in the Iron' that makes up our industries

4.4.1 Industry is the Backbone of our Country:

American corporations when ethically managed have provided the iron in the vertebrae of our nation. This is in terms of the industries they serve, the American citizens that they employ and the shareholder value they contribute in the economy.

Smelting iron was one of the duties and activities of pride for the people of Maoist China. The fault they eventually confronted was the impurities discovered in the iron that was so depended on for the strength of their nation. There were limited controls in place to assure the true quality of the resource intended.

Fundamentally, our corporations are creating the scoliosis in the backbone of our nation when having a near sighted approach to quarterly reports. Corporate high crime has been mostly in misrepresentation of share holder value, industry abuse, M&A manipulation and in off shoring of labor. In oversight, settled monitory measures can be viewed as the *net costs*, where the gross costs are generally in the areas of national and economic security, environmental impact, cost of human life, and / or human health, and in under minding the viability of the actual industries that they serve. This is while impacting the standards of work and living, of employee communities.

American corporations must have their ethics continually held accountable. They must serve their respective industries, and provide incentive for quality employee loyalty, and to provide an accurate representation of shareholder value.

The New Deal, an Election 2008 Primer

When uncompromised through sincere lobbyist reform, the American people can be assured of the federal and state government's due diligence and absence of complicity in dealing with corporate reform, the assurance of standards for true industry excellence, and the regard for fair labor representation. Corporations are to respect the environment and communities that they operate in.

A- Verification of Shareholder Value

In many cases, the smoke and mirrors *perception of shareholder value* has taken precedence above and beyond the ethics of corporate governance. This ultimately impacts the industries they serve, the people they employ, the communities of their employees, and therefore, their actual or lack of real contribution to the U.S. economy.

The '*perception of shareholder value*' is a *near sighted outlook* which only serves the immediate conveniences of corporate governance, and not the shareholders of a publicly held corporation, nor the employees and the communities that they operate in.

The values of corporate governance in the 20th century had become diluted in scope to "me, myself, and I". This ultimately short changed itself in the long run while undermining the quality in the industry of its focus. To get away with what one can in only having to meet minimal standards in best practice and compliance is not excellence in an industry or fair labor rights. It's just very expensive 'lip service' in offering the perception of a packaged sound bite termed '*excellence*'.

The federal government has the responsibility to ensure, in an unfettered manner for the American people, as well as our neighbors, that best standards of practice are clearly established at a very *high bar of sustainability*.

Settlements can be considered only part of the minimum in resolve, where restitution can call for the freezing of assets, assurance of Employee benefits, and pay out to shareholders, and those in class action suites; removal of patent rights; removal of listing in the Stock Exchanges; Prevention of diversification of the corporate vale into other industries, and M&A interests from other corporations; prevention of further business in the United States, or from an offshore alias; and serious jail time for entire corporate boards, and others identified for their complicity, as well as their personal assets confiscated for lost employee wages and related creditors. In less severe cases, settlements can be structured into funds such as to help finance municipal investment bonds. As a Government Investment Bond they will be tax exempt, and empower reconstruction funds for infrastructure and transportation investments.

For the Strategic Future of Our Nation

B- Industry Abuse:

Recent examples of corporate abuse are Enron, Arthur Andersen, Worldcomm, and CitiCorp. Others also fill the rosters of litigation such as Philip Morris Tobacco that was converted to Altria, which is becoming further diversified before legal action can find its teeth. A growing list includes the chemical industry, energy/oil, the food and airline industries, tobacco, pharmaceuticals, banking, credit and insurance. Some of the most notorious are Union Carbide which would not disclose the formula for a pesticide that killed over 15,000 people in India, and has affected the health of an additional 500,000 there; and General Electric who polluted the Hudson River with PCBs.

The bottom line is simply the 'quality in the iron' that makes up our industries; and therefore, the viability of the communities and how they must rely on the resultant economy.

Disasters: When disaster occurs from the near sighted actions of corporations, State Attorney Generals are typically the first to be called to champion the issues if not the NASD. The result is typically one to two 'fall guys' are picked. Fines are imposed on the corporate entity which then is back to *business as usual*; or where necessary to use a new corporate name.

These costs, although translatable to a settled monitory measure, are also expressed in ways where their measures cannot be ultimately assessed.

> **Industry Abuse Bond**: A viable application for fines can be for specific industry abuse, where this can be a mix of Social Welfare and Program Development bonds. The funds are to be used specifically for re mediating correction of the abuse.

Exploitation: In reforming predatory lending, where the amount of unscrupulous profits can be established and from what banks lenders, can then be structured into bond investments to pay back exploited consumers. Additionally they can be used to leverage in the markets as institutional investment instruments on behalf of the US Government.

> **Banking Taxes and Penalties** are discussed in detail later, but suffice to note, that this money can eventually be paid back to the exploited consumer. This further corrects predatory creditors as in needing to stand behind their debt in the banking community. It adds the incentive to have investments perform well on behalf of the government.

The New Deal, an Election 2008 Primer

C- M&A Gluttony:

The M&A *big fish/little fish* practice must be further regulated. This is to limit monopolies from occupying the economy. This occupation limits growth of employment in the United States by having less employers and roles available. Regulation is to further limit the growing unemployment due to the disappearance of companies that have been swept up as M&A victims.

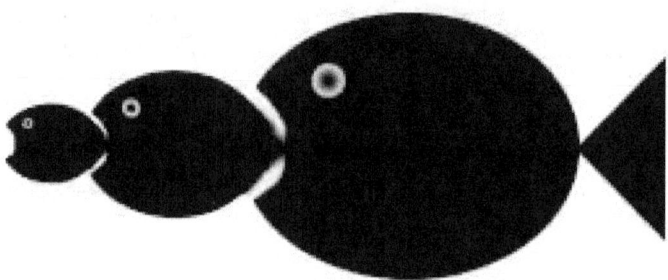

Ultimately the big fish will starve once the little ones are all eaten. It's a matter of curbing corporate gluttony.

M&A Restructuring Settlement: I propose that industries which become non-competitive will be decomposed into new market members.

Any bank can be decomposed like AT&T which might have to embrace this again. Companies can be formed that can reenter the economy where with more players there is more market volatility.

For the Strategic Future of Our Nation

D- Corporate Offshore Sanctions and Usage:

Further, U.S. corporations must be prevented from doing business with foreign countries where there are U.S. sanctions. An example is once again Halliburton through a subsidiary shell getting around the loop holes of current law. It prevents the sanction from having the effect of its purpose. It also demonstrates that corporate policy has no allegiance to the country (USA) that it is based in.

Offshore Tax Act: For US based companies whose resources are off shored, or who do business directly or indirectly with countries that have US sanctions, based on the Balanced *Trade Policy*, are to pay an offshore *operations tax*.

For Sanction Abuse, corporations are no longer allowed to do business, nor operate within in US borders, or must forfeit all profits as a tax for any business benefit with the sanctioned country.

For Non-Sanctioned Abuse, product prices of large conglomerates like Wal-Mart can then offer a fair purchase parity with local based conglomerates which then drives a greater volume of municipal sales tax volume.

4.4.2 Compliance Management:

For State Attorney General filings, federal and state government need to have reciprocity to access corporate documentation and for case management. The State Attorney General's Office is normally the first place where issues of compliance occur. In order to avoid post facto case load (disasters), and to assist in early detection of non-compliance, corporations should be required to file corporate compliance documentation on a quarterly basis with the State Attorney General's Office in the state of incorporation.

Through Federal Corporate Records Management, Attorney Generals from other states where a corporation conducts operations, other than the one they are incorporated will be able to access and file issues pertaining to the out of state corporation. It is up to the State Attorney General to provide the industry specific compliance forms, and it is up to the federal government to maintain such records on behalf of the states. For industry audit filings, corporations in the industries they serve are to file on a 6 month basis with the State Attorney General's office. This is for compliance ranking with state and federal standards for the specific industry(s) that they serve. This compliance is to include in scope, all on shore, and offshore activities in the industry in question, where compliance is based on 'on shore standards'.

4.5 Trade Reform Plan

'The right of every businessman, large and small, to trade in an atmosphere of freedom from unfair competition and domination by monopolies at home or abroad' , FDR - The Economic Bill of Rights

To achieve fair trade, it must be balanced. Trade can be balanced or imbalanced. Trade regulated by volume and not by price enables trade to become economically balanced in parity.

4.5.1 Today's World of Trade in the United States of America

Trade, the exchange of goods, or goods for moneys is in our history books as to when culture has first been documented. In history, it is what distinguishes a culture such as in establishing trade routes.

Simple examples are the Silk Route from China to Europe, and the spice routes in later history from the Americas to Europe; and the slave trade routes to the colonials.

When looking at my PC, television, appliance, or even my clothing, I ask myself, what was actually made in the United States? When looking for a company's help desk on line for a product or service; one must realize also that the call is answered by one most likely in India. During tax time, we also have to realize that someone over seas will be more than likely preparing our returns.

Years ago I preferred a Japanese car over any other as getting more for the money. It was also a more reliable car.

For the Strategic Future of Our Nation

If you ask yourself the question: 'What body of Congress is responsible for our position in World Trade? , it is somewhat of a head scratch. When going to both the Senate and House web sites you will find committees where part of their mandate is US Labor, where another deals with agriculture, and then there is the subcommittee on China.

When looking at the Department of Commerce website, one finds that focus is on exports, and not regulating imports.

Bush Statement on Leveling the Playing Field

"When you hear me talk about negotiating trade agreements, really what we're doing is leveling the playing field. What we're really doing is making sure America has a chance to compete on the same terms that people can sell into our market. And if they don't respond . . .we'll use the tools necessary to make sure that the playing field is level."

President George W. Bush
Appleton, Wisconsin,
March 30, 2004

Consider, there are over 7,000 idle shipping containers on our shores from imported goods.

Shipping containers sit on our shore going no where

They can also be used these days to build houses and structures, and/or sold at discount to the steal industry to recycle. But otherwise, due to trade imbalance, this idle count will just continue to grow.

The New Deal, an Election 2008 Primer

Bush can spin the naive and the foolish, but facts are that we export raw materials that are imported more than a magnitude back to the US in finished goods. As our economy and costs are inflated, what finished goods we could export would be too expensive for other third world economies.

About exports, if you are looking for a job these days, it could already have been off shored. It can also have being taken locally by a friendly visitor, through a guest worker program, at half the expected wages who sends this money back to their home and family.

On the up side, we can pat ourselves on the back in saying how we are really helping other countries in developing their economy, although it is at a cost to our own. If looking at the down side, we can say philosophically that manufacturing is tending to be more economically accomplished offshore, as well as everything else.

But if we need to refurbish our military with equipment, would the Government based on the lowest bid, offshore this as currently how cost effective and resilient are our steel and manufacturing industries when under demand to serving our nation ?

This is all well and good for offshore entrepreneurs who have profited in helping us out. It could appear that they have our best interest in mind by providing inexpensive products and services. We are really saving purchase money which we should do as in earning less these days due to this. This ultimately though provides diminishing returns like our current sales tax.

Wal-Mart, as well as its suppliers, have gone offshore in order to provide high volume imports at 'below market prices' in order to serve American consumers better. For the accountant, it makes good business sense when looking at the books.

When caught up in economic downturn it is also unfair for anyone to 'have to buy American' in the US when the offshore solution/alternative saves serious money. As individuals, we the consumer are survivors before being philanthropists.

But given our eroding manufacturing, agriculture, and service base; and given the unbending growth of debt in this country, the question is 'who are we as the consumer ?' Eventually our industries, and services will impact all of us when our job is replaced by a foreign visitor or offshore alternative.

This means, eventually, regardless of volume import at cheap prices, if you don't have the money for them, it won't matter really how cheap, or inexpensive they are. Predatory lending in the credit card industry in the long

For the Strategic Future of Our Nation

run also won't help us out of the jam that we are getting ourselves in as a consumer, but instead compounds this further.

In a similar manner when hearing that automating will save on labor costs, one has to ask the obvious question, who will the automation serve if we are all automated out of our jobs ?

When continuing on our present course, more and more of us will wonder even how to afford a cup of coffee. We have to realize that this is a Gordian knot that we are all apart of and will be eventually affected by before we can actually be willing to look at viable solutions.

Vague solutions offered on podiums by politicians talk about 'new education' and training for the 'worker' whatever that might mean. This is while others talk about new industries and others just want to import guest workers.

I believe that this is all well and great when wanting to blue sky for tomorrow's world, but the growing many of us are confronted with how to pay the rent or mortgage and put food on the table right now.

Further, why would it not occur to these speakers that any new education is also something that offshore and guest workers would like too ?

The most demonstrative action by government has been to place artificial price increases on some imports. This only lowers the price of offshore labor to make up the difference. Other US business, that off shore everything but the 'home office' in the name of the 'free market economy', just cry fowl to Congress.

In affect, our government is not providing a solution for 'trade' that can really deal with our tomorrow. This is partly due to our representatives finding, in a similar manner to the clothes we have on, that most of the lobbyists that are willing to pool towards the next campaign fund do represent offshore import interests, regardless if their official place of business is in the US.

Irony also is that the home office of many business's in making good business sense are also off shoring their home office for tax purposes like Halliburton.

The 'one for all, and all for one' viewpoint cannot grab a foot hold in the changing playing field. That is unless we really examine the mechanics of supply and demand where it is from the standpoint of volume instead of price; where in the case of volume we look at managing it from the standpoint of domestic, or import.

The New Deal, an Election 2008 Primer

4.5.2 Balanced Trade Plan:

The premise in balanced trade is that trade regulated by volume and not by price enables trade to become economically balanced. By limiting import volume into the United States, the price of the import will increase due to level of availability and in order to obtain a reasonable profit margin.

Regulating import volume makes it costly to offshore. This offers business two incentives to hire American labor.

Proposed is an Off Shore Usage Tax for those institutions which offshore their labor. This is to encourage hiring Americans locally. This tax can be applied towards unemployment benefits to American workers. It should become un-American not to hire US citizens. In addition to *offshore usage taxes,* this will dampen volume and provide less incentive for moving manufacturing operations offshore.

This leaves the choice of not doing business in the United States, which represents the largest base of consumers or doing it in compliance with Balanced Trade.

By loosing the offshore incentive, US manufactures are encouraged to make domestic infrastructure investments and will need local US workers.

The same principles of 'trade volume' in manufacturing and textiles, can be applied to agriculture, as well as the outsourcing of technology labor. There are a multitude of work visa based visitors in the US, where in fact most institutional banks use them for their IT needs. Additionally, this compromises free market trade in terms of pricing for the technical labor pool in this country.

Any company that so wishes to import foreign labor, should be required to not under price going rates for the standard of living in the United States, and prove to the Department of Labor, and not the State Department, that an American cannot fill the job.

4.5.2 Formation of the Trade Committee:

Congress will have to step up to the plate in terms of forming The *Trade Committee.* This must include as its members and representatives that also sit on the labor, industry and agriculture and services committees. If there is no cross representation within the Trade Committee, its formation will only serve for the purposes of lip services in managing fair trade.

For the Strategic Future of Our Nation

4.6 Economic Solvency

Putting Wall Street to Work for The United States of America

4.6.1 Consideration:

I would never suggest nor recommend that one take a crap shoot in the financial markets I also do not believe in private investment accounts for one's Social Security. In suggesting this, the Bush administration is throwing the people an artificial sense of empowerment in determining their own destiny. It's like putting you in a row boat in rough seas, and then saying, *now you are the captain of your own ship. Best of luck !*

Simply, it's okay to be in the markets as long as you can afford to, but most can't and shouldn't gamble their future. Also most of us will simply need as much money as possible before retirement age. This is regardless if smart enough to make the right investments at the onset.

But then the question remains, 'why not *put Wall Street to work for us as the United States of America?*

Given the gamble and the scandal, the lack of SEC over site in the past few years since the ".com implosion", and its backlash on levels of investor confidence, we could easily dismiss considering this. The stymied lesson learned by some who are now broke, is that only the corrupt make money on Wall Street by fleecing the foolish.

But then consider, if given specific guidance with compliance requirements by the US Government, and managed honestly and ethically, what can Wall Street and its investment institutions really accomplish?

The New Deal, an Election 2008 Primer

Historically Wall Street had grown since the 70's into its own self serving world where regulation is after the fact. It has sophisticated technology that is specific for investment strategy management. It earns fortunes for those at the helm of its investment strategies.

Regardless if the deck is not stacked, those at the helm can not view Wall Street as another Las Vegas, or Casino, as their business is to make money with money, and not to lose it gambling.

In current wealth management, institutional banking private client services handle over $10 trillion in assets per year for the chosen 2% of the richest people in our country. These *private clients* obviously benefit, or they would not entrust Wall Street private client services in financial institutions to manage their money.

Consider that the Government is also about $10 trillion in dept which is growing. In lieu of how we have been doing things since the days of lords and surfs, because we have the *world markets* at hand I am proposing an *investment based economy*.

Specifically, I am not suggesting that anyone gamble in stocks but instead to look at how the world financial markets, international banks, and investment management firms actually operate. Then, to consider making the Treasury Department a *client with a guaranteed return*.

In financing our government, historically, taxes from the people have always paid the way. No matter how we want to look at it, this can only sum up to nothing more than 'tax and spend'. This model diminishes the original purchase value for goods and services when re-taxing the same dollars.

We also know from common Wall Street sense, that when given the opportunity, it is better to invest the dollar than to just spend it.

For thousands of years, there has always been the cart, and in the 20th Century, the automobile was invented. For thousands of years there has been taxes, where in the 20th Century, Wall Street was born.

The question now becomes, 'should our government, the people, and our economy be relegated to just carts, while those at the helm of Wall Street are driving Ferrari's ?'

Would it benefit to have the Government invest our tax dollars based on an assured return instead of just spending with diminishing returns?

For the Strategic Future of Our Nation

The question evolves to, 'could our government apply investment wisdom into a viable paradigm, where The Treasury Department is the most valued client on Wall Street, which acts as our proxy, the tax payer; and where quarterly returns on Treasury tranche allocations are to pay down the interest rates, and amounting debt, and where eventually this can allow infrastructure development, etc ?

If the Treasury maintained the circulation of liquidity in commerce it could obviate diminishing returns. By putting Wall Street to work for the US tax payer, as Wall Street works for the financial institutions that do business in the US, then we have also stepped into a new era of tax based managed investments.

A portion of our tax dollars through the Treasury, can be invested on a business quarter basis as an example, where eventually it can gain parity with our existing foreign debt interest burden.

Consider how we can put the world markets, and those at its helm such as J.P. Morgan/Chase, The Salomon's, the Goldman Sachs, Warburgs, and the rest of the market makers on Wall Street _to work for America_ by having the Treasury Department act as our proxy.

We have a means to deal with our foreign debt where the alternative is to each pay by 2014, about $45-60,000. Personally I do not have access to this kind of money and only wish I did for other purposes.

If we do not have tax reform as described earlier, and stay on our present course in tax and spend, while borrowing from ready foreign lenders the tax gap will become insurmountable. This direction has limited life expectancy as what will the government under such circumstances do. And how will it affect our lives.

Instead, we can establish a United States Treasury Trust Management System (USTTMS) where in acting as our proxy can become the most valued and respected client of these market makers.

The USTTMS is to represent an active participant in the world markets with an assured return. The world markets via approved banking and investment institutions is considered a perpetual investment engine for many government investment instruments. They are to include a portion of our current tax dollars; corporate tax, fines and penalties; and government program development and social welfare investment bonds.

The New Deal, an Election 2008 Primer

4.6.2 The Perpetual Investment Engine (PIE)

Earlier the Perpetual Investment Engine, *PIE* was described to incorporate 3 basic components. These are a 'market engine' that is made up of the institutional banks and market makers; the client user of the engine which is the Treasury on behalf of the people, and the Return on Investment, or ROI component for managing returns. They are summarized as:

1- A Perpetual Investment Engine is to be composed of the institutional banking systems of this world, commercial investment firms and companies.

2- The Government/People are a client of this Perpetual Investment Engine. The banks produce returns. If the market maker earns more on the use of the monies than was committed in the bid, then the market maker keeps the difference. Or the return comes out of their pockets.

3- The Return On Investment is a reinvestment, and then going to pay for such things as the interest, and then the principal behind the national debt.

A- In Tax Reform, obligation becomes naturally graduated:

In paying off foreign interest and debt, the road to economic solvency is paved. Its natural evolution enables returns to be shared with tax payers. This can be in dollars, or in benefits and programs afforded by the government.

Those that avoid taxes end up getting less of a return than those who don't avoid paying taxes. Consequently, roll backs for the chosen result in less investment return for them.

B- Rebuilding Market Confidence

If the market makers are given the opportunity to work within such a paradigm, they are given latitude they have never had.

In other words, they can be an integral component in building confidence in the capital markets.

Most of all, as the capital markets grow, so do we. Additionally, we the people will have more confidence in the capital markets if our government demonstrates its confidence. It is not a question of more regulation or ducking from stock hype advice, but instead a question of an earned trust by the people that the market makers can achieve when their greed has to innovate due to government parity.

For the Strategic Future of Our Nation

C- The Treasury Department's Success with Companies

In 1984 the Treasury Department had a Chrysler Management Group. Should we have airlines, and other industry bailout groups there now and in the future. Or should we have instead a management interface into the institutions that make up the burgeoning 21st Century world economy; and then be able to pay down our debt, correct inflation, and allow our industries a level playing field instead ?

D- World Trade Parity

World Trade can be financed on a level playing field for the benefit of more than a few, and industries which are allowed to be competitive will galvanize. Those that are not competitive will shift globally.

E- Assuring National Security

Consider we have much to pay for these days, and more to come due to September 11th. Also, in addition to our outstanding debt, we now have to pay future debt for the few wars that we have been creating.

National security is ultimately based on economic security. Who really owns our debt, which is currently mostly foreigners, own us. This is no matter how many wars we have. We can only demonstrate solvency through the payback of this debt.

F- Affording Community Programs

'Leave No Child Behind' will mean something instead of just 'endorsed lip service'. State budgets will not have to be slashed and educational programs will not have to compromise on the quality of tomorrow's America's human capital.

The government can also have the cash flow to afford vocational transition training programs for those who wish to evolve into other industries as described in chapter 5 in employment reform.

Basically, with ample real cash flow, Congress can have other things to focus on as opposed to how to get their particular part of a limited budget for one program over another. Earmarks will be obsolete, as they can represent their own Bill on the Floor.

More decisions will be based on nonpartisan agreements which means more legislation will be efficiently and cost effectively accomplished.

The New Deal, an Election 2008 Primer

G- Foreign Aid

Foreign aid will not compromise domestic spending. At present just how do we plan on providing foreign aid without compromising our domestic budgets ?

Consider this - we will actually be able to pay to feed our own starving kids and care for our own aging; that is besides others.

H- Sharing the Investment Model

Other countries can also key off of our investment based system.

4.6.4 Physics of the Perpetual Investment Engine

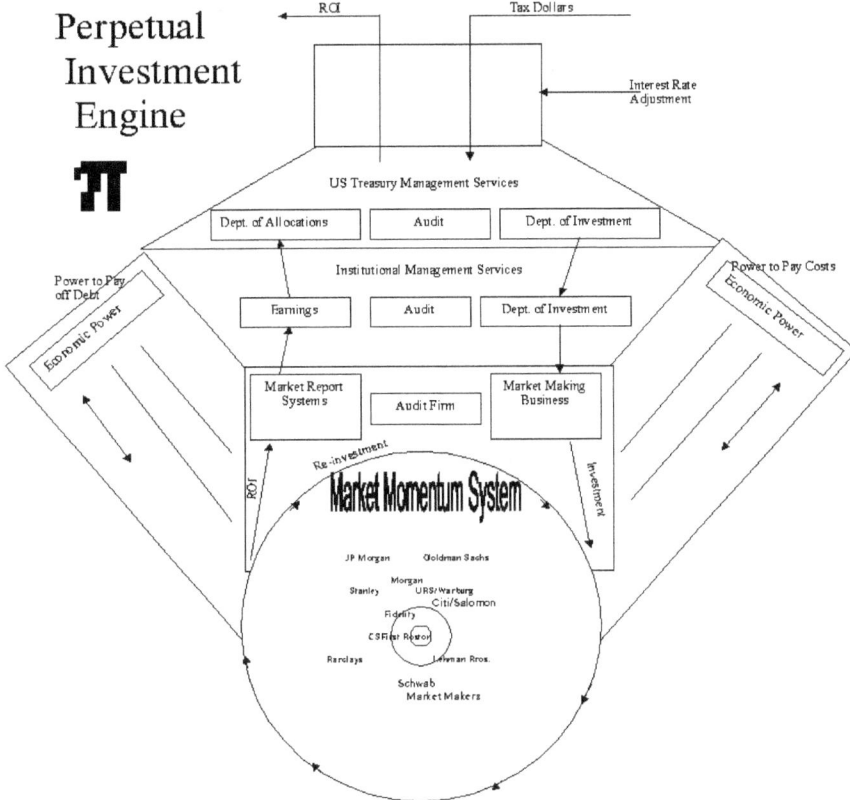

Perpetual Investment Based Engine

The United States Treasury Trust Management System (USTTMS) consist of departments of investment, audit, and of earnings. This is to sit on top of the Perpetual Investment Engine.

For illustrative purposes only, the perpetual investment engine (PIE) above, appears in similar fashion as the combustion engine. For those who are not car mechanics, this could easily be depicted as an electric generator.

The principles are the same for deriving power for the economic gyroscope. Its source of fuel is the tax system and government investment vehicles. The application of the fuel is into the world markets managed by money makers.

The power derived is represented as the commited return on investment. The notion of momentum and torque for our gyroscope is a metric of power for fuel used in replenishing our economy. We can over come foreign debt.

The New Deal, an Election 2008 Primer

4.6.5 Perpetual Investment Engine Rules of Engagement

Market maker business is to consist of any form of lucrative investment management that complies with any regulatory requirements that are legislated through Congress and set forth by the Treasury Department for managing a financial market contracts.

The USTTMS management of PIE works like a plenum into and out of the market momentum system. It consists of two distinct and segregated layers. They are the US Treasury Trust Management Services, (*USTTMS*) , and the institutional management services that are unique and separate to each institution.

There are peer to peer functional areas with each layer in terms of funds flow. It enables the government side to communicate to the institutional side and from the institutional side to the government side

4.6.5.1 Cooperative Management Layers:

Co-operative management layers are between the institutional investment momentum services and the world markets which consists of accredited institutions.

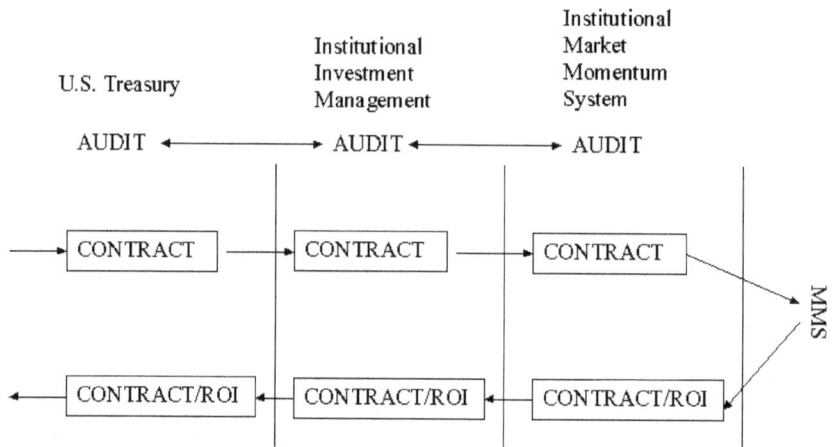

This provides assured layers of clear audit management where each layer reports to an external layer of audit management.

If not the lowest layer, it has a layer below which reports to it.

4.6.5.2 - The United States Treasury Trust Management System

The USTTMS is to be a unique department in the U.S. Treasury. It is to be responsible for the operational interface from the standpoint of the U.S. Treasury into the perpetual investment engine's contract management systems. It is to consist solely of government employees which are not permitted to have a conflict of interest with the business of the USTTMS.

The scope and focus in conflict of interest is to be defined, and where laws that do not exist, are legislated by Congress to maintain the standards of conflict of interest observance.

It is to provide the market contract bid/award system, and receive prescribed funds from the U.S. Treasury Dept. as determined necessary by the Federal Reserve.

For newer institutions, such funds can sponsor a pilot that represents a fraction of a percent of available for investment.

These funds can be furthered in volume and scope as time proves a refined and effective investment engine model that best meets the needs of the government.

4.6.5.3 USTTMS Audit Management

For the Treasury and the markets, a view of the layer below is accessible through the Federal Information Management System described in Chapter 3.

The view can be based only on a market contract, or view as defined as necessary. Each view has external counterparts that are separate and independent from it. Generally this is for the purposes of congressional and treasury oversight and for access by the SEC.

Expertise is to be adequately provided in each layer of audit. This is to carry out and maintain observance of audit controls and the observance of materiality for the business at hand.

Each layer of audit is to be accountable for the checks and balances of contract funds that are coming in from an upper layer, and return of funds, and related ROI to the upper layer.

Each layer of audit is to be accountable for the checks and balances of contract funds that are going to, or for return of funds from and ROI from a lower layer.

The New Deal, an Election 2008 Primer

Each interface component is to functionally receive, manage, and hand off funds between its upper layer, the USTTMS, and the market momentum system. In each case there is a higher and subordinate peer.

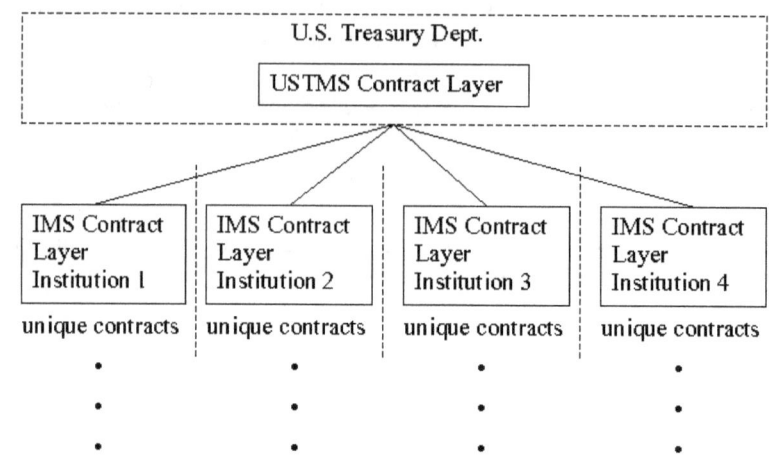

4.6.5.4 - Wall Street Transparency

For institutions and market makers, communication to the USTTMS is through a well defined interface consisting of the *Dept of Investment, Audit, and the Dept of Earnings.*

To participate, each institution maintains a separate institutional services layer. It functions as a cooperative interface between contract layers with USTTMS that is to provide transparency and segregation of job duties.

Transparency on behalf of the institution is with respect to the U.S. Treasury Management services layer (USTTMS) which is to have complete audit accessibility.

The USTTMS is to maintain controls in observance of securities fraud legislation and instituional market performance observance.

Segregation is to isolate the detailed business of the institution from other institutions.

4.6.6 Benefits to the US Treasury, The People, and to Wall Street

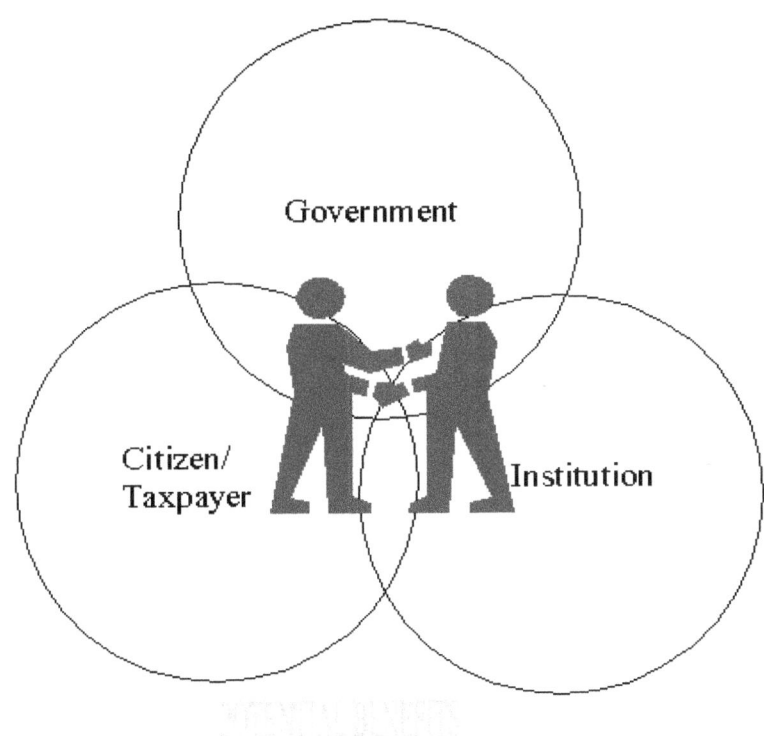

When well regulated, where there is profit, or restitution, institutions can perform for the U.S Treasury even far more profitably that for their private clients.

This is to benefit the US Treasury, and therefore, the tax payer. It is to then benefit Wall Street where they can make an honest and ethical profit.

These benefits are enumerated in the following pages of this section. Their order is benefits to the U.S. Treasury, the people, and then to institutions.

Demonstrated in these benefits is stabilizing and providing a proactive low inflation economy. This can afford program development for our environment reform and energy alternatives; and in building and maintaining our infrastructure and transportation systems that lower the cost of operations. We can further afford community, social, and personal empowerment programs like nationalized health care, quality education systems, employment, and assured Social Security at a minimum.

4.6.6.1 Benefits to the U.S. Treasury

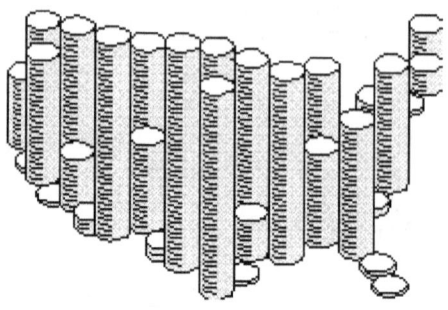

A- Obviating Tax and Spend Policies

Economic indicators are generally after the fact, by about a month. They can be misleading. The Gross Domestic Product and Consumer Price indices, with or without associated debt, can imply the same thing but have significant differences as real indicators.

With the USTTMS, new indicators can emerge based on projection of returns. This enables a more accurate commitment of "read my lips," based on forecast tax burdens with respect to national costs and national debt.

We can have 'Pay as you Go', as budgets on the floor can be proposed and debated more effectively based on such indicators and public sentiment in terms of overall ROI as opposed to furthered tax burdens.

B- Reinforce National Security through Economic Security

Being able to buy back debt from foreign owners', means that the US is less compromised by them.

In the Constitution, Section 9 on *Limits on Congress* states that '*no government official can accept titles by foreign powers*'. Removal or limitation of foreign ownership of national debt could limit claims of influence from foreign powers.

It further places a cap on escalating debt. By limiting the window of exposure for a particular debt issue, reassures credit worthiness while lowering the sphere of influence associated with its ownership. This empowers the interest from additional buyers. Debt which is bought back enables new debt to be financed locally in more productive ways.

For the Strategic Future of Our Nation

C- Ability to Stabilize Economic Cycle

The economic cycle is perceived ideally as a perfect circle where structured debt and leveraged liquidity are its points of balance. It can be viewed as a gyroscope in effect to balance the economy.

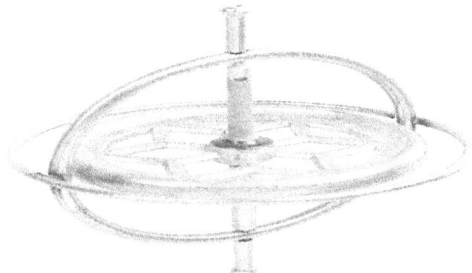

The Economic Gyroscope

Reality is that if a gyroscope is over compensated at one point or another, similar to excessively leveraged liquidity, then the cycle must rebound to conservative debt structure to maintain balance. But compromised by deficit spending, this re-balancing cannot momentarily be readily achieved. By being able to cap debt escalation, the cycle can be eventually re-balanced.

D- Demonstrate Confidence in the Capital Markets

After the '.com boom', personal investor confidence was lost in the markets. This further got exacerbated when Enron took its tumble that disenfranchised many of its employees and share holders.

In war, confidence and moral are obtained by having the opposing force on the run or retreat. A strong economic foundation puts recessions and depression in retreat.

In building a strong economic foundation, between the world markets and the US Treasury, rebuilds the confidence that was previously lost. Confidence is returned to the investor as it is demonstrated by the U.S. Government

This will help lower inflated market prices. Confidence is further assured by the ability of the Treasury to more easily recover moneys that have been erroneously lost in the markets. If and when there is a 'next Enron', the Treasury can cease capital assets when detecting market non-compliance. This will help encourage free enterprise to do its honest best in compliance and representation to its investors.

The New Deal, an Election 2008 Primer

E- Enable Unrealized Sources of Liquidity to Stabilize Debt.

Provides incentives, based on near term returns, for local debt owners to take on and finance new debt issues. The Equity Linked Note is a good financial structure to be evolved for this. It is described in the next few pages.

Debt which is financed for reclamation projects as an example, can be traded, where part of its profits pay bond coupons which can be placed in an enterprise's or new venture stock, or private venture grant fund, for a future public offering.

A mature and well gardened startup, that was managed through Government Investment Bonds, can be sold out of a government portfolio to mezzanine financiers.

This allows a path from government programs of bonds to grants for new business startups for possibly going public.

F- Expenditure Planning in Gains Expectations

Dealing with a deficit based economy in a recession is comparable to a race condition with hopes as historical evidence that a defense industry will aid to the recovery.

Wars have always created an industry for economic recovery, but it is not as strategic compared to the investment based economy.

Government budgets can be allowed latitude based on investment margin instead of a fixed amount of tax debt. This allows the flexibility to prioritize program funding where based on market performance budgets can expand accordingly.

This allows the ability to restore surpluses while lowering overall tax requirements. Restoring surpluses can be accomplished based on type.

As for Social Security annuity assurance, scheduled payments can be made toward the lock box and based on the % ROI which lowers the overall tax burden to make up for a dwindling lock box. Breaking out a % of ROI would be based on the overall ROI from an investment contract cycle.

Priorities can be reached, to afford more programs, by more efficient non-partisan legislation. This reduces government time and cost for legislation. It enables the ability to start giving back to the people.

For the Strategic Future of Our Nation

4.6.6.2 Benefits for the People

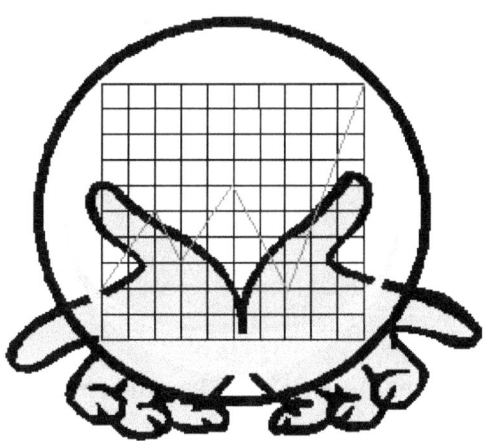

Benefits for the people are to further personal empowerment. This ranges from taxpayer benefits, ability to structure outstanding tax burdens, assurance in retirement income, and more confidence in one's financial future.

A- Tax Benefits

Consistent with the idea of tax returns, interest, penalties fines, and workable alternatives can be provided based on the *Return On Investment* (ROI).

Tax payers should expect ROI less than that which is allocated by the Treasury Dept. Here tax avoidance means less if not any ROI. It can be applied as credit toward outstanding interest and penalties.

ROI also provides a mutual insurance policy to avoid outstanding burdens by the tax payer while assuring the Treasury of an amount guaranteed by the tax payer. ROI itself is neither considered nor construed to be taxable income.

B- Remedy for Outstanding Tax Burdens

Tax burdens can be borrowed against from the Treasury based on normal debt interest rates. Based on the *Tax Reform Plan* earlier, interest is fair interest based on market interest rates. Penalties should be nominal as to promote investors and not tax cheats.

The IRS can borrow against profits to fund closing of the tax gap as described in Tax Reform.

The New Deal, an Election 2008 Primer

C- Retirement Income Assurance

Work harder is to imply working smarter for one's future retirement assurance. Currently this incentive does not exist. Today, working harder implies no win and working smarter implies shortcuts.

Social Security can be construed as a separate entity or a component of the investments (burden) by the tax payer. In either case the people are assured by Treasury financial statements that such surpluses are regarded and assured.

Surpluses likewise can aid in medical benefits as well as living income, rental/mortgage assistance, as is described later.

D- Confidence in the Capital Markets and Government

Confidence in the capital markets is obtained by observing the leadership's confidence, and observing this through the demonstration of accountability based on checks and balances. This is to be based on accountant/SEC oversight groups and councils that were legislated subsequent to Enron to assure the SEC's effectiveness.

In demonstrating accountability and oversight guidance the government demonstrates such virtues as purpose for trust and goodwill toward the tax payer. Good will normally begets goodwill.

E- Obviating Hostile / Predator Loan Market

As a vehicle when surpluses are available, loans can be structured through the government and then resold into a fair market place. The government will maintain a list of preferred creditors. Banks that demonstrate quality service, and long term fixed rate loan options are within the bounds of the US Government' s criterion for fair debt obligation.

This is described as in one example in later in Infrastructure Reform as *personal residential loans.*

F – Taxpayer Empowerment

Tax payers are intended to eventually become investors in the economy. As an investor, the tax payer is expected to gain personal empowerment and perhaps interest as an active community member. As quality of life improves, the tax payer becomes an investor in the economy. This also yields a sense of accountability while expecting it from their elected officials.

For the Strategic Future of Our Nation

People who can afford to be active community members generally want to vote more often and consistently, and seek to be informed as the basis of their vote. This avenue is further described under *The Economy of Active Representation* in Chapter 3, on Goverment Reform.

As active members, complacency in the "system" can be overcome where greater involvement is sought. As investors, reform where is determined as needed can be through groups that the tax payer associates him/herself with.

G- Improved Disposition for Investments

Disposable income is a luxury which today is only for a few. Pension funds today are also a non reality.

401Ks and IRAs or self directed IRAs are within reach given a liquid economy by being invested with confidence.

Investment incentives can be provided to apply ROI as principle in these vehicles and borrow against if need be without penalty as they are themselves tax exempt ROI.

A stable economy allows a more reliable market for retail trading that can boom even far greater than the .com boom.

As we have reliable foundations for investments and startups, beyond Day Trading, the public could benefit from the markets as active investors.

4.6.6.3 Potential Benefits for Participating Institutions

A- Opportunity to Increase Asset Portfolios

This provides additional latitude for the creation of investment vehicles that can improve overall profitability to institutions while minimizing tax costs.

Similar to how the GSA bid process works, accredited institutions are viewed in a similar manner as a vendor contract allocation.

For example, the Treasury has a % of tax dollars split into a number of tranches, or an array of investment opportunities in increasing amounts on a business quarter basis. Institutions then place bids on the tranches.

Contract award is then based on the amount of performance promised by the use of the funds for period of duration.

Consider if a tranche is valued at $200 million. When banks A, B, C bid, they are offering what they can do with the money for a period of a business quarter. If bank $'B'$ has the highest return promised, and can provide an assured return based on their asset value, then the market contract is awarded to them.

If *bank B* then promises back $220 million, the Treasury has made back $20 million on the transaction. If bank B makes $50 million on the contract, they keep $30 Million tax exempt.

If they do not produce $20 million, then this is paid instead out of their assets at the government's discretion into such things as *Government Infrastructure Funds* as is described later in this chapter.

This will drive bank incentives to want to produce profits for the U.S Treasury.

For the Strategic Future of Our Nation

B- Proactive Leadership Role in the Economy

Institutions can provide structured paradigms of all investment vehicles planned or intended for use. They are to be pre-approved by the U.S. Treasury and Congress.

This is to be based on such criteria as demand of conscious vs. market demand, historical basis vs new vehicle, levels of risk assessed by certified analysts vs. credit worthiness of institutions, and past performance of the speific institution in previous market contracts.

C- Demonstrate Capital Market Confidence / Improve Credit Worthiness

Institutions are to provide collateral for assurance of performance commitments. Institutions may provide tolerance of +/- percent of gain without affecting collateral.

- If performance falls within the *negative range of gain estimate*, the negative is carry forwarded to the next contract allocation.

- If performance is over and *above the range of gain estimate*, the amount is treated as a credit against the next contract allocation performance estimate.

D- Reduce Institutional Tax Exposure

Profits to institution, fees, etc. on PIE deals are considered tax exempt.

Participating institutions are not to be permitted to write off losses or offset losses via indirect write-offs.

PIE deals are also to provide incentive to institutions to avoid relocation of their place of business during tax reporting times.

In other words, business lines such as securities lending can be international, where actual business can be relocated to another country to avoid tax consequences. This has to be circumvented so that corporate tax that is due can be measured accurately, and collected into investment vehicles.

E- New Investment Vehicle Development

Institutional trading is generally based on profit due to taking advantage of ineffiencies. A simple example is to trade off a weaker currency for a stronger one.

Institutions have likewise built investment vehicles like the 'Equity Linked Note'.

The New Deal, an Election 2008 Primer

This is based on limiting investor risk where part of the investment is in debt instruments like bonds. They have a scheduled pay out, and on the equity side, one can receive beneft from the stock rise.

Investment vehicles that are considered within ethical and legal constraints that are productive in making a good return on the US dollar should be permitted in the markets.

F- New Sources of Liquidity

As long as institutional investment management is producing a garunteed return to the U.S Treasury that is not from ill-gotten gain, it should be permitted in the market place for others to invest in.

For the Strategic Future of Our Nation

4.6.7 Bank Financing Program for Government Infrastructure Fund

Banks do business, and pay taxes. Regulation of banking practices comes from Congress generally after some oversight has occurred.

To regiment banking and make differing investment vehicles liquid like the mortgage backed securities for the housing market, prevent predatory lending, and to avoid tax misreporting practices, there are two areas where current banking can make a contribution instead into dedicated fund plans. An example is the proposed *Government Infrastructure Fund* (**GIF**).

The banks in lieu of taxes and penalties, are to place *the equivalent* in investment vehicles that provide the government an assured return consistent with overall bank returns. All predatory lending payback likewise is to be invested in this GIF.

The GIF is later described in application like in *Infrastructure Reform*. It is to provide funding for commercial and personal real estate and related industries. This investment, except for the principal, is to provide in full circle, liquidity for the MBS (Mortgage Back Security) industry based on its return on investment. This will improve the housing market and home owner's credit.

Professional investors and money managers will make investments with a required spread of benefit for the government. This is where in making such a spread , these money managers are permitted to deduct reasonable fees. In short, this is equivalent to your landlord allowing you to invest the money you normally would pay in rent; except the differences are that the money managers are quite capable of making up to 80% gain. This is the institutional bank historical trend in leveraged investments.

4.6.7.1 Banking Taxes and Penalties

In lieu of actually paying taxes to the government for the right to do business in the United States, would it not be more viable for these institutions to manage investments whose principal represents what would be normally a 'tax' paid to the government. In other words, instead of these institutions actually paying such taxes for the right to do business, they put assets into funds managed for the government. This in turn increases the credit worthiness of the government too. Consider also that the banks, and financial institutions are required to be a managed participant in the investment strategy. In the following this can be referred to as the 'Primary Investment or Fund'. On a continuing basis, they are required to pay in a flat rate toward this investment (The Primary Fund) principal per month; or say every six months depending how Congress sees it.

4.6.7.2 Predatory Lending Pay Back

Since the late 90's, most of the commercial banks that are responsible for predatory lending practices also have an institutional investment side. It is my expectation that the funds that have been absconded will be instead invested in the GIF.

Consumers that lay claim to exploitation from predatory lending practices, may apply for reclaiming their losses through the Federal Information Management System described in Chapter 3.

4.6.7.3 GIF Expected Benefits

The investment community is expected to make the GIF investment perform in order to see their own profits. This is as opposed to losses and pay-outs due to poor investment strategies.

Banks that normally use their own money generally are more careful on how they make their investment strategies. This guarantees the actual investor, the government, of a high performance and low risk investment.

Banks should be permitted to provide mortgages and other property restoration loans to both the government, businesses and to the people. This is later described in *Infrastructure Restoration* and other reform programs.

4.6.7.4 MBS Liquidity through Debt and Equity Structures

Based on the real estate and housing market demand, the Mortgage Backed Security market can be funded by the **GIF MBS** (government infrastructure funded MBS) as an Equity Linked Note (ELN).

Part of the ELN will be a fixed income government infrastructure bond to cover the loan in the commercial and residential real estate markets.

Fixed Income Bond	Equity Fund

The bond side has a coupon that is paid based on interest rates, and bond performance. It acts like an assured return which partly goes back to the GIF for reinvestment. Attached to the bond is a synthetic equity that is based on existing publicly traded equities, and also a private venture grant fund.

For the Strategic Future of Our Nation

Venture grants are as described later in environment, energy, infrastructure and transportation grant programs. They represent the equivalent of private equity.

Their purpose is for providing tax exempt investments (*Government Investment Bond*) for different grant programs in the noted reform acts.

For program development funding, additional capital can be invested at a mezzanine level in a private equity grant program or private venture grant fund. This can then be part of the equity side of the ELN.

If there is an increase in value due to the publicly traded part of the equity instrument, then the private equity grant becomes less of an investment risk.

Given this structure, the Government can actually shepherd small start up ventures that mature based on program development focus. These shares can be bought by the public markets for pre IPO opportunities.

The government's gardening of venture startups provides a level of due diligence. It provides full transparency for early investor limited risk.

The government will receive an estimated profit on the investments in the Fixed Rate GIF (fixed income bond) as described on a monthly basis.

Where the banks fail in their delivery, the banks must settle to ensure the government its estimated revenue flow.

4.7 Environmental Reform

The forests on the planet create our oxygen base. The forest is getting shaved off the earth's surface. There is only 7% of the forestry that was estimated to be originally in Europe. We also have a lust for wood and pulp, and for clearing land for development. In conjunction with the concentration of fossil fuels is our global warming issue. Our federal government is even telling insurance companies that they should be worried about losing money due to rising global temperatures.

On our way to global warming, there are a number of contributing environmental issues where in total is making ' mother nature ill'. This means that our health is at stake, our safety is put a risk, and our welfare is not assured.

We could say that the earth for the purposes of sustaining life as we know it, is falling apart. It is not a matter of 'if', but when. Consequently there are justifications to become a '*do it now*' activist for all or even one thread of environment issues, and especially on behalf of business development. Then there is also the opposite side which gives the main argument, that to wait is more cost effective.

It is not a matter of being our fault, or due to natural causes for the inevitable demise of the earth, but what we contribute, and in leadership , what example we set.

The bottom line is, that unless we stand up we are sitting on the issue, where it should be an action in momentum instead. For our health, we must make tactical investments in our environment. Our safety and welfare are achieved in strategic investments.

For the Strategic Future of Our Nation

4.7.1 Tactical Initiatives:

To overcome the '*do it now*' or '*wait till later*' contention, simply imagine if we all were to no longer litter. That alone would establish the United States as the leader in environment.

Caring about our environment requires nothing more than a true since of self esteem. With this, we can even exceed the standards of the Kyoto agreement.

A- I Swear not to Litter Campaign petition

To work toward that end, there is a petition on line at both http://unity2008.org and at http://care2.com. The intent is in obtaining and presenting 3 million signatures to the US Senate Environment and Public Works committee.

Its purpose is to create a domino affect in putting the environment on our action radar ! Signing this petition is to empower our representative government to help take the next steps necessary for making a cleaner and healthier environment.

As we are not littering, leaves no room for industry to litter, pollute, or lay waste to our environment and ecosystems. All environmental issues can now be pro-actively on the radar of law makers !

Like government, industry will get the clear message of our expectations for the environmental standards that we expect for ourselves now and how this is to be respected and regarded.

This encourages industry to also help shepherd tactical and strategic investments in environmental reform projects and for energy research and development.

B- European Mileage Standards

Although hybrid vehicles are on the fore-front, they have some time to go before taking a critical mass for transportation use.

Europe has a 45 mile per gallon standard which some advocate that if it is met here we could forgo a relationship with OPEC.

In effect, we could reduce our emissions, the cost of fuel consumption, and also our exposure to an *energy security* issue in dealing with destabilized nations.

The New Deal, an Election 2008 Primer

4.7.2 Environment Reform Plan

The Environment Reform Plan is considered tactical and strategic. It is applicable to federal, state, and community managed programs. The scope is to include cleaning up of infrastructure, land, water and air; and providing strategic means for maintaining our environment.

As being on our active radar for also producing cheap and clean energy, we can also exceed the compliance with the Kyoto agreement. This is for reducing emissions of pollutants, green house gases, and reduction of acid rain. Its impact is not major globally when other nations ignore compliance, but does matter in terms of providing a clean place to live. As a standard in living, its value is also what others eventually envy.

4.7.2.1 Exceeding the Kyoto Standard

I am willing to follow Kyoto's lead. But this is for only until further notice as its standards can soon be surpassed as in the following example.

Carbon trading is part of the Kyoto deal. This is where one polluter may sell their 'carbon credits' for polluting less to another polluter who is polluting more. On the surface this looks like a way of balancing with carbon mission caps, but strategically it does not lead to lower pollution, has no incentive to seek that direction, but does have the incentive to cost consumers more for the same or more pollution.

If this example is a coal based energy company that shared a 'grid' with other sources, it could end up going out of business as not being competitive. If it is a smelting plant for steel, then it becomes non-competitive. In such cases, it will pay if we set up underground plumbing for obnoxious gases. They can be directed to industries that need them such as oil fields that can pump such emissions at oil shale to loosen the oil component for liquification.

This is merely a plan for the Department of Energy, Environment, Interior, and others to collaborate on in order to create state projects that can be funded by bond grant programs to build such a plumbing system across the United States.

Through this, we are recycling our emissions and exceeding the Kyoto agreement in terms of a standard. Carbon trading can then be initiated with international counter parts that will then have to rethink their strategic emission reduction goals or pay into our economy for credits.

4.7.2.3 Emphasizing Programs

We must clean up our past abuse on the environment in order to live here longer. Environmental impact is compromised by the amount of carbon we emit into the air. The water and ground that we pollute, and the lack of replenishment of the resources that have been taken from our land, must be corrected. Commitments are made for proactive pollution prevention and environmental clean up and recovery; and in particular to not duplicate, but activate current and pending legislation such as on water resource projects.

Environmental Advocacy Groups if they collect money for their efforts or government grants, are to register and be regulated as lobbyists. To qualify, efforts have to be assessed by the Senate Environment and Public Works committee for their legitimacy with respect to funds collected.

Pollution Laws are to be reviewed for the scope and effectiveness, and related remedies.

Existing accountability will be reviewed in terms of violations to the laws, and due diligence to be enacted on accordingly. Pollution laws will be revised for effectiveness, and empowered where not empowered.

Program Definition and Scope for existing pollution laws will be a single component. Remedies are in terms of cost of clean up. This will be financed as bond funded grant programs based on fines and assets of those considered contributors to the pollution problem at hand. In a similar manner, where the land has been compromised, such as forestry and land erosion, timely remedies for replenishment will be sought by the contributors to the problem.

Zoning ordinances will be reviewed for the necessity of the development in its relationship to the impact on the environment. Ordinances that appear to be lopsided at the cost of the environment will be revised by federal statue.

Program Deployment will be monitored by the Congress, and the EPA, and other related federal industry oriented agencies. It is expected that this deployment due to its scope of effort will be in stages, and as areas of focus with stated milestones of accomplishment. It is further expected that deployment in one thread of the program can be in parallel with other threads that are in the definition and scope phase of planning. Government Investment Portfolios can maintain many similar projects.

Program Measurements are viewed by the administration as key to keeping the promise for clean up and recovery. They will be made public via the Federal Information System, as described in chapter 3, as deemed in review by Congress.

4.8 Energy Reform Plan

Energy alternatives are key to the how we impact our environment. It is also a matter of our national security to remove foreign energy dependencies. Economically, through safe, cheap and clean energy, we are making our environment far more cost effective to flourish in.

In the provisioning, this strategically saves our environment, while can helping to lower our costs of operation. This lowers the cost of transportation, goods and industry at a minimum. Like dominoes, this lowers the cost of infrastructure which enables jobs to be created.

Programs will be sought to determine the best alternatives for energy. All alternatives are considered as on the table. Not one is to be considered to the exclusion of others. It can even be in a combined solution in some cases which provides benefit over cost, and in other cases opting for one over another for the purposes of producing electricity, and powering our transportation systems, infrastructure and homes.

Government Bond Funded Grant Programs for energy solution development are intended to instill a new era of investment in our nation's future. This is to be based on *Program Development Bonds* as earlier described. It is intended to provide incentives to entrepreneurs in answering many of our needs, and to finance sustainable solutions for them.

The development of energy alternatives is considered to provide opportunities for economic boom when handled in an ethical and regulated manner. It also invites venture capital from the private sector when seen as proof of vision. Debt financing for bonds, and equity financing of venture capital can be structured further in the institutional markets.

For the Strategic Future of Our Nation

4.8.1 All Solutions are considered to be on the table

A- Nuclear Power

Nuclear power is considered clean, but in having its history of serious problems in its pioneering is frowned on by those who do not want it in their back yard. This also can be put in the context of pioneering a new technology, such as early airplanes. When the nuclear power plant can be made safe and cost effective, it then becomes a matter of where you want to put it. We also must consider that the use of energy efficient light bulbs alone used in every home would cause many existing nuclear power plants to store off excess energy which then lowers cost for consumption. Then other questions exist such as needing upwards of 10,000 plants to power the world if it was the only solution. Additionally, we still have the matter of world contention about who gets to have nuclear power that we must overcome.

B- Green Energy/Bio Fuels

Green energy is a new frontier that should be developed and calls for more investment. Bio fuels can in some circumstances be more applicable when its cost and efficiency are achieved over and above a nuclear power plant.

b.1 Solar: This type of power is typically used in two ways. Additional ones can be explored through innovation.

One current use is in the absorption of photon energy by photo-voltaic cells that produce electricity. The cost of manufacturing can come down significantly when in true consumer volume as solar paint for covering buildings. The second is in the heating of water to create steam for turbine generators for producing electricity.

This second means, in some cases can be a competitive alternative to nuclear power. It accomplishes the same positive result without the downside of hazard risk. In other words, where solar energy is abundant on open plains across America, the cost per kilowatt can be much lower than of a nuclear power plant. But then, a nuclear power plant might have competitive advantages elsewhere in the country. Further they can be switched on to the national grid to make up for cloudy days and at nights elsewhere.

b.2 Wind: Wind power can be considered a stand alone cost effective solution. Additionally it can be used in conjunction with other alternatives in application.

b.3 Hydro-Electric: This source has been with us for a long time. It can be leveraged even further in some cases when in concert with others such as wind and solar. Given that a hydro dam is in an open area, it can generate a maximum amount of energy. Its location might also have valuable wind currents and long days of direct sunlight. Could this facility be considered ideal for the additional complements of wind, solar, or both? It's not recommended for Niagara Falls, but other cases could be considered where aesthetics are not a tourist issue.

b.4 Geothermal Energy: The heat from our earth has to likewise be exploited as we have a significant source just a few miles below our surface.

C- Clean Coal: The actual meaning of Clean Coal has to still be realized. It is a new technology which merits accelerated research. In its next generation it can be seen in providing a clean source of energy. This also provides a strategic path for its job force to play as a sustainable role in our economy. Many believe that through science, clean coal can be achieved, thereby allowing us to continue use of this abundant source of energy. This is while limiting its impact on the environment. Communities that depend on this industry for income can remain empowered through this industry.

D- Yet to be discovered: Newer technologies like hydrogen fuel cells over the next 10 years should have cost effective benefits as an alternative fuel for powering vehicles. Perhaps this someday might power our cities. Through Nano technology, even greater discoveries for batteries could be also realized.

E- The Smart Grid: Proposed by former Vice President Al Gore, this thinking will also be sincerely considered for its benefits in energy distribution, and assured availability. This is by obviating the dependency of one source for any local or regional area. It further provides incentives for the deregulation of the energy industry by allowing many participants including private consumers to sell off excess energy.

F- Enhanced Oil Recovery and an Emissions Delivery System

In the 40's, the US built the 'Big Inch Pipe'. It was placed in a canal that was 3 feet wide, and 4 feet deep and stretched between Texas and New York.

Enhanced Oil recovery is based on CO_2 being pumped into the ground. It excites the oil from shale which liquefies it so to be pumped.

For the Strategic Future of Our Nation

G- Industry Emissions Capture System

If we were to capture all industry emissions across the United States into a plumbing system very much like the 'Big Inch Pipe', then we can deliver noxious gases to where they can be used, from anywhere in the United States.

As emissions represent many gases, these can be distilled in route, where the chemical industry could perhaps find use for fabricating industrial binding agents to recombining with others to produce other energy saving products and services.

Further, we have fundamentally reduced our carbon emissions by using an *Emissions Delivery System.*

This also obsoletes the need of carbon trading for a nationalized brokered waste management system.

As a plumbing system, distillation facilities can be in route to many destinations. Further distillation can be accomplished by geothermal means. Where different temperatures burn off exhaust to raw compounds, they can be collected for re-use. Others can be burnt off entirely by joining a geothermal generator return duct.

Carbon is a basic building block in nature and can be used for many ways. Further what is considered as the combination of toxic gases, as compounds can also be allied for reuse through the chemical and textile industries. Carbon nano tube technology is one area of research for this.

This enables a complete new avenue for resource recycling where local industry can flourish.

The New Deal, an Election 2008 Primer

4.9 Transportation Systems

Earlier noted, high speed electro magnetic rail means at over 200 mph. As the cost of energy declines, rapid shipping and transit become within reason. This also allows infrastructure to be spread out further than existing metropolitan areas which lowers the cost of living while being within their reach.

Electric Rail: With lowered power costs, electric and electro magnetic rail becomes a cost effective means to rapidly transport raw and finished goods across our nation. If the timely delivery of steel from Pittsburgh is at a lower cost, then its costs is lowered. Industry in general can benefit while alleviating the impact on our transportation systems infrastructure compared to when transported using carbon based fuels. *Automated Depot Points* can be used for loading and unloading to tractor trailer rigs for local, or within 100 mile delivery destinations.

Rapid Commuter E-Rails are used today. As transportation, they should be considered further in application due to the lowered costs of electricity. Areas like LA and San Francisco can stand further commuter traffic relief of their highways and byways. Further consider connecting these cities by a 200 mph electro magnetic commuter rail. The reduction of traffic reduces the amount of carbon emissions and fuel consumption. Rapid commuter E-rails can be far more cost effective while also reducing traffic fatalities from congested highways. When accounting for population growth this is one of the more reasonable strategies for meeting the commuter's needs. Stations in the future, unlike normal urban subways, can be spread apart by a factor of 10 to 20 miles. A Telecommuter E-train could average 150 miles in an hour. This is while making 10 stops in between. As an added benefit, preventative health is afforded for the relief of the stress and strain of normal commuting.

Highways Byways, Bridges and Tunnels: It is critically important that our roads, bridges and tunnels are maintained. State taxes, municipal bonds, and tolls normally are what pay for this. To assist states, per the development and use of E-rail transportation alternatives, federal bond aid will be made available to subsidize the costs of this aspect of infrastructure.

Commercial and residential building should have tax benefits where econ-energy systems are used like solar paint and reducing carbon emissions.

The Automotive Industry should likewise be expected to do their part in both mileage standards, and adaptive fuel systems such that geographically, where fuel alternatives are available, the fuel system can be adapted. In other words besides makes and models of cars, we should have versions of them. Innovation could even reconsider the Chrysler Turbine Engine that could run on any fuel including perfume !

For the Strategic Future of Our Nation

4.10 Infrastructure

The scope of infrastructure must cover state, city, commercial and residential focus.

The Government will use a sizable portion of added revenue flow from the GIF (Government Infrastructure Fund discussed earlier) for infrastructure support and replenishment.

Availability of funds will be applied in the following priorities:

- Emergency / Disaster Recovery

- Government Properties

- Commercial Properties and business development

- Personal Home Loans

Banks will make loans based on debt notes against the GIF and managed as a GIF MBS structure. Commercial Properties and Personal Home Loans are described in chapter 5, *Personal Empowerment and Social Welfare.*

4.10.1 Emergency / Disaster Recovery

The GIF base of liquidity is to be on a demand basis made available firstly for infrastructure disasters. This means that there must be enough in the GIF base to afford normal commercial and personal property and loan funding, while being robust in stature to recover a city if necessary such as New Orleans, or an earth quake in San Francisco.

Financing is based on loans and grants. All loans are to be fixed rate investments into existing government assisted businesses, and commercial and residential real estate.

In addition, the GIF revenue flow is to be applied to the costs of restoration of properties. They could require necessary reconstruction, operations, and financing work programs; and related educational grants.

4.10.2 Government Properties

Government property restoration as a priority is to be based on its need to serve the people. This is to be prioritized by Congressional review.

4.11 Agriculture

The right of every farmer to raise and sell his products at a return which will give him and his family a decent living - FDR

Agriculture support ranges in need from basic commercial farming to the development and production of bio energy sources and fossil fuel supplements and alternatives. This can also be for providing additional cost effective solutions for public utility use in supplying electricity.

4.11.1 Agriculture Support Loans

Agriculture support programs should be considered consistent in scope as for disaster, social welfare, program development, and commercial real-estate and commercial business grants and loans. They are to be managed under the same terms.

4.11.2 Agriculture Emergency Support Programs

Emergency support is to be considered when in the state of disaster. It is to have the same constraints as Infrastructure Emergency / Disaster Recovery

4.11.3 Agriculture New Energy Research Assistance

This will be in the form of federal grants and loans that is consistent for any existing industry, or burgeoning industry that can demonstrate new avenues of cost effective energy development, delivery, and use. *Supporting industries will also have the opportunity to qualify for federal assistance.* In addition to agriculture, there are supporting industries that serve agriculture such as producing biodegradable fertilizers and soil enhancers in order to produce crops. If it can improve our health, and our environment, and can be provided cost effectively then it must be considered.

Chapter 5

Personal Empowerment

and

Social Welfare

Communities as local municipalities are represented by the work of civil servants, police, fire, emergency, and medical services, teachers and education systems. Communities are then represented by the commerce and employment level that are made available within them for our personal empowerment.

Communities that do not have adequate Homeland Security funding cannot meet the needs of their *first responders*. Education programs when compromised financially can not serve their communities. Commerce when absent cannot provide employment opportunities. When our health care and Social Security become the objects of free enterprise, our fundamental needs become financial luxuries. In addition to what comes home with them, this is also what our veterans must confront.

Federally subsidized programs are proposed to enhance the viability of the needs at the local level for community safety, health, and welfare.

Most projects and solutions proposed in this chapter look at government social welfare and program development bonds for funding. Their basis is discussed at length in Chapter 4 on Economic Reform.

Intended for our communities and personal empowerment, the government bond / grant programs are tax exempt and are only considered to be used for their specific purpose. The federal government will not manipulate these funds from specific program initiatives for other purposes.

The New Deal, an Election 2008 Primer

These bonds are to be available to the public at large for investment. Being purchased with pre-tax dollars and income lowers the actual federal taxes to be collected.

There should be no hiatus in federal government for the delivery of subsidized funds to states; and that funds and related programs are not cut; and where signed into law are not shorted; and where states deem the need for more support, that the federal government hears and responds to the stated needs in a timely manner through funding programs.

A- For Crime Reduction

The reduction of crime reduces the cost of enforcement for both community and personal safety. It is my expectation that communities will understand the need for compliance with fair commerce practices within their communities while setting standards for the expectations of their members. This will enhance the effectiveness of federally subsidized budgets overall.

B- For Education

As much as Education is the key to the future for personal development, communities suffer from the impact of its absence in its younger generation.

Moreover, communities should be empowered to develop the skills and abilities of its local youth such as in after school programs, tutoring where necessary, and other areas of focus that reinforce the sense of self esteem in the youth where attraction to gangs and frustrated groups of kids become less of an issue for communities.

C- About Third Party Participation in Communities

When we re-enfranchise our citizens, we build stronger communities. By communities providing support services and safety nets, the government should pursue tax incentives and further subsidized assistance to support this effort.

It is vital that organizations like the ACLU, NAACP and AFL-CIO have further involvement in assisting communities in developing such programs, in addition to after school care programs and faith based followings. Per the non exclusion of different faiths, any non-profit community oriented organization should be able to acquire many further bond funded grants for worthy purpose for community empowerment.

For the Strategic Future of Our Nation

D- Fixing our Social Welfare Policies

We are currently missing many needed safety nets in our communities and in our social welfare policies. Our communities can be multicultural, have different adult sexual orientation, and/or customs and faiths that we might not be aware of, familiar with, or are perceived as something else like oil and water with our own outlook on life. Tolerance with diversity is essential in understanding our communities, and its needs in communication. Communication is critical in bridging gaps and empowering our cultures to cross great divides to each other within our communities. In addition to language barriers, there are many challenges that we face today in our communities.

The *aged* deserve the most respect and consideration. Today our value systems consider the aged to be something 'out dated', and therefore, obsolete. Let us consider ourselves obsolete in lacking wisdom if we view the aged as obsolete for they have been either directly, or indirectly our teachers.

Our veterans are hailed as heroes when they march in uniform, but when they are fortunate enough to return, in many ways they may still be where we sent them. When you provide vocational technology training assistance it is simply one less hill for them to climb.

We should keep in mind that the reintegration of our Vets from the Vietnam war was basically not considered relevant, and that this also represents the original critical mass of the homeless on our streets. When we have people that are fortunate to return from our wars, we must take the responsibility to have them reintegrate into out communities.

Rehabilitation assistance for abuse is needed by many, where each can have their own set of unique reasons. Offering the hand of compassion is the expression of one's sense of self esteem. It can inspire others for theirs. The jobless and homeless can be anyone, and in most communities can be viewed as an inconvenience. The homeless has become a population since the early 1980's where the proliferation is in coincidence to the *trickle down economy*. Life can trickle down on any one of us with little notice or warning no matter who we think we are at the moment.

Justice is to be blind when it comes to being equal under the law, but its heart must see when dues are paid. When ex convicts have paid their dues, it is our obligation as fellow citizens to offer the road back. An Ex Con who originated from a community should have that opportunity offered by the same community to earn their self esteem back based on the standards set in the community.

The New Deal, an Election 2008 Primer

5.1 Leave No Vet Behind

Veterans Services will be further augmented in scope for the dignity and benefits of our veterans and their families. This is to include but not be limited to medical benefits, financial assistance, veteran family assistance, and vocational training. Services are to further provide a network into state/community level support programs.

Veteran's hospitals are to be further funded to adequately provide assistance in case load. Veteran's hospitals will not be short on supplies nor required staff to serve our veterans.

Veteran hospital workers are to be rated by the patients. If the vets believe that the worker serves them, then they are welcomed to retain their jobs. If the ratings are not acceptable, the worker is to be replaced by one who will care about the vets. It is more than a job of employment in taking care of the vets, it is to be considered an honor.

Returning to duty is to be a veteran's choice when and if the government determines that he or she is fit for duty. It has been a voluntary military force, and should remain that way.

Vets will not have to wait until sometime in the future for assistance. They will get the assistance programs when determined needed by the vet or their family.

For the Strategic Future of Our Nation

There will be *no deductibles* for vets of any category. Medical, psychological, and sociological assistance will be readily available by the government.

There are to be no *injury ratings*, as injury is injury, and this is not about car insurance, but about American people. Disabled vets are not to be covered as some form of property or Government Issue, but in how they are to recover and get back to life as Americans.

Wounds are wounds. Discrimination is not to be permitted in terms of combat, or non combat related injuries to the self when in active military service.

Both grants and loans will be made available for vets who seek financial assistance and demonstrate use in the vocational training and community support net level programs. Loans will be below normal bank interest rates for equivalent loans.

Veteran family assistance is to be provided in scope, but not be limited to the grants for family assistance, and qualification of family head of household to assume veteran benefits when loosing an immediate family member in active military service.

The New Deal, an Election 2008 Primer

5.2 The Progressive National Employment Plan

Post 1929 Stock Market crash bread line.

5.2.1 Correcting the Unemployment Problem of Our Nation

President Franklin Delano Roosevelt (FDR) noted in his 'The Economic Bill of Rights' that for all, to have "The right to adequate protection from the economic fears of old age, sickness, accident, and unemployment".

Today, to be unemployed is to be disenfranchised in our capitalistic system. We cannot blame corporations for wanting to save costs. But by off shoring, or by *wage gouging* in local hire through nickel and dimming for cheap foreign worker has caused an earthquake in our economy. Its domino effect is the quality and quantity of employment opportunities for US citizens.

Currently, I estimate $800 billion is shipped offshore per year . This is by businesses that are technically head quartered in the US, but who operate offshore. This is where worldwide spending on information technology is expected to reach 1.48 trillion by 2010.

There has been the exodus of our industries, their infrastructure, and labor needs in exploiting world trade policies.

For the Strategic Future of Our Nation

Over the past few years our economy and jobs have actually been impacted by foreign labor forces. They are willing to work at even less than previous market rates. Can we say that our identity can be stolen in more than one way when what represents us is being off shored?

More than likely when you call a US based Internet service help desk, you will be speaking with someone in India. When using a franchised tax preparation service your very personal tax forms can be prepared by a stranger there. In some industries, like IT, market rates have been reduced to where they were in 1993.

It is a matter of wage gouging, and not a question of available American workers. By lowering the actual wage rate, only those without roots in our country can afford them. For most guest workers, wages are shipped back to the country of origin with minimal local living expenses. In many cases, such visitors room up with many others as this meets their temporary and cost effective stay in the US. In the case where a visa offers a limited time this arrangement is ideal for them. For their 12 month home budget they only need to work 4 of them on our shores.

Like the automotive and tool makers industry, where possible, for many businesses today, offshoring is the way to go. It gets around labor unions and enables US based companies to theoretically compete with other offshore manufactures. For example, the U.S. machine-tool industry won't soon recapture the 50% of a $9-billion domestic market lost to import makers in the past 15 years, but in off shoring themselves puts this industry near a level play field.

In white collar employment, most financial and insurance institutions in New York offshore most of their labor, and hiring locally foreign visitors at below fare market rates where possible. Wall Street, also, is not exactly the way it use to be either.

For blue collar employment, corporate outsourcing of foreign labor and in investing in offshore manufacturing has been the answer to union representation. As this ultimately undermines both our economy, and the level of employment in our country, it is addressed in the *Balanced Trade Proposal*.

Where there is no union representation in an industry in the United States, our economy and jobs have actually been impacted by foreign labor forces that are willing to work at even less than previous market rates and ship US dollars out of the country.

The New Deal, an Election 2008 Primer

What is very serious is that the American US dollar is not trickling down into our local commerce. This further compounds the unemployment problem in our communities. This syndrome is addressed in *Balanced Trade* in *Economic Reform.*

It is considered a significant issue in impacting our economy as opposed to benefiting it, and therefore, employment opportunities in our communities. To deal with this earthquake, we must achieve balance in our industries, and government help for the employment of qualified US citizens.

5.2.2 The National Progressive Employment Plan

To further quote FDR, he believed in:

a- "The right to a useful and remunerative job in the industries or shops or farms or mines of the nation"

b- "The right to earn enough to provide adequate food and clothing and recreation"

To deal with the job plight since 2001, I propose the *Progressive National Employment Plan.* I see the right for livelihood to be a given when exercised in a legal and ethical manner. This right must be supported without limiting it to the following proactive components. 'Balanced Trade' initiatives and corporate reform will help prevent lost jobs, discounted wages and unnecessary layoffs domestically.

5.2.2.1 Affirmative Action Policies and Practices

Affirmative Action policies and practices will be pursued for compliance by all employers that operate within the United States. All United States based employers will further be in compliance with polices and practices for the hiring and employment of U.S citizens that work, or are employed offshore on behalf of the employer.

Affirmative Action has to be examined for its effectiveness and relevance in protecting jobs for all US citizens over and above foreign visitors that have visa sponsored labor offerings at below market salary value.

For the Strategic Future of Our Nation

5.2.2.2 Union Empowerment

When it comes to labor issues, the employees have to rely on the strength of their labor unions. Federal government entities are to work with these state elected officials, and unions; and where and when required, senate investigations and legal trials are to be pursued.

Labor unions in of themselves have been the subject of abuse, but have for the most part served their purpose in providing an important representation for their workers.

Some of the early examples are the evolution of the union for coal miners and the automotive industry. Today, there are a number of labor and service unions that represent America's labor.

The bottom line is: *where there is a union for an industry, the labor force has a better chance of not being exploited by employers.* It helps further to ensure that our economy is directed into our communities.

The AFL-CIO, and other Union initiatives will be supported with respect to the need to afford union dues by non union workers within union places of work where union labor is performed in an *equivalent manner*, focus and scope in employee performance and responsibilities.

These union dues on non union workers are to ensure for the non union worker, the same representation, rights, and benefits that are afforded to union workers of the same classification within the same work place of employment.

In non-union workplaces, union petition is to be permitted in all industries, and US based companies. Union formation is to be only accepted by a 2/3 vote by employees within the workplace in question.

Voting is to be held in privacy such as in the manner of government elections. Vote counting is to be performed by impartial and objective means by a notary public that is not directly or indirectly related to the industry or union in question.

Where there is and where there is not union representation, the federal government must be more proactive in managing wage rates, where wage gouging can be avoided by commercial interests.

5.2.2.2.1 Union Empowerment Loans

One of the biggest limitations a potential labor union has is in its ability to fund its startup or a strike action when required. For government assistance, caveats are that unions cannot have outstanding issues with their members, such as in cutting health benefits, or otherwise at the time or during the duration of empowerment loans and for ten years post loan payment.

A- Union Formation Funding

Union empowerment for startup is to be considered equivalent to a commercial loan. While under the duration of the loan, the unions may not strike.

B- Union Strike Funding

Union Empowerment Strike Action is to be recognized for mature labor unions, or one that is not under an Empowerment Grant/Loan. Under consensus of its members strike due to a lack of a contract with an employing industry, empowerment grant/loans are to satisfy the cost of employment compensation for its members.

This is to be for a period of 30 days. This type of empowerment grant/loan is considered a longer term commercial loan where the union, once its workers are back to work can pay it off over a period of time.

5.2.2.3 US Wage Base

For *living wage*, minimum wages are to be examined based on the 'living wage' and what is defined as the 'Poverty Level'. Wages are to reflect the actual cost of living for the community where the employment, and residence, occurs and subject to the *inflation index* as opposed to the *take it or leave it* wage gouging tactics of today's typical employment offer.

Wage gouging is to be circumvented by using the *Federal Government Wage Pricing System Information Service*. This can be an enumerated service of the Federal Information System described in chapter 3.

Fixed Price and overtime is for every worker regardless of whether directly employed, or via third party contract. Workers must be paid for work done. For direct employment, overtime is to be paid as 'time and one half'. For contractors, time is to be paid by the hour. The professional day as set to eight hours does not obviate the responsibility of the employer to provide monetary compensation for overtime.

For the Strategic Future of Our Nation

A- Rights to Work for a Fair Wage

The Right to work for a fair wage applies to US citizens. It must take precedence of green card and visa based workers. Employment opportunities are defined as both vacancies, as well as employment positions, whether temporary, by contract or permanent that are currently occupied by foreigners on US soil.

B- Poverty Level:

This must be set based realistically on the 'cost of living', and the 'Inflation Index'. Minimum wage must be accounted for as in being above the poverty level for the local area.

C- Unemployment Benefit Extension

Argued many times over in Congress is whether 'unemployment benefits cost the tax payer'. How ever the better argument is that employed people are tax payers.

Our government can make an investment in its people with the proviso that when offered a job it is compulsory to accept it being that it is sound employment and meets the same, at a minimum, of the unemployment payments made to the unemployed.

It is the responsibility of the unemployed to improve themselves from this starting point, or to forgo unemployment assistance from that point on.

5.2.2.4 Additional Program Initiatives

A- Proactive Marketing of the Unemployed

Through the Federal Information System, employment/vacancy opportunities are to be reported for federal, state, city and private sectors.

If unemployed and when given a starting point, it is self esteem that is to carry us forward. This does not intend for employers to provide employment opportunities at below market rate, but does intend that employers will make an offer at market rate for an employment position that could even be currently filled by a foreigner with an active visa or green card that is currently filling the same position on US soil.

The New Deal, an Election 2008 Primer

B- Vocational Training Assistance

Programs must be made available such that people can have a starting point for a career or new career, as opposed to just a job, if desired, or needed. There is more on this in the *Education Reform Act* which follows.

C- Work Programs

C1- Co Sponsored Work Programs

Work programs are to be stewarded by our government. They can be co-founded by financial institutions and other businesses for the purposes of tax relief, et al.

In the case of private enterprise stewarding work programs, it is up to our government to determine the terms and conditions of related benefits to these non-government companies and enterprises.

What is most important is that such private enterprises have the capacities to identify needs for professional skills in their specific industry, thereby enabling skilled workers who are citizens to fill their needs.

C2- Government Solely Sponsored Work programs:

There will be Government sponsored work programs. They are to meet two purposes:

a- To train non-working, or unemployed individuals in job and career related skill sets; where this can be both blue collar, and white collar in nature; thereby allowing them to eventually achieve the status of formal employment within a profession or vocation.

b- To apply the unemployed for the benefits of the communities infrastructure restoration, and in developing the preparedness of the new century.

There is much work to be done in the restoration of cities, and certainly in the improvement of highways, and byways, and improvement of living conditions in more rural areas of the country.

For the Strategic Future of Our Nation

D- Foreign Labor Policy

U.S citizens must come first if we are expected to stand on our own two feet and make a contribution in our economy.

It is not in our interest to disenfranchise a foreigner but it is the intention to empower the US citizen in the United States.

Foreigners who wish to immigrate need to get a fair deal in being able to immigrate, if in fact they plan on becoming US citizens.

Guest workers with legitimate visas and green cards should be welcomed to work on US soil where it can be proved that there is not an equally qualified U.S citizen available for it within the geographic region of the job and where there is no evidence of wage gouging that prevents the citizen from working at a fair wage.

Foreign corporations, institutions and enterprises that operate on US soil are not to be exempt from this rule.

Any country that so wishes to import their labor force should be required to not 'under price' going rates for the standard of living in the United States, and prove that an American cannot fill the job, and provide the US with an equal export monetary value.

For those institutions which offshore their labor, such labor should be taxed in order to encourage such institutions to hire American labor.

The New Deal, an Election 2008 Primer

5.3 Commercial Real Estate and Commercial Business Loans

Commercial real-estate and business loans in the USA are normally issued by banks under terms of eligibility. Currently these terms could, or might not apply to what's needed in today's high risk debt based economy. GIF funded loans can be more flexible where at a minimum eligibility accounts for:

1- That the owner/owners regardless of being incorporated
are not in default in personal liabilities and in good standing with creditors.

2- That the owners although rated credit worthy in of themselves can
not reflect the credit worthiness of the company, regardless if they,
the owners have invested their own personal assets into the company.

3- The company is established as a revenue bearing business for a minimum period of time, say six months, prior to applying for the loan.

4- Business owners do not have a history of short lived, and failed startups as described in *Default* later in this section.

5- That no new additional partners are permitted during the period of the loan.

6- No company may obtain such a loan for an acquired company or for purposes of creating an imminent domain take over strategy.

7- Packaging of loans can be made as an addition using other funding sources, but must be approved by the funding bank, or institution in question.

8- This intends also in no way to prevent a business to accept funding from other sources which are unrelated to the proposed here. But if other sources are to be pooled, such pools must be quite clean in mix to prevent money laundering sources, etc.

For the Strategic Future of Our Nation

5.3.1 Commercial Business Mandatory Upkeep Policies

Commercial business, in order to remain viable in offering goods and services on a sustained basis while in use of a commercial loan, must have an upkeep policy. Such a policy should dictate that at a minimum:

1- When a commercial business has obtained a commercial loan for said business, the loan monies are to be used for the sole purposes of the loan as stated in the loan's application.

2- The purpose and size of loans are based on a clear business plan that has been reviewed and due diligence performed by the Government.

3- The business that is taking the loan is obligated to maintain the quality of its service(s), product(s), and premise(s).

4- The businesses level of up keep, and maintenance is considered all inclusive, regardless of that part of the business which was funded by commercial loans as described above, and/or in combination of funding through other sources.

5.3.2 Commercial Business Loan Defaults, Remedies and Settlements

Any business in any economy can have hard times, and subsequently default on loan payments. This can be even to the extent of bankruptcy as described as 'Chapter 11, / 13' in US corporate business code.

In the proposed, for such cases where companies are not able to make payments towards their loans for a period of 3 months (90 days), the government is to be obliged to become a participating watch dog partner. All accounting books are to be audited and maintained for the company in question.

5.3.3 Conditions for Government Acquisition of a Failed Business:

The government will have the right under certain conditions to assume eventual ownership of said defaulting / failing companies, and for auction of its assets. This applies where fraud by the company's current owner(s) is clearly identified through due process and stewarded by audits of the legal courts of the government. In this case such owners shall loose ownership, and could, based on the laws and justice of the land, incur prison sentences. This condition also applies where a company has continued to fail in the following three months, where the government has become a scrutinizing partner after the first 3 months of loan payment failure.

The New Deal, an Election 2008 Primer

5.3.4 Remedies and Settlements

The Government upon complete acquisition of a failing company, may at its discretion sell its related assets for the actual 'liquidation value' with the following limitations:

That it is sold only to a citizen of the United States and where such monies for the purchase from a citizen is not derived nor construed directly from any loan from the loan pool, nor from grant monies as described later for non-working citizens.

5.3.5 Repaying Outstanding Debts of a Failed Business

Creditors who are located as the primary business location will be credited such outstanding sums owed to them towards any loan payments. They in turn might owe to the GIF MBS for an existing loan.

Creditors who are not under any loan agreements/contracts with the Primary Fund will be offered alternative discounts for the costs of doing business such as to be applied against taxes.

Employees of these failed companies less the owners, are to have any outstanding debt applied towards loan payments. They may have outstanding payments that are about to become due from the GIF MBS.

The employees are to have, if needed payments from the assets applied to their personal loan needs and payment to their own creditors for payment that is due.

5.4 Personal Real Estate and Related Loans

The right of every family to a decent home - FDR

A- Government Financing for Working Citizens

Citizens who maintain consistent employment for over a period of ninety days meet the criterion to take loans from the government for commercial and home real-estate restoration, and for necessary improvements. Further, the loans are to afford the purchase of a new home where this purchase could be from a private owner or from the government. This type of loan is intended to be negotiated eventually from a government portfolio to a fix rate at banks who want the reliable and stable business.

As in residential bank loans, the working citizens may resell their property and outstanding government mortgage loan when desired in order to move up in their standard(s) of living with respect to property value and other assets.

B- Grants to Loans program for Non- Working Citizens

For head start, non-working citizens are permitted to take government loans for home or home purchase and improvement. This includes the homeless which are also provided rental assistance described later. In all cases, residential *grants to loans* program is to be based on the potential for earning an income when given the opportunity. This is based on the individuals earning potential skills and experience. Government improvement grants should call for up to a 15 year duration and require the borrower to dwell in their premises for at least that length of time. Grants are to be converted to loans based on employment that exceeds 90 days. The purpose of the caveat is to provide the non-working citizen with the incentives to work when the opportunity avails itself. Given 6 months of payment history, banks can assume these government grants as loans and thereby allowing such citizens the opportunity to prosper as in above. This is while unburdening the government of such a grant and while providing additional business to the banks.

The New Deal, an Election 2008 Primer

C- Homeless Rental Assistance Program

In our military, we have *leave no soldier behind.* In chapter 5, you will find the program called 'Leave No Vet Behind'. What is also important is that we as Americans, if for no other reason except our national pride, have to have 'Leave No American Behind'.

The federal government has the responsibility to subsidize states for not homeless shelters, but for state managed rental assistance programs or SMRAP.

With SMRAP, let there be no homeless person in our great nation.

D- Working Citizen Loan Defaults

For working citizens, under the condition of a legitimate default, as described in the following, should not be penalized in loan obligations for loosing their employment based on economic conditions or upon a business failure.

In these cases, payments on the loan will be suspended for a period of up to ninety days. This is for the purposes of allowing the citizen to re-obtain employment.

In the same period, referred to as a '*postponement of obligation*', their loan will be converted into "*government grant status*", with the caveat/a priori understanding is that this 90 day postponement will be added on as outstanding loan payments without additional interest nor penalties once the debt is returned to loan status.

Re-activation to loan status only applies when the re-employed citizen remains employed for the subsequent 3 months once re-employed.

No-Fault / Default applies if the ninety day period is exceeded where the citizen has not been able to obtain work at no fault of their own. Examples of this are the case of disability, or lack of work and divorce or death. This loan would be converted back into a formal grant as noted earlier in *Grants to Loans program for Non- Working Citizens.*

For the Strategic Future of Our Nation

E- Legitimate Defaults

Legitimate defaults **a**re to be defined as *'no provable fault of ones own'*. This definition is to account for circumstances which are ordinarily beyond one's own control with respect to preventing due diligence in addressing personal responsibilities.

This is to accommodate defaults due to physical disabilities, and loss of income from a job where one is an employee or had loss of income from an act of 'God and nature'. This further covers unexpected legacy costs from previous health and medical issues prior to the 'Peoples Health Care Plan' enactment as described later in chapter 5; and from divorce or death as described below.

E.1 Divorce under Abandonment, Abusive Partnerships, and Mutual Agreements

We have a high rate of divorce in our nation. It is a circumstance that all societies must deal with. It must be accounted for in this plan.

Loans must not be attempted where there is an intention knowingly to subsequently divorce or separate from a spouse. But this circumstance can and will occur while under loan agreements.

In cases where there is m*utual domestic partner abuse:*

For the abandoning party which abandons the other party (except if the abandoning party is considered to be decreed as the abused party) will forfeit the property to the other party.

Who is proved to be the abusive party is considered by default to be the abandoning party.

In these cases the abandoning party will still remain solely responsible for the payment of such loans until payments have been completed; and will be considered in-eligible to obtain an additional loans (personal or commercial) until such time that the personal loan is paid off.

In these cases, if one is not employed, and the other is, the employed is liable for payment against the loan.

E.2 Mutual Abuse and Intent to Divorce:

Under such circumstances both parties will be responsible for the payment of the loan where both are working, or can elect to forfeit the property to the Government if it can be established that they mutually elect to do so, while not under duress from the other party.

The parties in question will become under the status of 'Non-Legitimate Defaults'.

E.3 Default Due to Death

Loan defaults due to death are covered under two categories:

Category 1: Death of a Non-Married Working Citizen

All property rights will be assumed by the government, where related assets are for such things as non-commercial government sponsored charities, etc.

This is when the deceased does not have relatives or a *last will and testament,* where identifying such exceeds the time of 90 days post the event of death, and where due diligence has been demonstrated by the government to identify relatives and/or 'Wills'.

Category 2: Death of Married Working Citizens:

Under this circumstance, property will be assumed by the spouse and children, who are alive and remain. This will override any 'Wills' that do not include these family members with respect to the property that was obtained by such loans. This applies *if and only if* these members have, and had been living as part of the deceased residence where it was under full acceptance, and desire by the deceased prior to their death. Hence if a 'Will' differs from family claims, then family claims have reason to be scrutinized.

E.4 Non-Legitimate Personal Defaults

Non-Legitimate defaults are defined as '*provable fault of ones own*'. This definition is to account for circumstances which are ordinarily within our control and with respect to ones due diligence in addressing responsibilities.

Non-Legitimate defaults must be identified as in having two categories: criminal and non-criminal intent.

For the Strategic Future of Our Nation

There must be a clear and clean line of definition to segregate what is considered criminal, and non-criminal. In all circumstances of either non-criminal, or with criminal intent, under the condition of 'non-legitimate defaults', a citizen who becomes under this category will forfeit their home if in fact improvements have been applied via such improvement loans. At which point they will be issued a home that is solely government owned and considered at less value than the one forfeited.

It is to be assumed that in cases proved to be of criminal intent, that the laws of the land would further reconcile with the individual in question.

Criminal in intention is to be based on the laws, and subsequent laws of the land. What this is to account for are acts that demonstrate the intent to knowingly mislead, acts of fraud and misrepresentations, or attempts to exploit, or leverage using the use of the GIF MBS Fund through unfair advantages.

Examples would include taking home improvement loans where commercial reasons are intended under a personal home improvement loan. In other words, misrepresentation is construed when and if an applicant does not have a dwelling, or is intending to buy, fix-up and sell without paying such loans, properties where they do not actually have their 'single place of residence'.

Misrepresentation can be where two partners cohabitant, non-married in the eyes of the law, where both partners sharing the property take out two separate loans for the same home improvement purpose, and where only one of such loans is actually used for such purposes, and where the other loan is used for unrelated purposes.

Individual cases can be where one fully knows that one is going to retire from formal employment or knows prior to taking such loans, that they are about to be laid off or dismissed.

Additionally when knowing full well that one will die due to natural causes or disease, within a year or two, but wishes to take on a loan for one's families home improvement, thereby allowing the state to absorb the loss of loan payments where the other living parties are not employed, nor intend to be.

Further, to claim one is employed where one does not really have an actual service, product or legitimate consumer base. For instance gambling and Equities Day Trading by an individual would fall into such categories as well as peddlers.

E.5 Non-Criminal Intention:

This is not to imply or state that all classifications of non-legitimate defaults are based on fraud, nor the attempt to mislead, such as the case of domestic partnerships which has irreconcilable differences between the parities, where both parties wish to end such a partnership such as mutual abandonment as described above where this mutual decision was not an intent prior to taking a loan with the *Primary Investment Fund.*

For the Strategic Future of Our Nation

5.5 The Education Reform Act for the United States

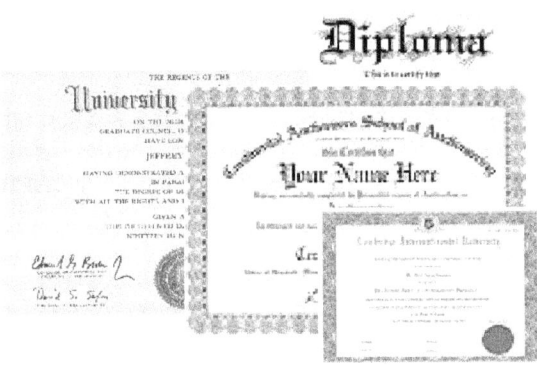

In the 'The Economic Bill of Rights', FDR noted : 'The right to a good education'. The following is to address this objective.

The *Education Reform Act* is to empower the *No Child Left Behind* program. It is to be made available on a graduated scale of requirements as opposed to an all or nothing merit system. Most of all, the program should be considered paramount.

All education financing programs are to be scrutinized closely on an ongoing basis by Congress of private enterprise profits and conflicts of interests.

Education ranges from the very young to the aged. Funding priorities are proposed in the order of state assistance programs and larger grants and loans. Focus is to be on the following for US citizens:

* No Child Left Behind

* Vocational Grant Assistance Programs

* Higher Education

* Ongoing Education Programs

* Optional Education Programs such as for professional certification

The New Deal, an Election 2008 Primer

5.5.1 How to Pay for Education:

Affording education must be a Federal and state funded initiative. Federal funding will be expanded significantly by way of tax exempt social welfare bonds for education.

Their maturity for redemption will be available within a K-12 and other education periods. This is to allow parents of students to make an investment in their child's later education needs. They can be used as collateral for additional student loans if needed, or for living needs of students during their higher education period.

5.5.2 Availability

Education is viewed differently by many. Some see it as a basic K-12, sometimes vocational, and then there is higher education and ongoing education. My late grandmother once said that there is 'no excuse not to have an education if there is an available library'. Although quite dogmatic, in a way she was quite right. You can always go to the library, and now we also have the Internet.

A- Regarding Early Education:

If there were only the library or the Internet, disciplined learning skills would still be required in order to benefit.

These skills must be developed at a young age. Starting at a young age, we are confronted as consumers with an overbearing amount of distraction from advertising and television.

Combined with junk food, this causes a shrinking level of cognitive bandwidth for our young. By the time they are in the second grade their learning patterns or lack of them have been established.

Amongst these patterns are ADD (Attention Deficit Disorder), and ADHD (Attention Deficit Hyperactivity Disorder) Syndrome, where the more popular remedy is in the use of drugs.

In high schools, adolescents are required to put a full day in at their desk, where their bodies are distracting them. Due to lack of actual movement, or body exercise, the young become increasingly distracted. In urban school systems, teachers become behavior referees in contrast to their purpose as teachers.

For the Strategic Future of Our Nation

Exercise is critical for the developing child and adolescent. Further, obesity has become an issue in our communities. A strong youth A- lowers the level of <u>future health care issues</u>; and B- works off excess energy that allows a student to focus on their studies.

If subjected to poor quality education, a student's horizons are limited in what they see for themselves. Additional challenges placed on school systems are that at least 10% of the students need to learn English, and due to the rate of immigration we can assume in the next few years for this need to increase.

The **'No Child Left Behind Act'** requires certain performance standards for community schools to be compliant with in order to obtain financial assistance. It's a safe bet that many schools in our nation cannot currently qualify.

Community empowerment is required to bring schools to a standard where many are not capable of this. This is due to needing a jump start in the first place. In other words, even for the 'No Child Left Behind Act' to have value, education must overcome the inertia of circumstances that it must embrace to gain momentum.

The *opt out* plan of school vouchers is attractive for this reason if you feel your child might have a chance elsewhere.

5.5.3 The Early Education Strategy:

A.1- Pre-K

Pre-K is a critical period for children, as well as for the parents who need childcare while they work. Pre-K tuition can be as expensive as college tuition. This is especially true when parents have to leave their children for extended periods such as during a work day. Pre-K children are generally from young families, where working parents additionally have the challenge of new careers, and in making ends meet.

To rectify this, Pre-K learning centers will be able to obtain Federal funds for assistance directly based on number of children they are managing at a max capacity of 25 per learning center. States are required to provide the standards for the environment of the learning center, viable capacities for children in the location, and in pro-active learning practices. The learning center must be in compliance with this state standard for practicing pro-active learning skills for Pre-K children. Learning centers that accept such funds are not allowed to receive additional funds from parents.

The New Deal, an Election 2008 Primer

A.2- No Child Left Behind

'No Child Left Behind' must become available on a graduated scale of requirements as opposed to an all or nothing merit system. This is to help jump start early education where we must become pro-active about disciplined learning skills.

Communities can arrive at a level of empowerment which can be based on gradients of achievement. Where schools still fall behind, the responsibility must be on the state, and its representatives and Senators in Congress to make their case as to what further is required to meet certain academic standards for full community empowerment.

A.3 -School Vouchers

School vouchers have to be community based. There can be some communities with very well developed public school systems, and in other cases where there is a better offering from private schools. This must be addressed on a case by case bases, while having the graduated scale of requirements for public schools to overcome inertia. It is wrong for a child or young adult to have to be boat anchored where they can accelerate, and it is also, for other students to stagnate.

Every community, through its state representatives and Senators in Congress must make the case as to what best suits its needs. In some cases it might be only school vouchers, and in others none may be needed, and in others there could be a mix. This can be a very much a reality where the federal government itself cannot have a black and white policy of either/or.

A.4- Vocational Grant Assistance Programs

It is important to account for those who wish assistance in paying for vocational training. Young people starting from the age of 18 or as a high school graduate should be able to acquire loans and grants for vocational education programs and training services that are offered in the communities that they reside in.

Currently, educational loans are available, but their terms can be predatory. It is important that our federal government provide its fair share of assistance in this area. States should be able to match educational grant programs and facilitate additional loans as necessary.

For the Strategic Future of Our Nation

A.5 - College and University Education

State colleges and universities are to be further funded on a per student basis. This is in order to lower school tuition and enable additional scholarships.

There will be the return of Pell Grants and making education affordable based on a person's economies of scale. Tax deductions will be made applicable for student tuition. These tax deductions can be made by institutions, organizations, empowerment groups, and families. Regardless if a college student is of 18 years or older, those who demonstrate that they have contributed to the student in question can apply for such deductions.

A.6 - Ongoing Education Programs

Student grants for graduate school, law and medicine will be made available to help pay for tuition at state universities where it can be demonstrated that the student's work is 'for the good'.

A.7 - Optional Education Programs for Professional Certification

Below interest rate loans will be available for professionals who return to school to be certified in new tools related to their profession.

A.8 - For our Vets

Education for veterans will be free of charge, provided that the course of study is in preparation for a career, and they attend a public university or vocational school.

5.6 - On Correcting Social Security

"no damn politician can ever scrap my social security program." FDR

5.6.1 Summary:

In examining hear say and the so called doom's day predictions about Social Security I want to summarize this concern. Then I want to introduce the 'Plan of Action' proposed to put it back on the course as was intended by Franklin Delano Roosevelt.

Additionally, I propose that our government to dedicate a $10.00 savings bond to every child that is born. Upon retirement age this person will have a nice investment in addition to their Social Security benefits.

In fact, if we took the earmarks for just one year, we could set aside enough savings bonds for a population growth for years to come. This will be advocated by my administration.

For the Strategic Future of Our Nation

5.6.2 Divisive Issues

Since Bush's reinstatement, one of his focal points has been warning us about the state of Social Security, and its questionable future. He and his administration claimed to be well informed. In their spending they have also stated that 'deficits do not matter'.

Putting this concern aside, it appears that Bush's administration has prompted the Democrats to take a position, or offered then another reason to 'chase their tails once more'.

Both positions appear to be based on hear say. They claim to have the facts about Social Security, but the facts seem to be quite different where the Republicans foretell the downfall of the current Social Security system, and the Democrats speak of its lasting future.

I want to look at each position for the purpose of posing questions where for the sake of argument *see how to agree* This is to help understand agendas behind this 'sudden overwhelming concern' about the Social Security system. It is not for the purposes to agree with their positions what so ever but offer a better alternative.

5.6.2.1 Republican's Position

If to agree with Bush, we must ignore their earlier position of "deficits don't matter". But then ask why do they promote the idea of privatization in the first place and why was the Social Security Trust messed ?

They speak about empowering us with our own investment destiny. They also imply that the Democrats don't believe that we are capable of this.

I would rather put the partisan noise aside, and simply ask the following questions:

1- Why not have the Treasury Department step up to the plate itself, and structure a similar investment paradigm as in Chapter 4. This is where the onus is on the Treasury Department for the investment performance, and not the U.S citizen ?

I do not believe it's a question of trying to blame *big government.* I view that it is the responsibility of the executive and legislative branches to make a more cost effective government, and not use it as an excuse to promote private enterprise. It is simply dysfunctional and needs to become cost effective as described in chapter 3.

The New Deal, an Election 2008 Primer

2- Why not have the Social Security trust fund for only Social Security, and nothing but; or better yet, why hasn't our government been responsible enough to do this in the first place in serving the people ?

Should we forget that the trust fund just has a bunch of "IOU's" from raping it since 2001 by those who have controlled the Senate and House until 2007?

These questions concern me, and should you too. They are not being answered, nor even asked by either of the two major parties.

5.6.2.2 Democrats Position

To agree with the Democrats, I need real assurance besides charts and long winded speeches.

1- In their due diligence, and in order to support their position, why not call for a true audit of the U.S. Treasury Department as opposed to just accepting its reports ? This way we all know what the real deal is. After all, who can claim that we are not just down right flat broke ? Deficits have not mattered to the Republicans. The Democrats I believe have a limited understanding of what the real deficit could be. My example is in how corporations normally sugar coat their liabilities. We cannot afford to do this with our budgets, and funds that are managed by the government. The Democrats take on a considerable risk otherwise. When not believing those about a concern who also state that 'deficits do not matter' is like ignoring a pyromaniac who yells Fire. Responsible Democrats and Republicans should demand an audit!

5.6.3 The Politics of Hedging Social Security:

If the Democratic position wins out, and the Social Security system turns out to be in jeopardy, then the Democrats would have been set up for a fall in their creditability. This means that we as the baby boomer, X, Y and Z generations also take this short fall thanks to the Democrats who were set up by the Republicans.

The Republican's then can say "We are responsible and tried to tell you so!". This would be a great CYA for the administration if nothing else at the cost of many generations of Americans to come. If the Republican's win out, and Social Security becomes privatized, then what happens to all of those "IOU's" that were to come due sometime soon? Further, if told that we are the captain of our own row boat suddenly, and put into rough seas, I view as a contemptible disregard for the very purpose that our elected leaders and representatives were put into office.

For the Strategic Future of Our Nation

5.6.4 Correcting the Social Security System for the Strategic Good

If our government is to serve the people well, my over all question is - Why not be transparent and accountable through a comprehensive audit?

The Social Security issue demonstrates the need of government and economic reform. Taking action specifically to correct the Social Security system for the strategic good of the people is dependent on this.

Franklin Delano Roosevelt intended for Social Security to have a good purpose and not be raped with IOU's. It still has that good purpose. It's a matter of putting it back on track. In other words, what has been taken out and replaced with IOU's has to be put back in. The audit tells us this.

If we are able to borrow fortunes for financing 'so called American interests' in Iraq or elsewhere, our first responsibility is to shore up our 'American interest' in our people.

If we do not address this, then what is to prevent the federal government from borrowing and not paying back from other needed programs. Agriculture is becoming another victim of this more recently.

This is the same as ultimately putting every program in some general fund in the way that Homeland Security is structured. Special interests can grab first what they want, and leave government departments with no alternative but to provide lame excuses as to what they share in having a short fall, and why services have to be further diminished.

Saying that more money is going out than coming into Social Security has to do with IOU's. This can be said about any government program if we do not respect them for their purpose.

There is no question for me that there should be considerable audits on the Treasury, and other government departments, and that the un sanitized results to be posted publicly, and discussed openly in public forum with Congress. This is how we can get to the bottom of 'more money going out, deficits do not matter, IOUs, and the cost of funding offshore American interests'.

It is my commitment to correct this. We must make sure that Social Security in what it was intended for by Franklin Delano Roosevelt. It is a guaranteed annuity and must remain so for all generations to come. We will not jettison gutted programs like Social Security, but correct the issues that have compromised them. Additionally I do propose a $10 dollar savings bond for each newborn in this country.

5.7 The Peoples Health Care Plan

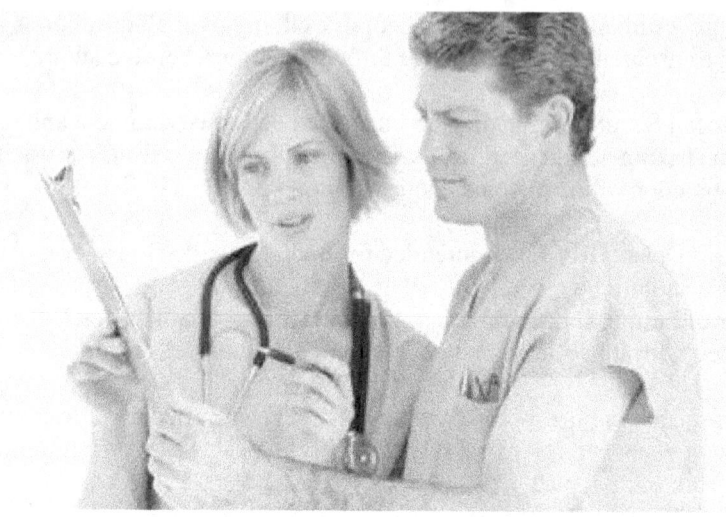

5.7.1 Health Care Reform

FDR noted in his 'The Economic Bill of Rights' that for all, to have 'The right to adequate medical care and the opportunity to achieve and enjoy good health'.

Today, for a major part of America, the choice is food or health care costs. The scope of health care is typically limited, and sometimes filled in by insurance programs that do not serve their stated purpose. There are several penalties in providing stated coverage or it is variable based on market price and demand.

Today's health care is complicated, expensive, and only provides diminishing returns. The government offers its token minimum, and then it is left to free enterprise. Government Medicare (Parts A and B) is for retirement onward. Medicaid is limited by the ability of a state to financially cover the poor. Then there are HMO's, and insurance programs from the private sector to capitalize on your needs.

Government based Medicare and Medicaid offerings are limited. The private sector offerings demonstrate an open volatile for profit business market where paying coverage is at their loss.

The insurance companies invest profits in the financial markets for themselves, while charging a small fortune for providing very little.

For the Strategic Future of Our Nation

The private sector is not intended to serve the people, and the government offering is intended to only provide a bare minimum. There is a myriad of health care insurance offerings. They can be as complicated as cell phone contracts. They are meant to serve the insurance provider. There are limited offerings for just emergencies, and then others for office visits. Then there is co-pay.

What ever these deals really add up to, not everyone gets one. Company Employee Health care plans are negotiated with providers. The coverage is inconsistent between companies. Insurers have to price their offerings based on the demographics of literally millions of policyholders. The bottom line is if you are not fortunate to have a company health plan, then it will cost even far more for less coverage.

For America to demonstrate world leadership, health care reform must be accounted for.

> Consider the *Breast Cancer Patient Protection Act* which will require insurance companies to cover a minimum 48-hour hospital stay for patients undergoing a mastectomy. It's about eliminating the "drive-through mastectomy" where women are forced to go home just a few hours after surgery, against the wishes of their doctor, still groggy from anesthesia and sometimes with drainage tubes still attached.

5.7.2 The 3 Step Workable Peoples Health Care Plan

What is proposed is to provide a government based National **Federal Care Program.** This is where community contribution can participate in preventative health care and the private sector can compete in order to offer even better health care coverage. This is summarized as:

* The Federal Care Program is required to afford fixed health care infrastructure costs, make services available when needed by any US citizen, and cover health treatments and remedies adequately up to 100%. This is to include but not be limited to chronic care, emergencies, restorative health, post operative recovery treatments, and generic prescription programs.

* 'For the Good' community based offerings are to address the economically disadvantaged, where health issues can be circumvented before becoming of significance. Practitioners may take tax benefits based on quota and level of service.

* The Private Sector is welcomed to operate honestly by offering competitive alternatives for such things as elective surgery and post operative care.

The New Deal, an Election 2008 Primer

Step 1: The Federal Care Component:

* Medicare and Medicaid funds will be shifted into a general federally managed pool for the **Peoples Health Care** fund. Half of what employer/employee health insurance normally pay will instead go to the government fund. There will be no need, but optional for private sector employee/employer health insurance. A partial contribution by employer and employee payroll tax will be added to the general pool; with a balance of about what employer/employee health insurance use to pay. For example, if you paid $400 per month for health insurance, you will pay only $200 per month instead into the fund as an alternative.

As insurance policies expire, the requirement can be moved to the Peoples Health Care Plan. For the uninsured, it should be made immediately available upon its implementation.

* Health Care Bonds are to be the financial underpinnings in financing the plan. They are considered tax exempt in being in the category of a social welfare bond. They will be offered to the financial markets, and to the public for investments. They are in of themselves to cover the same costs as employer and employee payroll tax contributions. These bonds will provide a financial robustness to the Peoples Health Care Plan. One forth, or 25%(¼) will be available for liquidity, and 75% or 3/4ths to be reinvested for the people.

Additionally, working people who invest in these bonds do not pay tax if taken from their gross income.

* The Peoples Health Care bond is based on social welfare bonds. It is to fill in the immediate financial gaps in health care costs, and partly reinvest to build surplus. The bond buyer can trade them like other government bonds. Being Tax exempt, means that financial institutions do not pay tax on benefits returned from the bonds there by providing a fine investment vehicle for the institutional banking markets.

* The Peoples Health Care bond removes the financial burden of costs and lowers employer and employee payroll tax requirements if used as a personal investment. This means that you have lowered your reportable gross income, and there by pay less tax; and can use the bond to hedge annual employee/employer health insurance payments that have been made toward the 'Peoples Health Care plan'. This enables you to make back the money tax free that you have paid into the 'Peoples Health Care plan', while taking a tax deduction on the original employee/employer health insurance payments.

For the Strategic Future of Our Nation

* The Peoples Health Care Plan is also a 'Safety Net' that will cover balances for extended veteran's coverage, unemployed, and other welfare needs. For the economically disadvantaged and veterans, our government is to cover the cost.

It is not to be a matter of a minimum time frame or other of being uninsured for eligibility, or otherwise.

- Eligibility is a matter of strata. When one's health care benefits would run out, then there must be a safety net where convergence to other eligibility occurs. This is based on the individual's economies of scale. In other words, as they might become re-employed from a point when unemployed, their method of coverage is realigned.

* Government Generic Drug Coverage is to drive the costs of drugs down in the prescription market. Any pharmaceutical provider will have to meet required government standard pricing models, or will not be selling on behalf of the government. The incentive for the pharmaceutical provider is in delivering volume over others who did not get contracted and endorsed by the government.

Step 2: For the Good Community Watch: Additionally, in the way that our schools require community services from students, I also see no reason as to why private practitioners, given guidelines, cannot write off a percent of their services against their normal taxed income that are afforded to the economically disadvantaged. This aids in preventative health care and employs people.

Step 3: Private Sector Plan: The Plan is to further encourages industry to match and exceed in quality or stay out of the way of the Peoples Health Care Plan.

In business, the imposition of government regulations generally is responded to by innovation. Unlike before, the government is to set a standard for the private sector to innovate through for more competitive offerings.

This standard is to meet or exceed the **'Peoples Health Care Plan'**.

As much as Wall Street demonstrates innovation in dealing with any new SEC regulation, why can't the health care industry do the same ?

This is to compel the health care industry to lower costs while competing against a universal health care plan that can serve all.

5.8 Immigration Reform

"Give me your tired, your poor, your huddled masses yearning to breathe free, The wretched refuse of your teeming shore. Send these, the homeless, tempest-tost to me, I lift my lamp beside the golden door!" by Emma Lazarus

Today, I get hate email about Immigration. An example is <u>Human Events</u> whose message is that "liberal media is advancing an open borders agenda that is threatening our sovereignty and security".

Immigration has suddenly out of no where become an overly important issue in the media and in advocacy groups. We heard in the news that *Terrorists can access the United States easily* at our borders. Then the ones that are caught *are just sent back* to try to get into our country again.

Other messages promoted are 'there is a lot of *human trafficking* of illegal immigrants'; and *drugs come with immigrants* and some are even used as mules; and that *immigrants take our jobs away* by working for less; and allot of times they *come here to go on welfare by having a child born in the United States* and *just bring their ways and do not respect ours*.

For the Strategic Future of Our Nation

This could sound alarming, and in the media, and in advocacy groups is intended to be. Finally our sitting president after 6 years in office has presented a policy to address his alarming concerns. Part of his policy is in building walls on our borders, and wanting immigrants to periodically leave, and pay hefty fees of over $10,000 per year just to work here. I think George Jr. over looked the fact that 'immigrants' are not intending to just be visitors but want to become US citizens.

Definition of immigrant from dictionary.com: "a person who migrates to another country, usually for permanent residence."

Foreign Visitor Labor does not represent immigrants.

Immigration has some real outstanding issues that are not being addressed. It is used as a smoke screen instead to distract from other pressing issues and to make barter deals in Congress to import foreign non-immigrant labor.

The issues that it is supposed to distract from include the War in Iraq, that we might end up going to war with Iran but yet still have to find a reason; that our economy is on a serious Herbert Hoover like slippery slope; that we do not have a real nationwide health care plan in place, and that Social Security is in quasi state that the Bush administration would prefer to jettison away instead of taking the responsibility for its gutting; that there is a serious unemployment issue; and that the tax gap is getting insurmountable. Then we can even consider that the stock market is getting critically over inflated like in Hoover's times; and that the Bush administration is being perpetually scrutinized by over sight committees in both houses of congress over an endless and perpetually growing laundry list of alleged corrupt polices. With this in mind, then how should we account for the *real issues* on immigration ?

Unfortunately, like another bolt coming lose that holds our country together, immigration has become a real issue like everything since November, 2000. This is due mostly to the current state of our economy. We can no longer afford the spirit of Emma Lazarus that is written on the tablet of the Statue of Liberty.

To be Americans, we must strive to be able to do this again once more. For if not, then what do we stand for?

What does Liberty Stand for, if we are to ignore the history of the American way in light of the 'no mans' land in principles that we have been led into since November 2000. In other words, if we follow our current leadership, where have they not said, cut your losses and run ?

The New Deal, an Election 2008 Primer

In the following there are:

> **A-** 8 Noted Issues in the Media

> **B-** What are seen as the Real Issues in my opinion

> **C-** The Proposed Immigration Reform Plan that I would like you to consider

A- The 8 Noted Issues in the Media

There are 8 that are noted. This is not to say, that there are 20 more, but are the one's that have pushed my buttons the most.

1- "Terrorists can access the United States easily"

If this is such a major issue, then should we build walls on our Canadian borders too. After all, could this have prevented 9/11, and can it actually slow down the volume of immigrants wishing to find a future life here ?

> Any organization that wishes to terrorize us can easily forge documentation and papers to get through the airports. This is not to suggest that we should not use prudence at our borders, but perhaps have a better relationship with our borders and our foreign neighbors.

> Immigrants are generally not terrorists but instead, wish to obtain US citizenship.

Okay, so let's instead consider bar coded passports. Besides preventing *identity theft,* the bar coded passports can be verified as authentic from the country of origin when given reciprocity.

> Countries can easily provide a reciprocal data base access where anyone can be authenticated as to who they say they are. The bar code can translate to a finger print record that also includes your travel history. It's a matter of collaboration and does not need to go to any extremes such as DNA prints, etc. If we do this with our passports, and allow other countries such an access service, and prevent others who do not offer the same, eventually, it will attain parity. What's more, why not login first to airport security to announce your travel plans and purpose. All flights normally do this, and if in question, limits the lines of travelers who need to be scrutinized. Can you imagine the amount of money saved at airports, as well as the amount of your time when traveling ?

For the Strategic Future of Our Nation

Additionally, the National Guard is to be used as is intended by the US Constitution for protecting our physical borders and ports. Instead of erecting walls , why can't we just put the National Guard to proper use to assist border guards ? Considering that we are supposed to have a Homeland Security issue, who else should we depend on in such a perceived crisis. You can dig under a wall, which is costly to put up in the first place, and this does not protect our ports from WMD or containers which can be loaded unfortunately with people who wish to disparately arrive in our country.

2- "Immigrants are just sent back with no penalty and return again"

To correct this, being caught and sent back by our border guards and National Guard, or being refused at the border over and over again can be regarded like getting driver license points. Consider that each and every time one is caught illegally 'entering' our space, that it's a matter of time consuming process of fingerprint verification as opposed to a quick return.

> The purpose is to discourage, and not for inhumane treatment. Each offense requires that one is processed for a period of time where they are photographed and finger printed. There is no fun in this when one's intent is to get into our country. We also get to learn about each one more. When sent back, if one gets too many points, say starting at 10, then they will be locked up instead for a period of 60 days and then sent back. This should help dissuade coming through our borders illegally.

> This is not intended to conflict with Amendment 13 of the Constitution on involuntary servitude or to imply some form of slavery. Although not also intended to be a paid vacation to a country club, those retained for a period of time are to be treated in a humane manner as all visitors to the United States.

Please note, that this is not to say, do not let one apply for citizenship as one should if that's their sincere intent. This is something that we should acknowledge in all sincerity. But it must be on terms that we as a nation can currently afford !

We must also take into consideration the health, safety and welfare of the people that surge to our shores, and are they actually seeking asylum. People that have survived crossing from Asia in shipping containers, or in an over burdened boat in reaching the coast of Florida, can not be regarded the same as crossing over the border from Mexico, or Canada where they can be returned easily; and where their lives are not threatened by their place of origin. I hold that justice must be blind, but its heart must see.

The New Deal, an Election 2008 Primer

3- "Human Trafficking:"

As this is unacceptable for a humane society, such business enterprises have to be dealt with effectively. There is no question that our prison systems are filled with people, but we should first fill them with the right ones. I am glad that I am not a judge and jury as I would want to lock up those who cause such misery for the remaining part of their lives. This is something that our laws we must rely on, and rely on them, we should.

4- "Drugs Come with Immigrants"

This is addressed in #2, and 3 above. Drug Trafficking can be viewed as the same as human trafficking. What has to be in mind, is that people who are used as mules, can be under a threat of their life by human traffickers. Hence, guilt by association cannot be assumed, but clearly scrutinized.

> While operating in trust and ignorance that someone is going to get you to the promised land where you have paid a hefty fortune for it, the price can change, and one can, when compromised, be put in a life threatening position to do the bidding of the trafficker. Further, one's children or loved ones can be at risk.

5- "Immigrants Take Our Jobs Away"

5.1 - This is some what of a misnomer. Thanks to the IRS, we know of at least 10.2 million unregistered immigrants that file with an average annual wage of $20,000 US dollars. They pay about $5,000 in Federal Income taxes. Annually, this adds about $50 billion to our government and an over all $200 billion into our economy.

What is more important is to know actually how many unregistered immigrants are on our shores today. If there are 20 million, then the contribution noted is cut by half, and if 40 to 50 million or more, then those contributing to our economy are negligible compared to those who are not.

For the Strategic Future of Our Nation

5.2 Most first generation immigrants are hard working people in this country. Many are entrepreneurs who just need a little help. This picture of the *Subway* shop represents some European immigrants. In New York City, most small business owners are first and second generation immigrants.

They are committed people that are not just visiting in order to send money out of the country to return to some other home someday to live off of their earnings. The majority wish to become, if not already, American citizens.

5.3 - Over the past few years our economy and jobs have actually been impacted by foreign labor forces that are willing to work at even less than previous market rates and also have no interest in citizenship. They can also be mistakenly called immigrants which they are not.

Technically, an immigrant cannot work here legally if they are taking a job away from an American person - that is the State Department rule. Further, visiting labor should be held to this rule and in back of the immigrant in line for the job.

In terms of the foreign labor market, for many businesses today, off shoring is the way to go in order to save money. I would hazard a guess that there is not a financial, nor insurance institution in New York that does not offshore most of its labor; and hire locally foreign visitors at below fare market rates. There is a significant volume of temporary visitors that work at below competitive wage rates in this country that do send their money back to their home.

6- "Immigrants come here to go on welfare by having a child born in the United States"

Not every one wants to go on welfare, and people do have their pride. This elderly lady has seen the Maoist regime in China, and today searches in garbage cans in NYC for redeemable bottles and cans.

She is a proud and gracious woman who at the end of her day has two very large bags of recyclable garbage tied onto a poll that she carries away on her shoulder.

For her this is better than earning 5 cents a day from where she came from. How she got here is also of concern. More than likely, she could have arrived in a shipping container. Besides the National Security issue about this, there is also the humane one that we also have to account for. Then we also have to account for what it really means to want to come here in the first place just to dig in our garbage.

She is no less of a human than you or I, and has no reason to look at herself less than we. She works for her living and does not ask for any one's sympathy. She is happy to have gotten here in her lifetime.

Do we really think that people come here just to live on welfare ? This is the country where people can make something of themselves, where as noted, 10.2 illegal immigrants have made over $200 billion in revenue in this country, where most of this is invested in this country, and $50 billion of this is paid in federal taxes.

Compare this to the $130 billion that is to be borrowed from our Asian lenders for the 2007 supplementary war budget that we as tax payers must pay back for our American commercial development interest along with brave American blood and lives in Iraq for 2008.

Immigration has also served as a new target to vent hate. Promoting the image of the lazy, worthless, *going on welfare* immigrant message can be like a new form of racism. To make the point, consider this thinking compared to how the Afro-American was viewed in WWII when our forces were segregated.

For the Strategic Future of Our Nation

Afro Americans were considered lazy and worthless, yet they were the Tuscany fliers who protected our day light bombers, and those who worked hard on building the Alaskan Highway. Given the opportunity anyone will rise to the occasion of dignity. Racism comes in all forms and immigration should not be regarded in such a trite manner.

At Universities, where higher learning is considered paramount, this form of racism is becoming apparent as in our country today. We should look at it for what it is worth and not let it cloud the actual issues about immigration.

In March 2007, like a mob, NYU Republican Club Students went out to find 'the Illegal Immigrant'. It turned out to be a foreign student, and not an immigrant. The student's papers had expired by about a week. This student was humiliated as this NYU political group decided to be the Department of Immigration in their own way.

These students overlooked the fact that NYU is located in a city, where its neighborhood business are for the most part owned and operated by immigrants. If these students use the copy shop, pizzeria, or otherwise, it is rare to find a non-immigrant merchant.

In higher learning, it demonstrates a dysfunctional student body where more history teachers might be helpful. The history teachers can start with Civil Rights and roll back further into history. This might help the level of introspection of these students when it comes to listening to their political icons. These students might realize that, like the drug traffickers that use human mules, they too are being used in a similar way to spew hate for the sake of other's agendas.

Simply, what is the difference between the hate demonstrated in the 'We Got Him' focus compared to McCarthyism, KKK, Nazi Germany, or what even is the attitude found currently in the Middle East. Can they aspire to more noble goals ?

What ever their issues are with immigration, perhaps they should put more study into economics. If you have a boat that fits 10 people, then putting 20 will capsize it. The size of the boat is based on *economy of scale*. This spells out the maximum number of passengers. Can these student political groups learn to build better ships ?

When we hear that the economy is booming, and yet have immigration issues, it might help to question who this economy applies to. As it is lopsided, perhaps the young leaders of political clubs might want to embrace an issue that will confront their future where immigration is only a symptom of it. Perhaps they could find a cure for the cause ?

The New Deal, an Election 2008 Primer

Being rich in the United States with a weak American dollar while heading towards a third world economy does not say much. It is a luxury to be a college student compared to what awaits one after words. It is also an opportune time to get an education.

What ever their political affiliations, hopefully its purpose is for a better tomorrow, and not to use these students as mules for political polarization.

7- "They just bring their ways and do not respect ours"

The United States is made up of culturally diverse people. As language is culture, most all have customs. Sometimes it is apparent that it is 'not like the old days when most of us looked like each other'.

One of the bones that Campaign 08 candidates can toss at us is that immigrants should learn English. This can be a legitimate concern, but I do not advocate that we can only speak English, as this puts our First Amendment rights at risk.

Newt Gingrich is well known for promoting the idea that the official language of the United Stated should be English. This is like selling you a house that you already own. English is already the official language.

Let's also consider what speaking English means. If you were to put natively born US citizens from different areas of the country in the same room, it would take some time for each to understand the other due to local accents as is the case in every country.

To press this point, unless you are a literary scholar of Shakespeare, and have studied the 'Tempest', then you, like I, do not know what "Bate, I beseech you, widow Dido" means ? Our next greatest challenge is to listen to English spoken with a foreign accent, besides from regions in the US itself.

In some cases, we should define 'what are our ways, and what are not our ways'. In the spirit of the First Amendment, we should further consider those ways which do not prevent other's ways that do not conflict. For example, one of the biggest issues we have today in our communities is a matter of tolerance with each other.

This is also not due to immigrants, but can even be due to politicians that want to create a red and blue divide in our country; or even others that create such divides to distinguish themselves while tossing the hungry for guidance and leadership, sugar coated illusion.

For the Strategic Future of Our Nation

An easy example is comparing the 'Newt Gingrich **Conservative** Green position' in accusing others as being the '**Liberal** Environmentalism'. Newt's message is that the others are not real environmentalists, but he is. So much for being a uniter and not a divider.

We can also look at what immigrants see when they get here as our ways. Part of the issue is how we are cast in terms of our diminishing self image. It is not social or personal empowerment. This is another reason why we must never forget the Dignity of Human rights as a principle.

With the message, 'let them eat cake', it becomes easier and easier to defer on true regard, and responsibility by those responsible for upholding standards for our nation. A tangible example is how FDR gave a damn compared to Hoover which brought in his wake 'Hooverville's across our nation.

For a government that is supposed to serve the people, like any service, it is easier to provide diminishing returns when led by criminally incompetent management. This is then compounded by the growing complexity of our social structure that is left to Capitalism at its worst to take advantage of.

An earlier example is Reagan and *big government*, and how private enterprise should run our lives. Since Reagan, we now have a population of disenfranchised citizens called the homeless, and a government that is inept in serving such fundamental needs as health care.

Consistent in form , today, the Government does very little for us, and we are given immigration as a focal point to vent our frustrations. Hence, we are told that the *American Dream* is only a dream.

The more we are told to lower our expectations and standards, the more we ultimately devalue our own sense of self esteem. In other words, why are we told in media that we must have such a low value of life ? It is simply easier then to offer only diminishing returns by our leadership and those who they serve.

Once upon a time when buying gas for your car, attendants would clean your hub caps check your oil, and clean the windshield. Like today's gas station attendants, election 08 candidates don't even have to demonstrate a plan, but press the message instead that you are lucky with what you get as leadership. So much for *hopes and dreams* , as under the hood it is vapor !

For the state of the nation, we have to look at collateral influences in our social structure and to whose and what purposes are served. Hence 'Transparent and Accountable Government' is a mandate for us to have any viable future.

The New Deal, an Election 2008 Primer

The only means of social welfare is through government reform, which will require in its evolution, corporate reform. We are taught by them over time to be self serving for our very survival. For me this is so much the case as it explains why street crime ultimately is the prodigy of white collar crime.

For Standards, it will take time, as we have been led into No Man's land. The road to return to personal empowerment is in Chapter 5.

8- "Should We Follow the Bush Plan"

On the books, for an accountant, it would look great to send illegal immigrants back to their place of origin each year, and then charge them a $10,000 if they wanted to return.

> "Under the plan, undocumented workers could apply for three-year work visas, which the plan dubs "Z" visas. They would be renewable indefinitely but renewal would cost $3,500 each time. The undocumented workers would have legal status with the visas, but to get a green card, making them legal permanent residents, they would have to return to their home country, apply at a U.S. embassy or consulate to re-enter legally and pay a $10,000 fine. " Source CNN.com

There is a constitutional hurdle that George junior, and his council will have to address.

> a- Section 9 Limits on Congress: 'The Migration or Importation of such Persons as any of the States now existing shall think proper to admit, shall not be prohibited by the Congress prior to the year one thousand eight hundred and eight, but a tax, or duty may be imposed on such Importation, not exceeding ten dollars for each Person.'

In addition to the constitutional issue, in doing the math, 10.2 million people are expected to leave the country, their stores, place of business, and homes, then jeopardizes the $200 billion annual revenue, and $50 billion in federal taxes, just so they can return to where they originated. They need to then come up with an additional $10,000 (or $100 billion) somehow without their stores, places of business and homes in order to return to the world that they built which could be ransacked while in their absence.

Early on in George junior's presidency, he noted that living in the White House was like being in a fish bowl. Perhaps this is where he was correct in his thinking.

For the Strategic Future of Our Nation

B- The Real Immigration Issues

Our real issues on immigration pertain to:

a- Our current economy which can or cannot support the influx of immigrants

b- Who really wants to swear an allegiance to this country and who really does not

Lets keep in mind that in addition to the 10.2 million unregistered immigrants, that there are registered foreigners that are shipping about $800 billion dollars out of our country every year legally.

We can also expect at least 7 million Iraqi refugees who are to immigrate here, that like the legalized foreign work force, don't have swearing an allegiance to this country in the forefront of their minds. Instead they will be waiting to when they can return to Iraq.

From the standpoint of Education, we also have to account for 10% of young students who do not currently speak English, and that this is expected to increase to about 25%, or 1/4 (1 quarter) of young students in the next 10 to 15 years. We also have to account for the fact that many adolescent age immigrants do not have any education from their country of origin, and that many adults likewise do not either.

This also fits the case of many native born Americans, as after all what is speaking the English Language, and how many native born Americans do even get a High School diploma?

Speaking English does not say that we are literate, or that we have enough education to understand the exploits of '*binding arbitration agreements*' even in *cell phone contracts*, *balloon mortgages*, or how not to be entrapped by *pay day loans* from predatory lenders.

As a nation, we have much to improve in our quality of life. We must put the breaks on in becoming a third world economy in the next few years or we are due to many new Hooverville's. And that's regardless of any immigrants that arrive on our shores and borders.

In the meantime, we are faced with an ever more rush of immigrants that want to live in our country, and must have workable solutions for this as we recover what we once had, The American Dream.

The New Deal, an Election 2008 Primer

C -Proposed Immigration Reform

1- Send Visitors Home for Now: Before we can competently address immigration with respect to our economy, we must first address other aspects of how we are affecting our economy in terms of labor.

From Balanced Trade: There are a multitude of work visa based visitors in the USA that are not willing to swear an allegiance to our country. They are cheap labor, and for the most part, send their money home.

> This compromises free market trade in terms of pricing for the labor pool in this country. Any country that so wishes to import their labor force, should be required to not under price going rates for the standard of living in the United States, prove that an American cannot fill the job (at the wage level that is, and has been for the job in question) at not below earlier market rates; and provide the US with an equal export monetary value. For those institutions which offshore their labor, such labor should be taxed in order to encourage such institutions to hire American labor.

2- The Laws: Consider what are 'fines' and what is 'amnesty' when it comes to the existing residing unregistered immigrants. We have to look at what law was actually broken, and what purpose does it really serve; and do we really want to know, actually, how many unregistered immigrants are in the USA. Consider, we could even have 20 million, where our infrastructure and economy is not prepared for this.

I view that it serves no real purpose to penalize those who are contributing to our economy such as the 10.2 million taxpayers that bring in $200 billion each year into our country; and that we need to understand what we are really dealing with in terms of immigration. Witch hunts will not serve this purpose as people normally hide when in fear.

As the economy is the primary factor for the level of immigration, in volume, that can be allowed, and in compliance with the noted proposed criterion (a - e) below, The Immigration Reform and Control Act of 1986 so shall be proposed for revision to Congress. This is to allow the United States to have fare and just law for immigration subject to the level of economic burden that can be supported by our nation.

a- For those who are paying taxes, should be able to register without fear of reprisal. They are contributors to our economy, and therefore, our country. For those who are not paying taxes, are in fact taxing our economy. In both cases we have to know, who is willing to swear an allegiance to our country, and who is not.

b- Those not willing to swear an allegiance to our country, and are employed, must leave until our economy can support their presence. In other words, when Americans are no longer out of work, can we afford to have foreigners here that want to ship money out of our country; and not before. That is regardless if they pay taxes or not. The jobs can be for Americans at realistic and fare market rates, that are not suddenly below earlier market rates, who can also pay the taxes, where this reduces the need also to collect unemployment.

> For example, as an IT specialist previous to 9/11, I could earn upwards of $90-100 dollars per hour. The same job description is now filled at $40-$50 per hour by foreign labor.

c- For those who are employed, and willing to swear an allegiance, allow them to do so. They want to be Americans, and this is what our country was built on.

As immigrants become citizens, labor unions can be strengthened to maintain fair wages.

d- For those who are not employed, and willing to swear an allegiance, they are to register with the Government for employment; If below the age of 60, and able bodied, they are allowed 60 days of residence, and if not gainfully employed by then, must be sent to the country of origin if not hostile to the US, where they can await notification of employment. If they are not able bodied, and/or over 60, I think we really have to search who we are, if to want to send them away.

e- For those not willing to register, and employed or not, demonstrate no intent to work with the constraints that we must have for immigration. This includes Iraqi refugees, or anyone who is not natively born in this country. They cannot be permitted to live here. In our current economy, we can only allow those who are, or intend to be Americans, the right to live here under our laws as a civil society.

As noted in 'd' above, each offense requires that one is processed for a period of time where they are photo graphed and finger printed. When sent back, if they get too many points, say starting at 10, then they will be locked up instead for a period of 60 days before being sent back.

Further as noted, this is not intended to conflict with Amendment 13 of the Constitution on involuntary servitude or to imply some form of slavery.

The New Deal, an Election 2008 Primer

3- No Open Borders

We cannot just have open borders. Our borders must be secure. In our current times this is where the National Guard should be deployed. We can build walls, but this becomes a permanent fixture that closes us in, as much as keeping others out. The current administration has done this over and over again. This is not in our history, and it is not the American Way.

Noted earlier, in our current economy, we also cannot afford the spirit of Emma Lazarus that is written on the tablet of the Statue of Liberty. But we must strive to be able to do this again once more, some day. For if not, then what do we stand for. What does Liberty stand for if we are to ignore the history of the American way ?

We must strive to better our country. Challenging times makes it that much more important that as a united people we do stand for what we stood for.

But just as much as the hungry can not feed others, in our current times we must accept the rude fact that we must shore up the standards of our way of life in order to have the American way.

In this manner, we can return to being able to afford others in the way that the Statue of Liberty has stood in symbolizing our American way of life and freedom for others as we care to have for ourselves.

Chapter 6

Foreign Policy

'Talk softly and carry a big stick' Theodore Roosevelt

6.1 Summary

From the 'Art of War' '- the single enemy's cart is worth 10 of one's own'. The wisdom that can be gleamed is that it is easier to make friends than to deplete one's resources in maintaining a front line to achieve the other's cart.

Foreign Policy is the state of the relationship that we have with other nations. This can be in terms of trade and commerce, and in what state of peace and/or war that we are involved in.

In both cases, foreign policy is a matter of ground. We can be on the high, low or on contentious ground in a state of peace, war, or in between with others. Economic solvency removes compromise when claiming ground.

Given a road to economic solvency, there is a road to chosen ground or what was referred to in the late 19th century as manifest destiny. In the 21st Century, this road is first built or repaired by willing to work with other nations where they share in our benefit in foreign policy.

Trade and commerce are addressed in the Balanced Trade Proposal in Chapter 4, Economic Reform, and is tangentially related to the following that addresses the basic practices of war and peace.

In diplomacy, given that we demonstrate mutual respect as a standard for how we respect ourselves, this is the standard to expect from others. It is the standard expected in our relationship with the UN and the countries it represents.

For others, it is the respect that we back with our level of defense and/or strategic alternatives and capability for taking preemptive action when considered necessary.

The New Deal, an Election 2008 Primer

6.2 - In Declaring War

When in peace, we seek certain objectives, and when in war, we seek others. During peace options for war can be put on the table and during war, options for peace. In either case, the question is how strategically are we considering them?

History can resemble a full circle. When we think of war, do we think of stated missions and exit strategies. Do we consider what affects a war and loss of human life will or can have at its completion compared to the intended purpose. Or is it viewed in terms of the victor within the scope of battles alone. Are we conservative or liberal in our latitude for thinking of its outcome? In order to do this, foreign policy must be able to shift in either case as needed. In all cases, its diplomacy must have teeth, and its defense the faculty of reason.

6.2.1 Habeas Corpus and the Strategic Right to Chosen Ground

I view that *Habeas Corpus* is to apply to all including non-citizens. The only time it does not apply is when under invasion, or insurrection.

Consider that the colonials could have been viewed as spies or illegal combatants by the British if we wanted to use Donald Rumsfeld's arguments. On the other hand, the Al Qaeda, Taliban, nor the Northern Alliance have uniforms, yet two of the three were/are considered enemies and one, an army of allies. This of course could change, as the others were allies once, and the third was previously the enemy. Consequently, all prisoners in war are prisoners of war and the Geneva Convention must be regarded..

If necessary, what I would have done different was to allow said prisoners to congregate, as opposed to separate, or isolate them. In this manner I could eventually identify the officers, and then separate them as a group. These are the ones to focus on. If there are crimes that they are accused of then they must have fair justice. The remaining body does not in its entirety need to be tried for crimes. The body without a head has no purpose. Hence, a new head can be offered for the body.

The question is 'if necessary' as we *dropped the ball* in Tora Bora. Could we learn anything of value from the ones left behind to be killed or captured ? Osama bin Laden had already escaped. I am convinced that bin Laden is in Sweden. This is discussed later in addressing the question if he was really the only player.

For the Strategic Future of Our Nation

6.2.2 The Right and the Wrong

There was both right and wrong in the use of the atomic bomb when war was declared on America by Japan. In our defense we must be capable of using power which is the right in addition to saving many more American lives; but was wrong in having to use it in the first place on humanity. When confronting the possibly of declaring war and its avoidance, it is not a matter of thinking out of the box, but not letting ourselves get stuffed into one. It could be a matter of what we believe is right compared to what we see as very wrong. But does this in of itself place us in a box of the 'hear and now', where right and wrong can ultimately be measured as a future result of our actions ? Present day Japan is a close friend, business partner, lender and ally. This was catalyzed by our strong defense. But in not seeing the future, what does 'for the greater good' mean ?

If defense is managed by reason, it is conservative in purpose, where its ripple affect can be like a tsunami. In the absence of reason, it is an unmanaged resource in its untold ripple affect and eventually depleted. Power has its limitations. If diplomacy were to have the same dynamic, in having teeth, could we then say that 'let war not be an option on the table before all other options can be considered '. And if our diplomacy lacks teeth, can we conclude that it could not see options to consider ?

A: Options and The American Civil War

We must be capable of using power correctly, or be subject to its limitations. Consider the *American Civil War* as an example. What were the other options? War was considered necessary in response to the succession of the South. This succession was based on both the North and South believing that they were in the right and the other in the wrong.

The American Civil War was a noble effort for both sides of the country regardless of who was right, and who was wrong. Although its apparent cause was the succession of the South, it set the precedent to abolish slavery; which is morally right, or can be considered 'for the greater good'. As a young country of less than 100 years old, for Congress to be able declare war against its former colleagues required the division of the country where as a full Congress previously voted for rights against wrongs together.

In American lives, it cost 4 for every slave freed, where modest projections in war are 10 wounded for one lost. In total, there were 620,000 military deaths, and I estimated 6,200,000 wounded Americans. Further, there is no statistic found yet for non-military deaths or causalities. It was, and is still considered a worth while sacrifice when left with no other option.

The New Deal, an Election 2008 Primer

This poses the questions: were other options looked at by President Lincoln, previous presidents and Congress before the South's succession. Was it a black and white matter of right and wrong. Were all means used at disposal. Did this prevent the option of war from being removed from the table, or could the Civil War have been unnecessary by looking at alternatives for those who felt right and those who felt wronged?

Previous to the war, the North was one of the major consumers of the South's cotton. A succession could hurt the South's economy. When in peace we can seek certain objectives. In war we cannot. War as a managed force must be missions based on a scheduled completion. In peace, missions are not limited to schedules and can endure. In diplomacy, it's a matter of going the extra mile.

For the South's labor force of slaves, workers just like today are only needed and can be considered over head when not needed. If the North could have helped to subsidize the cost of workers in the South, the need and cost of slaves could have been reconsidered by the South. This would have been an excellent debate in a Congress consisting of the North and the South.

In using all means at one's disposal, with the aid of government, financing a work force, can be accomplished through bonds. These bonds could be bought by industrialists in the North. The payment on this bond is based on the South or other, to pay for only labor used. This financing would allow the emancipation of slaves to become wage earners paid by the government. Where the price of the bond compared to the actual cost of labor paid differ is the value of the bond. The Government pays a coupon if the cost of labor is less than the bond. The bond provides the immediate sum of money needed by the government on an annual basis for paying labor. The bond is being paid in a monthly basis by plantation owners for labor used, where the balance of the bond can be invested for paying an additional offset. In other words, the government does not need 12 month coverage at one time. 10 Months of the bond funds could be invested. This adds to the value of the original funds raised by the bond. Based on estimated cost of labor and base value of the bond for a period of 12 months the return value could at a minimum pay for the coupons; or extend the base value for additional months of coverage; or a combination of both. Under such a structure, what was once a slave could become an independent contractor that seasonally could do work in the South and else where. For any independent contractor today, there is not always a labor union for every kind of contracting. Independent contractors are not assured of year round work, and are expected to obtain their next job. Consequently, the identity of the African-American as in parity, like self esteem, is something that we could have helped foster early on in our history.

For the Strategic Future of Our Nation

B: War for the Greater Good and Vietnam

Our undeclared war in Vietnam was triggered by an incident in North Vietnam waters called the Bay of Tonkin. It was announced by President Lyndon B. Johnson that North Vietnamese gun boats fired on one of our destroyers. President Nixon later had promoted the message that if we did not stop the communists there, it would destabilize the region and they would eventually invade our shores.

After years of war, and a compulsory military draft, upwards of 60,000 brave Americans lost their lives with an additional estimated 600,000 were severely wounded. Some represent part of the homeless in our nation today.

During that time, we carpet bombed Hanoi nightly. North Vietnam lost an estimated 5 for every one American lost. Their total losses could be estimated from 300,0000 to 500,000 deaths, and upwards of 3 to 5 million wounded. When leaving Vietnam, the US took on millions of South Vietnamese refugees, and Nixon wanted *peace with honor*.

China was our so called ultimate concern about Vietnam. As in having Vietnam could strategically place our defenses facing China.

When looking back today at our exit in Vietnam, many still feel that we had cut and run. But then we have to ask ourselves, if we had not exited from Vietnam, and given up what was considered our American interests in the region, could we have established initial trade relations with China in the early 80's. Consequently could China have become the financial super power it is today and who represents one of our major creditors for our national debt?

It would have been impossible to predict such an outcome but our defense demonstrated faculties of reason. The outcome of continued war can more likely be predicted as to continue with an average loss of life of American lives and a continued financial burden to fund the military effort, where there would be ultimately no progress in the region.

What also could have happened is that since China and Russia were supporting the North Vietnam position, could the war have further destabilized the region, and to a point of mutually assured destruction as we were still then in the Cold War.

The New Deal, an Election 2008 Primer

6.2.3 On Unilateral Action

The Bay of Tonkin as our embarking on the Vietnam war is considered unilateral action. Unilateral action could imply leadership to some based upon some stated principle for the action; but a principle that does not provide common ground in the United Nations normally lacks a shared foundation to stand on.

What is more than the case, is that unilateral action demonstrates a failure in foreign policy and world leadership. When this is the case, unilateral action in world affairs further compounds its own failures with non expected costs and collateral damage in our position as a world leader.

To inspire is leadership in the world, where to threaten is to isolate one's strategic place in it.

To be the world leader, we must lead it. This has to be not by coercion or threat, but instead through the continued demonstration of transparent diplomacy that brings others in world leadership to the table of common grounds.

The mandate of the UN is not to avoid or reason away world issues, but to address them. Leadership on a world issue consequently must expect the due diligence of the UN. It is not to give up on expecting this as it is the strength afforded by the UN.

Those that are inspired by sincerity will follow a leader based on their own due diligence. If common grounds cannot be established then it can be identified as to why they are not.

For all parties at the table, differences must be resolved, as personal agendas are to be put aside. The cost and the benefit are to be examined and horizons set as to the conclusion and then the tomorrow of joint action.

For the Strategic Future of Our Nation

6.2.4 Preemptive Strikes

I do believe in preemptive action when considered necessary, but also respect Congress as the one who actually declares war.

It is leadership as the president when obtaining Congress's declaration for war as this has the people's backing and therefore, the inherent respect for the president as commander and chief.

It is the *abuse of power* to disenfranchise congress from this decision when major commitments are ultimately required. The president should appeal to congress with the war plan and the *exit strategy*, or the cost of lives can become immeasurable.

When being able to just press 'the button', the Cold War was like a Hatfield McCoy syndrome that we knew as MAD, or mutually assured destruction. We are starting to forget this with the new escalation and related profits of nuclear weapons.

In the case of World War II, we in effect did a well founded preemptive strike on the Nazi's when Japan hit Pearl Harbor in an unprovoked attack.

Our policy due to the Pearl Harbor attack could have been so conservative as to say, 'Japan is our enemy at the time and that is where we should put our only military focus'. We could also rationalize that in putting our focus solely on Japan at the time that the pacific war could have ended earlier.

The New Deal, an Election 2008 Primer

We also had a moral issue to deal with. Our country, the United States is made up of the immigrants from Europe.

Foreign policy and world leadership called for us to join our allies in the war no matter if we had wanted to avoid it.

The logistical issue I believe would have also been accounted for. Consider that by the time we could have won the Pacific, the Nazi's could have overcome all our allies and be in Great Britain as well as all of Europe.

Their next appetite of conquest would have been the United States where we would no longer have allies. Here preemption is necessary without Japan's provocation.

In the case of 9/11, pursuing the Al Qaeda and the Taliban cannot be considered preemptive, and likewise had United Nations support.

Basically, preemptive does not mean unilateral where in today's world, preemptive attack can evolve to mutually assured destruction given the reason for doing so such as in the story of the Hatfield's and McCoy's.

For the Strategic Future of Our Nation

6.2.5 Causes for War and Due Diligence

In witnessing 9/11 first hand, like every American, I wanted to find and destroy the enemy. The White House has yet to prove who this was.

"Voice or no voice, the people can always be brought to the bidding of the leaders. That is easy. All you have to do is tell them that are being attacked and denounce the pacifists for lack of patriotism and exposing the country to danger. It works the same way in any country". By Hermann Goering, Nuremberg Diary (1947) by G.M. Gilbert

The 9/11 Commission Report was said to have accomplished much. I believe that more has to be accomplished in terms of the report; and then about the investigation of 9/11 and ongoing about it.

9/11 conspiracy theory is not a popular item for Congress. As why in the first place entertain it when being clearly informed of the cause ? But since it happened in my very own neighborhood and that most things seemingly did not fit seamlessly in explanation, unless you force fit them together, and that the scope of the 9/11 Commission report appeared to be limited to being within a fish bowl, rude inconsistencies about the reason for the *War on*

The New Deal, an Election 2008 Primer

Terror, purpose of the *Patriot Act*, and the state that our nation is in today, gives purposeful reason to question this part of our history.

In fact, unless being a slave, where we have given up the right to think, it can only be patriotic in duty to question the events that we are a part of.

We as America deserve clear and transparent answers no matter what the truth unveils.

6.2.5.1 Summary of the Commission's Accomplishments

The very first accomplishment was the formation of the 9/11 Commission itself. At the onset, the Bush administration had wanted to take on Congress's responsibility but eventually conceded to public pressure. Then ostensibly an independent non-partisan commission was formed.

Their mandate was to 'prepare a full and complete account of the circumstances surrounding the September 11, 2001 terrorist attacks including preparedness for and the immediate response to them. The Commission was also mandated to provide recommendations designed to guard against future attacks.'

The 9/11 report concluded with 51 recommendations.

- Both houses have passed their versions of legislation to address the recommendations made in the 9/11 Commission's Final Report. The bills now move to committee. 48 of the recommendations were further past in the Senate to be voted on.

- As of November/December 2004 this has been in idle mode. This is due to contention of different members of Congress that have prevented a vote on the floor in terms of their differing positions, and then there are differing positions in the representation of the 9/11 families themselves. Then there is budget/money control, management of Intelligence, and rushing through agreed recommendations with the concern of having, or not having further legislation in the future.

For the Strategic Future of Our Nation

6.2.5.2 Our Governments Due Diligence - *Personal View*:

When we talk of national, and /or homeland security, and about a 'War on Terror' that is without end, I find that it is difficult to consider the notion that the 9/11 Commission was a finite action.

It was also severely, if not criminally, under funded in only having $6 million dollars and was interfered with initially by the Bush administration. There would be no consideration or concern about follow-up legislation later, if not ongoing legislation; and in fact from 'lessons learned', the commission was not formed as a strategic body of oversight in our government. For me, it was to tidy. It looked like the issue was to be quickly put into the past and forgotten.

I believe beyond the contention in the *idle mode* that when considering the well promoted notion that 'attack is imminent', that we do instill government to continue the 9/11 Commission's charter.

Most of all, my concerns are that instead of speaking about "w*ar without end"*, that we have to understand far more about the roots and facets of its causes than just a few well chosen sound bites to toss at the public ear in a well manipulated media. Any war on terror has to be in mission statements, and not without an end.

There is much that the 9/11 Commission had not looked at and should. This could help further circumvent terrorism world wide in addition to it occurring on our own soil again. But any concern of this has been conveniently dismissed as 'Conspiracy Theory' when instead we should be asking ourselves just why there are so many of them on the Internet. Is it a matter of not trusting the sound bites?

For our due diligence in serving the American people, and in addition to the victims and families of 9/11, we must look at everything that could be directly or indirectly related to cause.

For instance, there was a lot of *big money made* upon the opening of the Stock Market right after 9/11, and that in war, big money is made, and that without an economy, war cannot make big money.

To account for the belief that hitting the WTC would be hitting at the heart of our economy and then to admit to ourselves that in the wake of an attack that it was more devastating than Pearl Harbor, we owe it to the American people to be as transparent and accountable as possible on going in our actions of "due process".

The New Deal, an Election 2008 Primer

6.2.5.3 In Retrospect:

September 11th, 2001 changed things for most in addition to killing over 3,500 helpless victims. Being located just up the street, the experience was first hand. But for you and me, and for many globally in addition to the United States, its shock wave is still being registered.

It took months for the smell of death, ash and PCBs to become thinner and the dust just to settle. During that time, like many, I did a lot of thinking. This was in listening to who took center stage in the <u>media</u>, what they said and didn't say; and what questions they raised, answered, glossed over, or did not raise, nor answer. In particular, there were still sincere questions as to why the Mayor of New York City, Rudolf Guillani would allow an open Halloween parade just a month later. It is attended annually by over a million participants where on every other day, dirty bomb awareness was promoted in the news.

In witnessing the World Trade Center as an inferno, the immediate question in mind was raised by another question -*who did it* , where mine was *why was it done*?

When John Ashcroft suddenly produced ample evidence of Arabic documents recovered from the debris of 9/11, more and more questions came about. What was witnessed could not leave anything behind much less intact and legible Arabic documents that could easily have been found.

I also realized that many under their breath, had questions. But with much of the empty hero worshiping by the media and government, for me it served as more as a political photo opportunity. The one message came clear was not to ask questions. Instead we were to just accept the answers that were handed out if to be patriotic.

If we fast forward to when the 9/11 Commission was formed, convenient explanations seemed to serve as the guidelines for their mandate. Back then, this created the next question for me, simply '*why once again?*'

As 9/11 is part of my immediate community, my concerns should be considered legitimate. The questions under my breath was simply, that since this was bigger than Pearl Harbor, then where and when was the next attack to occur? I was actually short on thinking that this was going to be a one and only attack. If so, then why ? Its just was not in the Art of War to make a single attack and run.

In other words, either you are being hit, or you are not, and one attack does not provide an enemy any military advantage, but in fact a disadvantage.

For the Strategic Future of Our Nation

Thinking back about it, may God help us if we do not ask serious questions about 9/11. Our patriotism should not to the issue by the federal authorities such as by John Ashcroft who so quickly was able to find evidence as to 'who did it'.

In history, it could help to look at similar events. One was when Hitler took power. He blamed a Communist at the time for burning the ***Reichstag.***

In living in the WTC area, I had deep concerns that my children could not go out on the street. There were concerns of 'truck bombs' as follow up in what we had heard of ongoing terrorist's attacks that had been occurring overseas.

I was more than surprised that the 2001 Halloween parade was not considered an easy target by our new enemy's. This is while Anthrax scares and dirty bomb warnings were occurring at exactly the same time. But then it was further confusing when other public events followed such as the New York Marathon. This served as another easy target when over 30,000 participants are located on a bridge in New York's harbor. Then let's not forget that these two events have occurred without incident every year since 2001.

Trying to ignore the obvious questions as what happened to our enemy and who were they was like trying to wear shoes that were too small. Specifically, why would just a ban of Al Qaeda 's try this in the first place who were in fact were considered to be Saudis?

I don't question that the planes were flown by Osama bin Laden's faction, but in just knowing that the US would retaliate overwhelmingly, the question remains "who really stood to gain by all this ?"

Since 9/11 there are a considerable number of observations and questions by many that any search engine can find. In the media, for the Bush administration to dismiss this as illegitimate concern and taking it with a condescending tone as just *conspiracy theory* does nothing to reassure anyone for the '*truth behind 9/11*'. With the awareness on the Internet, the 9/11 Commission appears to have performed their investigation in some fish bowl.

I could not ignore confronting questions such as, if the World Trade Center strike was to strike at the heart of our economy, then why not strike instead at the Mercantile Exchange that sits on the coast of the Hudson River. Then also why not the New York Stock Exchange. After all, this would halt the economy if that was what was really intended?

The New Deal, an Election 2008 Primer

When we face ourselves in the mirror, to recite what we are told without question, it is a disservice to our patriotism. We cannot overlook that wars have always had a profit motive behind them and that without an economy, obviously there would be no profit. In contrast, I view it as naive to think that some extremists really knew enough what to do and get themselves over here just for the sake of being nasty to infidels. Comparatively, this is only collateral to more compelling agendas for 9/11.

While Wall Street became compromised but not destroyed, I wondered who else but weapons manufactures could profit under such conditions. I looked at two stocks, Boeing and Lockheed. They are traded on the New York Stock Exchange. There was a striking relationship between what seemed to be complete opposite in their behaviors where 9/11 was the cross hatch.

6.2.5.4 How Profits are made at the cost of lives

Above, the Boeing stock snapshot for the week before 911, which was the manufacture of the planes used on 9/11, indicates a massive sell off in volume where its price plummets.

For the Strategic Future of Our Nation

When the markets reopened, Lockheed another weapons manufacture, charted below, in contrast took on the volume and value that Boeing lost just prior to 9/11. So it was an even trade from Boeing to Lockheed.

Boeing and Lockheed were in a head to head contest for a $300 billion defense contract prior to 9/11 but whose contract would be awarded that October.

On the Friday before 9/11, the Democrats were divided from the Republicans about the scope of planned defense spending. The Democrats right after 9/11 rolled over and agreed on deficit defense spending without caps.

By the end of the week, George Bush came off the ranch and got to have a *War on Terror* with a deficit based budget. Lockheed won the $300 billion contract that October, 2001 as in the chart spike above, and WTC reparations were estimated at $30-40 billion or just a little more than 1/10th of the defense contact's price tag.

The New Deal, an Election 2008 Primer

If we are to look at this from the standpoint of profits and losses, compare it to the far less profits made vs. lives lost in Vietnam. Comparably, this is a bonanza for the defense stocks and the futures markets. We also cannot discount ethics for some that could see that '*we all got to go sometime*'.

Simply put, if you knew to buy Lockheed just before 9/11 and say you were also smart enough to sell your Boeing at the same time, then you also could be one who is pulling some strings of some puppets!

Although circumstantial, observances can not be ignored as much as any other incident of possible evidence to be considered for the causes of encouraged terrorism on our shore.

To avoid, or even to minimize possible future attacks, it is imperative to view that the 9/11 Commission's work has only just begun. These types of commissions cannot be limited, but are to be regulated by Congress only. The Justice Department, nor the executive branch should dismiss, nor evade answering to such commissions that are appointed by Congress.

It is the responsibility of the Congress in the Constitution to form tribunals that are only inferior to the Supreme Court. It is not executive privilege of the president, or appointees to dismiss or to ignore them.

So the question still stands as to what was really accomplished by the 9/11 Commission, and by our government in its due diligence in doing the work for the people in understanding all the issues that surround 9/11.

It was the worst day in our nation's history, but yet did our government really do its job in addressing the prevention of another 9/11. Although Homeland Security and the Patriot Act were formed and we are now fighting terrorists of our own determination, does this serve our needs for security?

Do we know without question that our enemies are bin Laden and his followers or are they just the puppets of greater enemies that could even operate on our shores with a freedom that was taken from us in the Patriot Act ? We were easily handed the identity of the enemy by John Ashcroft in finding some papers written in Arabic, and told where we must go in order to fight our enemies. Is it treason to question this, or is it the complicity in treason not to ? When waging war, it is our duty to know our enemy.

In the Spanish American war, and the Bay of Tonkin we were given the same explanation but yet like today preferred to turn away from looking at questionable evidence that cost many American lives.

For the Strategic Future of Our Nation

6.2.6 Know Thy Enemy

About Osama bin Laden, where is he, and what ever happened to him ? In the future, looking at American history, it will seem unusual that the worst enemy of the 21st century was somehow forgotten about and that we sought after other conquests of manifest destiny instead. What really has our government done and what is it actually doing in looking for this enemy of the American people ?

There are many issues that must be addressed about both Osama bin Laden and September 11th, 2001. We owe it to ourselves to still raise the level of scrutiny specifically in terms of bin Laden 's eventual due process that he and/or the smoke and mirrors around him deserves. What ever becomes unraveled in discovery between truth and myth, full due process is deserved if we are to learn from 9/11.

Just after 9/11, bin Laden was on every one's mind. The Bush administration depicted him as the *no.1evil doer* . The message promoted was that Clinton is to be blamed for not getting bin Laden some time before. The Bush administration also did not have him on the radar prior to 9/11 and actually not until a few days after when George finally showed up at Ground Zero.

But the hunt was now supposed to be on. George Bush finally came back from his extended stay at the ranch. On network news he made his comments while standing on a mound of smoldering rubble where the towers had stood; and where perhaps rescue efforts could safely assume to still look beneath for remains once he stepped off of it.

Periodically, videos would arrive on the news, depicting bin Laden as the religious extremist behind the Al Qaeda movement, and that they were in Afghanistan with the Taliban who was once a US ally. In the video's, bin Laden's appearance would consistently be in his rag-tagged military fatigues, old dirty humble turban, and in having his machine gun within reach.

After an initial push into Afghanistan by US forces, with Hamid Karzai being anointed as president of Afghanistan, which amounts to nothing more than being the mayor of Kabul, bin Laden supposedly escaped through secret mountain paths in Tora Bora. This is where our forces were somehow understaffed, and our intelligence did not afford the knowledge of possible escape routes. Oddly, bin Laden then slipped off the Bush radar screen which then focused on Iraq.

Bush then decided to instead wage war on Iraq. Saddam Hussein was somehow bin Laden's friend and Iraq with its inept forces were the next imminent threat that was expected to somehow invade our shores!

The New Deal, an Election 2008 Primer

Periodically, press videos from bin Laden would still arrive on the news Sometimes in a timely manner he would support the Bush *war on terror* agenda with the message 'come to Iraq !' .

What bin Laden accomplished is in *bleeding a giant*, which eventually weakens the giant. Through our greed and pride we have squandered our people which has weakened us, where the sitting president has little political capital for true leadership.

The last time bin Laden showed up was during the Bush and Kerry election 2004 debates. It helped the Bush ratings the following day in making his case. This was actually the last video shown of bin Laden. In it, he was not dressed as usual, and there was no machine gun. In fact as was previously the case, he was not speaking from a cave. Instead, he was cleanly bathed, dressed in clean white linen, and stood in back of some alter. Behind him was some form of royal blue material backdrop. I thought this was odd, as it was a pious bin Laden like persona instead of the usual extremist bin Laden image.

He stated very clearly that the 'only country that was not under threat of the bin Laden redemption movement was Sweden'. It was the only country that he would not attack but yet this is not a Muslim nation.

I wondered why he would make this statement as was it that he was saying , 'so don't look for me in Sweden '? It would make more sense to me not to attack a place where one chooses to live. Sweden additionally would not need the national security program that other countries would require and therefore, there would be less of a chance of bin Laden being spotted there. I'm not sure what the reasoning was for probably ignoring this by the Bush administration as perhaps our intelligence effort shouldn't waste their time going to Sweden?

Could reasoning be palatable that intends that obviously what would bin Laden be there of all places when he generally liked to be depicted in a cave with his loyal followers in rag-tagged military fatigues and gun at his side?

Perhaps in 2004 it did not even make any sense to investigate every plastic surgeon in Sweden or who was visiting at the time that could operate there, as obviously there is no hint of a reason why?

A few years later it was promoted in the news that he was probably and suddenly dead ! Can we actually and safely say thank goodness the hunt is now over. If so, where is our due diligence in the forensic evidence, or is it just adequate to spread a well crafted media sound bite about it ? We are now told that there are greater enemies in the *war on terror* and that as noble our mission is, that it is without end.

For the Strategic Future of Our Nation

For our nation, this is not good enough for closing out the bin Laden issue. In representing a match head to ignite the *war on terror* we also deserve to discover what or who actually struck it and what and who made the kindling for the fire.

If we are to have a war on terror, we must know the true enemy, and it cannot be from a manipulated media.

American lives cannot be squandered on some nebulous enemy. The Bush administration keeps reinforcing the message that there is a growing population of *evil doers* throughout the world that we must fight continuously and endlessly to justify our very existence as a nation of liberty and freedom for all.

Will the message eventually be 'In the name of God and Country, be on the look out for all Muslims'?

Who is to put the brakes on this, and how are we to realign our focus in knowing what and who is the true enemy? This is especially true when considering how we have allied with enemies, and made enemies out of allies.

In Vietnam we could not tell if a native was friend or foe, and in Iraq for our military it is the same. We have been set up to defend ourselves against an enemy that is elusive and at tremendous cost to American lives.

The stealth enemy is one who will always eventually win. This is how we even attacked the British in the American Revolution.

It is in our Intelligence systems to find the core of our enemies. It is in a transparent and accountable government in removing this as a threat. In this we have the means for the roads to peace for our nation and the world.

It is in our leadership in diplomacy to avoid making further enemies who are not our enemies today.

Where we have peace, we must assure our commitments to it, and where there is potential for war, we must find the means to continue peace, and not to opt for reasons just to declare war.

The New Deal, an Election 2008 Primer

6.3 In Declaring Peace

When in war, to work for peace leaves one on contentious ground. In being in war, it is far more difficult to achieve a mutually acceptable peace between opponents; or there can be peace though compromise. Compromise is a matter of what ground that we are basing our pursuit for peace. In war, it can be defined by only the victor.

To have firmer ground for peace where there is war, we can first declare strategic peace as a strong diplomatic defense against other inevitable wars. This offers more ground to stand on.

6.3.1: China the Mediator, and Partner

Diplomacy has been in place between the US and China since the early 80's. They are one of our largest lenders for funding the Iraq war. Our relationship with China is commerce driven where our dollar becomes weaker with debt while they flood the US consumer with goods. The teeth of our diplomacy are not as strong when economically insolvent. This though does not matter if only chewing soft foods. Corporate America might think they are doing well but if their dollars are not strong then they could be doing better.

6.3.1.1: China's Little Brother, North Korea

Like defense, the power of diplomacy must be able to shift in its direction. At a minimum this gives us the ability to talk with China about other matters where it can benefit and profit. The stronger China becomes economically, the closer its currency can be like the Euro. They are currently even building a trillion dollar hedge fund and should be open to suggestion on how to further this.

North Korea could be viewed by China as a cost and not serve as a strategic investment. North Korea in a way could be viewed like a little brother to China. But as a little brother it has not yet grown up. China has to deflect complaints and in some cases admonish North Korea. One example was North Korea's testing of their nuclear bomb.

In contrast, South Korea is a mature market based economy that has a stock exchange. As our tenuous ally, China could make investments into South Korea. In seeing costs in North Korea, over a period of time, China could help shepherd an investment.

With encouragement from their big brother, North Korea can save face, retain its autonomy, feed its hungry, eventually offer its people their dignity, and then join the world a few years later.

For the Strategic Future of Our Nation

That's without having to have a McDonald's the way they do in China. In other words, North Korea can certainly follow China's economic model that started in 1980 which made it into becoming an economic super power today. The alternative is to shoot down North Korea's test missiles when they decide to lob them towards Japan in order to at a minimum to remind them of cost.

6.3.2 Give Peace a Chance

Where we have an actual war without a mission statement we must work to give peace a chance. As noted, we have to determine what ground do we really stand on when it comes to Iraq, and the Middle East over all.

6.3.2.1 The Value of Peace Protests against the Iraq War

As it is our voice that moves the nation, it is in this voice initially that moves governments in foreign policy. If it is not loud enough, it has no value. During the Vietnam war, I marched for peace in Washington DC. There was a tune that many sang. It was called 'Give Peace a Chance'. In one such event, over a million people had attended. Some say today that the Vets were resented back then for fighting in Vietnam. I never saw that as the case, and in fact marched in their honor. I was also '#3' in the draft lottery, and also had no desire to go to war for any reasons except if our nation was under direct threat.

The pro-war argument fostered by the Nixon administration at the time was similar to what is heard now about Iraq. If we did not win in Vietnam, then the region would become destabilized and the Communists would in fact invade our shores. After over 60,000 Americans gave their lives, and about 600,000 returned wounded, and where few returned without some form of scars, Nixon's claim never happened. The people in Vietnam today are more than willing to receive American tourists in Hanoi.

Unlike in the late 60's and early 70's, the protest marches against the Iraq War are far smaller in scale, and less frequent. There are many 'American Peace and Justice Coalition groups' that can be found on the Internet. Not one appears to function as a hub for the others. Peace marches are also not something that have any significant news coverage which leaves most of America uninformed of when they occur.

Below is an email letter that was sent out to a number of the 'coalitions and Vet groups for peace' on March 18th, and 19th 2007. It is suggesting 2 things that would make their efforts speak as a single voice to Congress. Although wanting to reach out, the email omits any suggestion of personal involvement. In being a candidate for Election 2008, such suggestion would intend some political gain which could undermine the stated intent of the peace coalition groups.

The New Deal, an Election 2008 Primer

The first suggestion is to aggregate into a critical mass through signatures on a petition that can be brought to Congress. This is not intended to be through a third party (527) on line political action group which has no land mail address, telephone number, nor direct email address, but willing to take your donations; and secondly to also provide a 'Peace Plan' where the Pelosi time table in of itself is good, but does not demonstrate a plan.

What the time table did provide collaterally, is that any election 2008 candidate can also safely state as their plan a phased withdrawal, which again as a plan offers no substance. For me, down-sizing of our troops offers the Republican counter argument more legitimacy in that when having less of a force makes for easier targets. There is a request to consider the 'Iraq Exit Strategy' as one of many that should be reviewed, but notes that what ever the plan that is collectively decided, that it should intend to bring all our people home from Iraq. In having an actual plan, a united coalition backed by signatures can obtain a Congressional hearing. Congress would have to take the action seriously. Without such an action as suggested, if there are future peace marches then the question is posed here, as what purpose is really served ?

Dear Peace Maker:

Wanting peace is not 'cutting and running' when considering that over 3,000 brave Americans gave their lives and another 30,000 or more were severely wounded in Iraq. This is what former NY Gov. Mario Cuomo pointed out at Cooper Union in NYC on Feb 28th, 2007.

In a TV show on March 18th, 2007, Tom Delay said that giving a date was unpatriotic because it would be telling the enemy when we would be leaving.

I do believe that time lines are critically important when it comes to milestones. For Iraq, besides telling the so-called insurgents, and so-called Iraqi government that it's time to act, it also affords the opportunity to start putting political options on the table which the Iraqi people in all fairness can and are compelled to consider. This is regardless of their leanings. It's a matter of what options are put on the table then, or to opt out, and let others decide.

The Congress has been some what responsive, but slow in addressing options. In the 70's the Vets confronted Congress with the war issues of that time.

Today, if the Vet groups were backed by the signatures of all the peace coalitions in America, they could bring this to Congress. Although peace protests are vitally important, this brings the face to face impact with

For the Strategic Future of Our Nation

Congress as it was in the 70's when millions had backed it by a march in DC.

If the Vets brought a plan, then Congress would then have to accept it as guidelines that they would have to align with.

This is in effect a rally, where the smaller coalitions can forward signatures, and perhaps recommend plans to the larger coalitions, who in turn forward the sum to the Veteran groups for peace, which then forward these to the largest of the groups.

Within a month, such a petition can be finalized, and an agreed upon plan can be brought by them for a Congressional hearing.

There are many plans, and one of which I do ask you to consider is what I call 'Peace with Dignity'. Like all plans, it's a straw man, and needs the minds of many to be complete.
http://unity2008.org/IragExitStrategy.html.

What ever the plan is though, it's got to bring our people home.

Please note, that there was no major email list for sending this. If it makes sense to you, please forward it on.

This letter got very little response. It reminded me of the 2004 election, where only 21% of the total voter population made their voice to determine the George Bush leadership, and its consequences.

In other words, to make this happen, does it require fan fare and since Gore could get to Congress on energy, would he or any other politician do the same for a petition from some Vets and thousands of peace organizations ?

This is why we do need to have participatory representation in government as is noted in Chapter 3.

It's simply much easier to vote on the Iraq war and have your representatives take that to the floors of Congress.

6.3.2.2 The Failure of HR1591

Congressman John Murtha of Penn, put together a great budget bill called HR1951. It would allocate $100 billion for Iraq; and then a balance of $25 billion of domestic spending such as on Vets, agriculture and other areas calling for attention. It got vetoed by Bush and could not get 2/thirds by both houses.

The real issues here are, the time (cost for the tax payer) to have this go no where as a test of power between the branches of government instead of enabling its spending allocation. No doubt, George Jr. will run on empty, but the costs of this only serves political posture at a great expense.

To communicate this in a constructive way, I put out a press release as noted below.

"Pullout from Iraq in 08 and Bush veto' is not a plan"

Orion Karl Daley believes that a time line for the pull out of Iraq in HR 1591 is not a plan, but does provide the opportunity to account for proposed plans. Mr. Daley suggests that by adding an amendment that a comprehensive plan must be provided that includes political solutions for Iraq as a condition, then the time line can be honored.

(PRWEB) March 30, 2007 -- Orion Karl Daley believes that a time line for the pull out of Iraq in HR 1591 is not a plan, but does provide the opportunity to account for proposed plans. He believes that without a real plan, given a time line, the Republican vision of a blow out in the region with an Iranian and Saudi dynamic is a reasonable probability; and that any anticipated American interests would also loose strategic ground.

Mr. Daley suggests that by adding an amendment that a comprehensive plan must be provided that includes political solutions for Iraq as a condition, then the time line can be honored.

Candidate Daley of the Balanced Party believes that for the Iraqi people to be considered freed that this means free from turmoil and civil war. In this manner, the United States would accomplish its stated mission to free the Iraqi people; and there would be no question from the world of American honor and leadership which has cost over 3,000 American lives, and severely wounded upwards of over 30,000 other brave American soldiers.

He does believe that time lines are critically important when it comes to milestones. For Iraq, besides telling the so-called insurgents, and Prime Minister Nuri Kamel Al-maliki's Iraqi government that it's time to act, it also

For the Strategic Future of Our Nation

affords the opportunity to start putting political solutions on the table which the Iraqi people, including the Sunnis and Shiites, in all fairness can and are compelled to consider. This is regardless of their leanings toward Iran and Saudi Arabia. It's a matter of what political solutions are put on the table.

Mr. Daley sees that the standing Iraqi government as a political solution is not strategically viable as it is part cause of the Civil war. He further views that phased withdrawal regardless of not announcing as to when, could make remaining American troops, in being fewer in number, even easier targets.

Mr. Daley suggests that as responsible interests, in parallel to the 08' time line, the United States should work with the UN to deliberate plans that can then be presented to Iraq for consideration. He contends that the 12 million people who did vote, given other options might have voted for something else, where there could even have been a greater turn out. Given plans that are ultimately sponsored by the UN, and backed by the United States for Iraq to vote on, civil war would at least have a cease fire from neighbor killing neighbor in the heart of Baghdad.

He also believes that this strategy would give Senators Hillary Rodham Clinton and Barack Obama, John Edwards, and other Election 08' Presidential Candidates, the ideal opportunity to provide clear, decisive and responsible plans even before the Election Primaries. For that matter it also tells the United Nations to get working !

Candidate Daley does propose a plan at his campaign website (http://unity2008.org). His plan accounts for the fact that like the Kurds, any culture, such as the Shiites, and Sunnis want their own Sovereignty; and therefore, have their dignity within their own autonomy. And that this should be the starting point of any plan to be considered for stewarding political solutions as it is the cause of the Civil War.

The Daley Plan, aka 'Peace with Dignity' (as listed in Google) was written in 2004. It proposes 3 sovereign nations of Iraq that have fairly shared their resources such as Oil; and that as sovereign nations, have full UN representation and protection from their neighbors, and are able to become part of OPEC; and that Iraq decides the government model for each new nation.

He believes that by having sovereign nations, there is also less potential of an Iranian, or Saudi dynamic compared to when in civil war; and the momentum of Jihad from outside interests will dissolve. Any presence of Al Qaeda would be come resented by the 3 nations of Iraq.

The New Deal, an Election 2008 Primer

In Mr. Daley's plan, each of the 3 nations being sovereign, are able to invite foreign interest as they see fit. The United States he believes would be a welcomed guest, and one of the more attractive investment sources and strategic partner in any one of their economies. This is due to having demonstrated an honorable interest in them as a people in the first place.

But at a minimum, he believes, to require a plan for the time line demonstrates unquestionable responsibility of Congress, where the $100 billion in additional spending toward military operations ONLY in Iraq and Afghanistan can be achieved, and where other needed and outstanding domestic funding is no longer viewed as pork by the Republicans.

He also dismisses the view that American solders fighting Al Qaeda in Iraq prevents terrorists in the war on terror from coming over here in boat loads in order to invade our shores. In fact for him it is reminiscent of the Nixon warning that in leaving Vietnam that the communists would invade our shores. The Vietnamese invite Americans now as tourists to Hanoi.

Further he sees that our National Guard better serves a much needed purpose in guarding and protecting our borders and ports as opposed to building walls between countries and leaving our ports unprotected.

Mr. Daley notes, that in not having the Time line 08', there is no budget, and without executive branch agreement, there is no time line. If we write to our representatives about this on both sides of the aisle then they are on notice that a responsible and timely solution is expected from our representation. ###

For the Strategic Future of Our Nation

6.3.2.3 In Advocating Peace Plans

From the standpoint of politics, it would be nice to see some real plans on the table. I had hoped this as early as May of 2004 when writing this email:

-------- Original Message -------- Subject: How to Fix Iraq Date: Wed, 05 May 2004 08:17:13 -0400 From: Orion Karl DaleyTo: senator@biden.senate.gov, senator_bingaman@bingaman.senate.gov, senator@breaux.senate.gov, senator@akaka.senate.gov, senator@dorgan.senate.gov, dick@durbin.senate.gov, russell_feingold@feingold.senate.gov, senator@kennedy.senate.gov, senator_leahy@leahy.senate.gov, senator@rockefeller.senate.gov, arlen_specter@specter.senate.gov

I'm missing why the obvious has not been addressed - please explain why we have had limited vision in terms of Iraq -
Example - To Fix Iraq

1- Split the land for three separate nations

2- Offer each a way to the UN - with Nonaggression rules

3- Allow each to join OPEC - with nonaggression rules

4- Provide Banking infrastructure in Saudi Arabia for the 3 nations

5- Provide irrigation services to instill both agricultural and oil Economies

6- Have the UN provide security against any one , or two nations against the other
------- ------- ------- ------- ------- -

When not hearing a response in 2004, I went to work on the plan called "Peace with Dignity which is in later pages of this chapter section.

Recently though, I was impressed when hearing Biden on the floor of Congress note his new cool plan for Iraq, as well as his move to run for Campaign 08.

The Biden plan can be located on the Internet as "The Biden-Gelb Plan for Iraq " . It is remarkably similar to the Peace with Dignity plan that I authored in 2004, which in my opinion is some what more strategic to what he calls his Partition plan for Iraq. In the following , I have outlined his which might not be totally accurate, and then mine for comparison.

In both cases, our troops come home, but in Joe's Plan, I see strategic limitations.

The New Deal, an Election 2008 Primer

In <u>Joe's plan</u>, although the land/resources are split into 3 separate areas for the Kurds, Sunnis, and Shiites there is still a central government. Since there is already a central government, with 3 separate cultures that have animosity for each other, in essence this appears to intend to 'just work your differences out' as the political solution.

Consider that Saddam Hussein was also a political solution. As of 2007, they are far from being able get along peacefully, but in Joe's plan like any other, intends that the US exits, and encourages the Iraq fix itself after a few thousand years of oppression from one dictator or another.

In any event there would be anarchy as there is now, which we have rightly washed our hands of in giving them due warning. I consider that fair, but also question if a weak government that we basically put in place, regardless of the vote that had been taken, can work as currently it has not.

In other words, it appears that not every one voted for the government structure, or for leaders that they have in place; and it invites alliances from outside factions to help 'get what is mine' which could include 'yours too'. It also does not offer any strategic protection mechanism such as making use of the UN as it is not a unified government, and hardly gets them to the table to discuss economics with OPEC.

In <u>Peace with Dignity</u> plan, they are regarded as '3 separate nations' that have representation in both the UN and in OPEC. The only one's that would not like this is the power structure which has its own manifest destiny in mind. The civil war there demonstrates this. The other real challenge is in the fair division of the resources.

This though can be worked out through the *league of nations* in the UN without the US being at the Helm. In other words, let the 3 separate cultures first vote their destiny and have the differences worked out by the UN. This also ensures no outside involvement by surrounding countries. This also avoids the need of inviting Al Qaeda by any one of them.

The 3 separate nations can have the governments which they choose, and is up to each to make it work if they want to be part of the world.

For the Strategic Future of Our Nation

6.3.2.4 Iraq Exit Strategy - Peace with Dignity

During the first air raid, Iraq left its lights on for us !

In 2004, the plan - 'Peace with Dignity' was authored as an Iraq exit strategy. Its intent is to offer peace with dignity to the Iraqi people, and to the coalition forces. It is based on the concept of having 3 sovereign nations in Iraq. It is only a straw man, but comes from the common sense that like the Kurds, any culture wants its own sovereignty; and therefore, their dignity within their own autonomy. I believe this is common for anyone.

In the name of our manifest destiny for the *American imminent domain oil interests*, there are rationales to dismiss this plan:

1- The Turks would not tolerate a Kurdish Nation.

2- Shiites and Sunnis could not have borders in that one can have relatives who could be the other.

3- The resources such as Oil are not evenly divided.

The 2004 straw man indirectly addresses these concerns without fore fitting American interests. In having sovereign nations, each is protected by and represented in the UN as well as OPEC; Just like in any country you can have relatives that live in another; and that resources of course should be divided fairly by the UN.

What style of government each would in being sovereign is up to that particular nation. If the style is not conducive to engaging in the world, consequently, that particular nation cannot not benefit as well as the others. Simply you have to get along with others if you are to have a future.

The New Deal, an Election 2008 Primer

The other question arrives as to why the Iraqi people did not vote for this in the first place where 12 million had voted ? On the surface this seems legitimate, but then the question is ' if this option was actually put on the table in the first place; and secondly, how many people did not vote. Thirdly, in given the lack of choice, did the ones who did vote, do so in at least finally getting some choice, if not the one that they could strive for ?

There could also be a dozen other reasons, like American interests, to dismiss such thinking, where presented with challenges to embrace it; and straw mans likewise have to be refined before they can take on gravity.

Strategically, we have to have economic solutions for world peace, but which have to first be built on mutual respect. This can only come from respecting others as we do ourselves.

6.3.2.4.1 Peace with Dignity from 2004

Presumably the invasion into Iraq was in the name of liberating the Iraq people. Elections in Iraq are intended to occur in late January 2004. The purpose of the election is to establish a formal Democratic nation called Iraq.

The acting government was appointed by the United States. This *acting government* now directs the military action of the United States armed forces in Iraq. Currently the state of Iraq is the equivalent of a Civil War, where elections by some seem doubtful to occur, or even if they do can really stabilize the nation.

The Bush administration has treated the situation in Iraq, where over 20,000 service people have been wounded , or in effect maimed for life, and over 1100 other young Americans killed as progress. The American armed forces are caught in a predictable urban war fare which the State and Defense Departments in their 'Bump and Run' strategy assume to ignore.

In forestry, the Bush administration also views that a control burn of a forest can clear out the undergrowth. He has treated Iraq in the same manner, but instead has created a forest fire. Meantime, in *no bid, no outsiders* allowed contracts, the US is pumping the oil out of Iraq as if it was its imminent domain.

For the Strategic Future of Our Nation

The Muslim population in the world has a growing view that in fact, the USA is made up of only infidels that are raping and pillaging Iraq, and that we are occupiers. This opens the door for the American armed forces lives to become squandered further in Iraq in the name of what use to be called 'manifest destiny , and now called American oil interests'.

In our manifest destiny for Vietnam, the NVA were willing to lose 5 for every American solder killed . They viewed it was their land, and worth fighting for. The kill ratio is basically the same in Iraq.

For Iraq, there is no stated exit strategy for the United States, as much as there are no stated plans for its place in the world for tomorrow. And all along the people of Iraq have had no say in any of the events that they have been subjected to. Civil war is predictable. The question is 'are we still ourselves naive about American policy on manifest destiny, and should we simply admit our real intentions?'

If our intentions were actually selfless, regardless of the Bush *Shock and Awe* preemptive invasion with the notion of liberating the Iraq people, would they be demonstrated in giving Iraq truly back to the Iraqi people?

Iraq is actually 3 separate nations of peoples known as the Kurds, Shiites, and Sunni's. Under Saddam Hussein, two of the three suffered the most.
To give Iraq back to its people, the most sincere way would be to put as a referendum, the option for the Iraq people to divide Iraq equally into 3 separate nations.

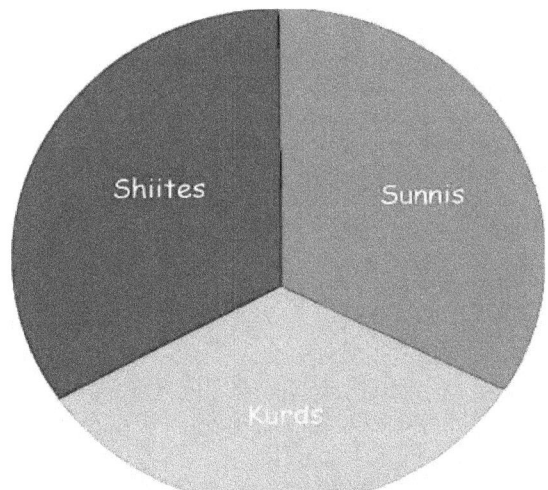

Sovereign Nations of Iraq

The New Deal, an Election 2008 Primer

6.3.2.4.2 - Sovereign Nations of Iraq

The *Sovereign Nations of Iraq* can be accomplished in a viable way. It provides each separate nation, their own independence. This is summarized as the following 5 guidelines:

1- Sovereign Nations of Iraq - Split the land for three separate nations

By dividing the land each of the peoples in Iraq have their sense of sovereignty. No matter which of the 3, each has the sense of their own dignity. In having a country with their own borders, no matter how they manage their government, democratic or otherwise, it should be considered their own government, regime, or how ever they choose to manage it. If they are fool hardy and not viewing their relationship to the world over all, then they have isolated themselves. As water eventually seeks its own level their particular means of governing themselves, if to survive and grow will evolve at their own pace.

In terms of *American oil interests*, for future reference, they can only thank the United States for giving them their own space, and are less likely to view the USA with as much animosity that they currently have. This serves our strategic interests.

Most importantly, no Muslim nation can fault the USA for doing this and those that were going to join a cause to 'fight the infidels' would have second thoughts behind the desire. As there is no imperialism demonstrated by us, "Jihad' in the current insurgents would be in question for which purpose it really served personally. In other words, we have removed the fire's fuel.

Terrorism as we know it, and its intensity as a fire world wide, could become eventually extinguished without the ongoing loss of life of American armed forces.

2- Offer each of the Sovereign Nations of Iraq a way to the UN

With non aggression rules, the path to the UN provides the next level of recognition and national pride and sovereignty for any country. It enables a country to realize the benefit in joining the community of nations, while obtaining peer recognition no matter how humble its beginnings are. Other benefits include assistance in the protection of their sovereignty, a vehicle or means to work with other nations in economics and in trade. With the primary commodity being oil that each of the sovereign nations can bring to the dealing table at the United Nations, enables foreign aid from many countries that would be willing to work with the new Sovereign Nations of Iraq.

For the Strategic Future of Our Nation

Each nation, in compliance with UN rules for sovereignty, can fully expect that their own independence and borders are protected from the other two nations of Iraq through UN assistance.

Regardless of history of the Bath parties aggression in Iraq, for any of the 3 nations that would express aggression towards another, would, I believe fall out of favor with the UN and the other Muslim nations. They would end up more than likely compromising their own sovereignty.

The United States Armed Forces at this point are no longer occupiers, nor should be considered for use by others. This enables our solders to return home safely even if it is through downsizing its presence, or by some agreed formula in exiting Iraq. Most importantly, American lives are no longer lost or changed due to Iraq and we can plan on their safe return home with pride intact.

3- Allow each to join OPEC - with nonaggression rules

The opportunity to join OPEC as a Muslim Nation has its given benefits, where each of the sovereign nations of Iraq can respectably join the oil union of the Middle East. Each nation would have the protection of OPEC price regulation. The opportunity would be *oil for money,* as opposed to oil for food. In turn , they could become low credit risks to the foreign aid provided in guide line 2 above.

This also regulates oil prices more favorably to consumers as more is made available and the 3 nations through volume output can build their economies.

Employment of otherwise previously impoverished and disenfranchised peoples that represent the 3 nations can become readily available thereby improving their standards of living as opposed to an eventual civil war where we could be the easiest of their common targets.

I see that terrorism comes from being disenfranchised. As much the French Revolution took off Marie Antoinette's head, in Iraq we should expect the same if the people there are to be disregarded.

When having the opportunity to be a citizen of one of the 3 nations, and to have food on the table in one's own house with the ability to have one' own car or vehicle enables a standard of living where one can offer a tomorrow for their children instead of just the burgeoning graves that are occurring now.

4- Provide Banking Infrastructure in both Saudi Arabia and Israel for the 3 nations

What is weak in the Middle East is the opportunity of competitive banking systems in what are not its non-allied nations. Given impetus for the Sovereign Nations of Iraq as well as other surrounding nations of the area, Mid East banking can actively subsidize involvement in the world economy. This is through debt and equity relationships such as is similar to municipal bonds for building infrastructure.

By offering the opportunity of having developing and competitive banking centers in the Middle East enables banking more momentum over all in the world economy of emerging markets.

Emerging market economics itself needs a shot in the arm, and in the Middle East peace plan, can get it.

5- Provide Irrigation Services to instill Agricultural Economies

Noted in the Middle East Plan later, agriculture can be part of the economies of the Sovereign Nations of Iraq. Each can develop their own agriculture bases for the need of feeding their own nations.

Irrigation can be accomplished in the same manner as described in the Middle East plan for Syria and Palestine that follows in this chapter. Further in being the original Mesopotamia and Sumeria its Euphrates and Tigris rivers can offer irrigation for a land of Eden.

6- Have the UN provide security against any one , or two nations against the other, and foreign nations

United Nations represents sovereignty, and it can't be stated in a simpler manner. As a league of nations, the UN is obligated to perform as one. Since it is hosted in the New York City, and is on our high ground, it can be encouraged by us to do so.

6.3.3 Collateral Peace Opportunities

There are many collateral peace opportunities that we can help develop in the Middle East and Iran. This accounts additionally for Middle East agriculture and Middle East banking systems where they too can work well together between previously contentious nations.

Consider that banking systems can be a strength that Israel can have if it planned it right. This could provide part of the path for peace in the overall Middle East.

If Israel is recognized by Syria and the Israel recognizes Palestine, then there can be peace between them. They simply need a common ground to tolerate each other on. It's a matter of what can be considered a common reason to do business with each other.

This also applies to Iran. When given the right common ground it can become the model Islamic nation for others to follow. It then has the potential to have multinational business relationships and retain its way of government unobstructed. It is a matter of a common reason to do business with others.

The following addresses Syria, Israel, Palestine, and Iran in proposing some collateral peace opportunities.

6.3.3.1: Syria and the Middle East

Syria is a key component in achieving peace for Israel and its neighbors. As much as they are weak points in achieving stability, they can be forged as strengths.

Like a vicious circle, Hamas will not recognize Israel's right to exist, but Syria can influence this. Our current State Department also has many issues about Syria that would need to be reconciled to forge this strength.

In other words, what could make Syria come to the table and oblige on working with the US as a partner in foreign policy? If we are caught up in being a jack in the box then we stay wired to the conditions that Syria offers. This consists of passive obstinance and US subtle threats. If our thinking is not boxed in, then there are means to collateral peace opportunities.

To approach this problem, there is a need to understand the potential objectives. If they are limited, then the partnership itself is limited. To not set a maximum objective why not offer a very valuable first step instead.

The New Deal, an Election 2008 Primer

In other words what is more valuable to Syria, but 'fresh water'. Fresh water can be worth more than oil as irrigation allows agricultural economies to flourish.

To provide fresh water, salt water can go through desalination. This technology is new, but quite real, and the General Electric corporation even advertises the business. But then the financing issue must be addressed.

Israel on the other hand has a potential of sustaining itself as a financial economy instead of as a persistent military aid drain from the US. If it provides banking services and banking centers then it can offer the Middle East the funding partnerships for the construction of desalination plants as an example in surrounding nations such as Syria and Palestine.

Here, neighbors are given a good reason to get over their differences and be good neighbors. It is based on their dependency with each other. It is the UN that can initially coordinate these business relationships between its contentious nations as that should be part of its very purpose.

People also get employed and eat better; and both the banking and agricultural economies can flourish together.

The relationship also offers parity as the loans must be reasonable enough to produce crops which Israel also needs. Israel can adjust the price of the loans based on fair crop pricing. Israel has a right to exist and Palestine too as serving each others needs.

This was based originally on a plan sent to Clinton some time back.

To : President William Jefferson Clinton   03/03/04
Fm : Orion Karl Daley
Subject : The Oil of Israel and the Middle East Economy

Dear President Clinton:

The need for Water is more vital than the need for Oil. Israel has an important area of the Coast that could feed water to many surrounding countries. This could allow these surrounding countries to become Agricultural Economies; which could also feed others besides themselves, and in particular Israel.

Israel has the sophistication of banking systems that can loan money for just the use of De-Salted Water for irrigation, and other uses; and could structure loans for delivery systems, seed, and other needs.

Israel has walled itself to the Sea, as much as it has walled out opportunity. Its ability to distribute water provides its leverage in the Middle East. This offers a far greater incentive for a road map of complementary economies; in addition to obtaining peace in its stride.

Kindly Yours,

Orion Karl Daley
212-226-8524

For the Strategic Future of Our Nation

6.3.3.2 An Economic Road Map for the Middle East:

I view that there are very simple and straight forward long lasting solutions to very complex and compounded problems in the Middle East that can benefit all there and elsewhere.

The simplicity is through vision if we are capable of putting our differences aside. The following example was originally named *The Oil of Israel*.

It is to give the incentive for having a Palestinian Democracy. This is by having an agricultural economy for Palestine; and Israel becoming a financial banking center. This can provide many incentives as noted below for peace in the Middle East.

The solution is simple. But implementing the solution requires a real leadership from the US to champion it through the UN. Please consider my thinking:

o The basic needs for water are far greater than the need for oil. Israel is also urbanizing and subsequently will need a more robust financial/banking economy.

o As a commodity, water allows agriculture to flourish. Feeding a nation makes a healthy nation and enables the creation for an agricultural economy.

o An agricultural Palestinian economy can go to the financial/banking economy of Israel for loan structuring. Such loan structures include the cost for the delivery of water.

The New Deal, an Election 2008 Primer

o The delivery of water from the Mediterranean could be canaled through the Gaza Strip to Israel's neighbors.

o Delivery would require the desalination of the water. This requires a plant and workers to manage it. Building *delivery canals* also requires the employment of many workers.

o Investment is considered significant until you leverage its future results. Compare it to oil refining. Further consider the cost of current alternatives in human resources.

o Market futures can also just as easily be structured in the commodities market for water delivery just like for oil. The technology can also become leveraged elsewhere. It could be viewed as an investment in the future of the Middle East.

o Allowing, and structuring financial products for its neighboring nations to flourish, Israel provides a road map where peace simply comes in its stride.

o Israel and its neighboring nations as emerging markets can create new banking products for institutional banks to manage.

o Israel can become the banking center of the Middle East and therefore, be able to compete against the oil markets while affording financial stability to many surrounding and emerging economies.

Moreover consider its influence on other Muslim nations in seeing this road map becoming realized. Simply, water puts out fires !

For the Strategic Future of Our Nation

6.3.3.3: Iran and the West

Consider what is achieved by what we are now offered as criminally incompetent leadership . On September 19th, 2006 at the UN, two presidents were condemning each other. This tied up New York for 3 days; but that's a minor issue.

Obama has stated that he would consider Nuking Iran and Newt wants to at least to bomb their gas refinery. The question is what's next as an idea in dealing with Iran ?

Most important is when did Congress declare war on Iran and what was the reason ? This is something that does not exist and while there is a window of sanity we should with the best of our diplomacy declare peace.

Consider instead if we and Iran could have brokered a settlement for friendship on 09/19/2006. Imagine how this could put out the fires that burn the unfortunate now. Imagine what it could do for world benefit.

Any incompetent dope can pull a trigger that can serve the 'hear and now' but life goes full circle like a shot heard around the world . Provoked we could take out their only gas station as <u>Newt Gingrich</u> suggests, but then we must account for newly purchased Russian missiles being shot at Israel, and at our Navy which spends a lot of time in the Persian Gulf. Due to Russia and China seeing Iran as a valuable oil supplier, the potential would be WW III.

e.1- Consider just a gesture of business friendship as one answer

To use any means at our disposal, consider that in the outskirts of a neighboring country, say just north of Iran we were to invest in building one to two more refineries. Then we could go to Iran and make the offer of refining their oil. We have helped them lower the cost in producing their own gasoline. Meantime the deal is that we get a discount on their oil -

Besides the deal itself, it has a ripple affect on the region. This includes OPEC pricing, the relationships between Iran, China and Russia; and on the many Iranian Jews that had to exit Iran once to save their lives. Iran's animosity toward the West will have to change disposition.

The New Deal, an Election 2008 Primer

e.2- Consider even a more dynamic gesture of business friendship as another answer

Proposed is that guided through UN leadership, Iran can be allowed to have their national esteem and a level playing field. This is in doing business with the world as a model Islamic Nation. All we have to do is help them with their efforts for nuclear energy instead of condemning them for wanting it. Iran has a current challenge in refining oil so their want for nuclear energy is not unreasonable.

As the earth itself shifts its magnetic poles, accomplishing peace in the Middle East is possible if we are not a jack in the box tied to artificial constraints.

This is addressed in the following press release. It was sent to Iran's Government news station the day before the 15 UK hostages were released. .

6.3.3.3.1 "Deal with Iran like Reagan"

Orion Karl Daley aka, OKD believes that Iran holding the 15 Royal British navy personnel as hostages is like acting out to regain national esteem. OKD further believes that Iran is reaching out to the world of nations due to feeling isolated and deemphasized in UN representative importance . He says that like in Reagan's time , we should be talking with Iran about mutual strategic interests.

New York, NY (PRWEB) April 3, 2007 -- Orion Karl Daley of the Balanced Party (http://unity2008.org) believes that Iran is reaching out and it's due to feeling isolated. He suggests this because the capture of the 15 British sailors and marines by Iran's Revolutionary Guard could have been resolved easily if Iran returned them. There was a question on the territory boundary, we all make mistakes, and Britain is apologizing for their side, so why not just fix this one ? OKD dismisses that Iran is really testing military waters. He also believes that this does not need to become another Bay of Tonkin .

Candidate Daley says that we know that Iran's obstinance could destabilize Iraq. The US military is threaded, the Brits have not spoken about theirs, and Iran always wants to demonstrate their readiness. But Iran has to be aware of an unlimited ordinance that could come their way from the Persian Gulf. It also does not matter that the Democrats demonstrated disapproval of the 'surge' and that US policy does not reflect 'united we stand' about Iraq. Iran could expect that the Executive and legislative branch to come together if it were to press the issue.

Regardless if Iran could figure that it has support from Russia and China its obstinacies can provide the UN Security Council incentive to get behind Great Britain.

For the Strategic Future of Our Nation

Mr. Daley points out that when President Reagan took office, he talked to Iran about hostages when our Tehran Embassy was compromised. President Mahmoud Ahmadinejad of Iran implies that it's a matter of principle in response to arrogance. Mr. Daley believes that what is important is that Ahmadinejad wants to talk. The UN should use all means possible to achieve active dialogue.

In Reagan's time and again now , Candidate Daley feels that it's a matter of talking about it. He believes that it is only natural that Iran wants to be recognized by the rest of the world, but its image has a stigma which requires a strong case for its recognition. OKD says that Iran also could have felt deemphasized in representative importance by the UN with its last mandate, and this is not much to take home in terms of national pride.

In leadership, Mr. Daley emphasizes that talk is a very important. This does not mean ultimatums. When given the opportunity in September 2006, this did not happen at the UN. When not being face to face, Presidents Bush and Ahmadinejad just condemned each other. OKD sees that Ahmadinejad can't lose face any further so he found another issue to bring to the table.

He recommends that for Ahmadinejad to lower his wall of pride, then the UN should as well. OKD sees it as a matter of horse trading, where the actual deal is Iran's Nuclear Power plant.

Assuming the legitimacy of any position about this, Candidate Daley notes that we have to recognize that still, it will continue to exist, and Iran is acting out. To manage a relationship with Iran, he points out is different than trying to control it.

OKD envisions that a responsible UN leadership can manage this relationship. His reasoning is that we have the opportunity to talk, there is a lot of horse trading that could go on the table, and the British, US and others as members of the UN should take advantage of it.

Since Iran holds the position that they are seeking clean nuclear power, Candidate Daley suggests offering UN member assistance in building a safe clean nuclear power plant for Iran. His reasoning is that Iran can learn of Russia's mistakes with Chernobyl, and then there are lessons to be learned by 3 Mile Island and US advances in safe nuclear energy; and then as partners, there is less of a concern also about inspectors.

He sees that Iran has the potential of making many multi-national business alliances if given the opportunity, and could even be used as one of the first examples of safe, reliable and clean nuclear energy. This over shadows any need for nuclear weapons.

The New Deal, an Election 2008 Primer

OKD sees that there is no reason why Iran can't be invaded with world kindness, which makes all UN members active participants in Iran's clean energy program, and therefore, in its future prosperity. Making business partners could also help stabilize the region.

Mr. Daley sees that although Iran's military is building up thanks to Russia's help, it does not really compare to a Nation becoming recognized as a strategic player in world leadership. Guided through UN leadership, Iran can be allowed to have their national esteem and a level playing field for doing business with the world. Military contributions from others become far less in importance compared to having national prestige for an Islamic nation.

I see that there is no reason why Iran can't be invaded by the UN with world kindness. This makes all UN members active participants in Iran's clean energy program and therefore, in its future prosperity. There is then less of a concern about inspectors where making business partners could also help stabilize the region.

6.3.4 Trade in Weapons for Economy

It is not far fetched to consider that nuclear prone governments can trade down their nuclear weapons count to enhance their economy given a common ground for peace. In poor countries that seek power and presence in the world it can be a means for restructuring their economies if they no longer feel the threat of other nuclear prone nations (NPNs). The basis of the idea is as follows:

1- What does it cost to maintain a nuclear missile per year ? For now lets say $1*X dollars.

2- If the NPN and the U.S. were to decommission 1 missile each jointly then there would be a reduction in cost of $2X dollars. Each side can save the cost of $1Xdollars that could be put back into the domestic economies.

3- By doing this, the U.S. has saved $1X dollars which can be loaned to the nuclear prone nation where the risk of the loan becomes a wash due to the fact that it was an actual cost previously.

4- By receiving the loan of $1X dollars, the nuclear prone nation can have a total of $2X dollars to put into their economy.

The New Deal, an Election 2008 Primer

5- The loan should be made into a government bond, where the companies which have either invested in the nuclear prone nation or have taken monies out of it are required to invest in.

This allows an increment above the original $1X value, so that the NPN can receive $1X savings in addition to $1X loan. That is plus the additional corporate investment benefits applied towards the bond.

The corporations in turn will have a vested interest to help affectively plan phase II of the economic restructuring along with the NPN, and the U.S.

To put this in perspective, let's consider the number of nuclear missiles that both countries have and that only a third if less would be required to provide any perceived defense posture against a hostile threat.

Consider as an example Russia, India and Pakistan consider themselves as our friends these days, and what better way to help one who is new to capitalism to survive, stabilize and mature into economic powers !

This can also be applied as an example for token bridge building with smaller NPNs like Iran and North Korea. Further, a symbolic decrease of weapons with even a smaller hostile nation can build similar bridges.

We do not need to be imperialistic to accomplish manifest destiny, as *good will* is a more sustainable investment.

For the Strategic Future of Our Nation

Chapter 7 – Personal Viewpoints

All US presidents have been different in leadership. Each has had some similar and then differing viewpoints about our nations issues. In taking the oath of office one's viewpoints must come second to that oath.

There are a number of issues today that we as citizens do concern ourselves with. They can be considered constitutional and can range from beliefs in personal privacy, the question if we should be allowed to own guns; to even more personal issues about a president's belief in God. Then there are views about good and evil, and how this is recognized in a president's outlook and policy. Like in 2004, many of the presidential candidates for Election 2008 will even use these to quickly identify who they are in order to reach a particular demographic.

The main core of these issues include the separation of Church and State, if a president is either a liberal or a conservative, and how they view abortion. The newest issues for contention are over same sex marriage and immigration.

These are not policies that US presidents are to focus their leadership on but are in fact to be taken up with the legislative branch.

The president is obligated by oath to manage based on the *will of the people.* This is represented by the legislative branch.

In the following I do not care to use these issues but present my own viewpoints on them. But as an elected president, in taking the oath to uphold the US Constitution what ever my own beliefs are come second to it.

I further believe that no presidential candidate should claim moral ground over another by using such issues as they do not serve the health, safety and welfare of the people, but can result in creating divisions instead in our nation.

A president is to be a uniter and not a divider where we all can have differing beliefs about these issues. The president in leadership must take the ground chosen by law.

What I do believe in first and foremost are checks and balances in our government's branches which empower the president to do his or her job as defined in the US Constitution, and nothing more, nor less. My personal view of the Constitution is that it is intended in the Bill of Rights to advocate the message *live and let live.*

The New Deal, an Election 2008 Primer

7.1 Personal Privacy and the Bill of Rights

I view that the rights to our privacy are applicable to all. Our personal privacy is held most dear to all of us. During the authorship of the 'Bill of Rights', the word 'privacy' actually did not exist.

I view that this right is demonstrated in the notion of allowing each our own sense of "personal space with the message of *live and let live* " as is demonstrated in authoring of Amendments III and IV.

I do not personally believe that the intention of these Amendments need to be second guessed due to the absence of the word 'Privacy'.

Public figures as elected officials are public figures. This should be considered in the context 'for the need of full transparency and accountability'. This is in terms of the work they do of and for the people as *public figures.*

For public figures to expect the right to privacy it must be for all on an even playing field. In other words, to respect everyone's privacy in order to have one's own respected.

Since 9/11, our personal privacy as citizens has been at a compromise where the executive branch has insisted to have its own extreme personal privacy. In contrast it should be more transparent. This has been based on the Patriot Act for our lack of privacy with the intent advocated that it is a national security issue for the executive branch to operate in complete privacy.

Although signed into law, I will advocate that it is to be rewritten carefully by the 3 branches of government into something that serves the people and which does regard personal privacy. It must assure our Bill of Rights.

This also goes for our public figures. In terms of mutual respect, public figures should also have their private lives and should be considered as other people are that are non-public figures.

Like for every citizen, this applies to their private lives where they must account to themselves and to ones in their personal lives.

Consequently, one's private life should be regarded as private when it is not at the public's expense or by personal imposition on the public. Otherwise, public figures, just like non-public figures, the term and right of privacy should not apply.

For the Strategic Future of Our Nation

7.2 The Right to Bear Arms in a Civil Society

As schools are easy targets, so are shopping centers and urban areas. Prior to Virginia Tech, other schools were victimized, and then the public from Beltway assassins. When having liberal laws about lethal weapons are these circumstances accounted for. And in their accounting do these laws indirectly suggest that we should all then carry guns for our personal protection ?

If this is the case, then how do local law officials and the police determine who is shooting in self defense, as opposed to one who is not. Simply should the law be *all or nothing*, or should they be more conservative where guns are legal?

America's heritage has the Kentucky long rifle. But this does not mean that our history must also demonstrate negligent laws!

To structure gun law, you do not have to be a lawyer to read the very clear English in the United States Constitution. But yet it can lead to confusion for law makers, judicial bodies, politicians and political candidates.

In terms of the right to have guns as a personal possession, Amendment II is often referenced, but not Amendment X. What's more, Amendment III accounts for our personal space, and IV, our possessions. Each can be considered part of gun law.

I see Amendment II for having a totally different purpose. It is intended to serve the security of a State, where Amendment X enables *ad hoc* laws to be realized. Gun law can incorporate the rights of Amendments III and IV because of this.

7.2.1 Amendment 2- *Right to Bear Arms* "A well regulated Militia, being necessary to the security of a free state, the right of the people to keep and bear Arms, shall not be infringed. "

When I read this, I look at the terms 'Regulate, Militia , Security, State " as being the conditions for the "right to bear arms" .

The Amendment appears to intend that for the' Security of a State, that a well Regulated Militia' is called for. During the times of the drafting of the Constitution, "we the people' made up such militias.

Today's state militias are the National Guard. This is supposed to be their only purpose. This is who I would want to see protecting our borders, and our ports, and when in full deployment nationally, they are quite capable of providing border and port security.

I do not see Amendment II stating that we as individual people may collect guns at will for the sake of collecting guns.

Amendment X, I would think can be used to make a stronger case for both pro and anti gun advocates. This is because it leaves it to state law.

7.2.2 Amendment X - *Powers of the State and People* "The Powers not delegated to the United States by the Constitution, nor prohibited by it to the States, are reserved to the States respectively, or to the people".

This Amendment enables each state to form its own laws. This permits Virginia to allow a transient to purchase a 50 Caliber rifle where New York State does not have to oblige Virginia's law. Consider that 'arms' can mean anything including 'C4 explosives' depending on the competence of the law.

So with a little imagination, the Constitution's Amendment II can also serve as a limitation to Amendment X's latitude in making laws. For the sake of argument, as a state through Amendment X can allow one to have any kind of weapon, Amendment 2 then calls for the state militia to prevent this from being a threat if necessary.

We can appease our desires for guns, respect the laws of other states for not allowing them, and yet not have one infringe on the other. In each case, the state in question has to live with the consequences of its laws.

7.2.3 Guns for the Good Citizen: Personally I have no issue with people wishing to have guns in wide open spaces, but in heavily congested urban areas, I do. In fact the very concern of needing a well regulated militia can be called for in the case of urban riots.

Here is what I mean. People should have the right to collect all the guns they want if that is what they wish. But it is not something for one's place as part of a sustained society. As much as Amendments III and IV allow our privacy, this is where our personal lives belong and not in public.

For example, in a congested urban area, or even in a crowded subway, there would be more collateral damage if we all pulled our guns in the name of the good when thinking that another had pulled theirs. Hence, I would never advocate that in a civil society that we are to all arm ourselves, as it would be pandemonium to all run around with our registered concealed weapons and mounting paranoia.

Do we have a mind set for this in the first place when considering road rage ? We live in a highly complex society where this has to be accounted for when we all have our own personal beefs and limited space.

For the Strategic Future of Our Nation

For my own beef and space, in being located 10 blocks north of ground zero, I looked for the local militia when 9 /11 looked like an invasion in our neighborhood. I wanted to know if they were adopting a citizens unit. With my family at stake, with ashes and death all around us, I also looked at anyone, and everyone to see what was in their eyes and hands.

It was instinct, and did not require thought. This is not a way to *live, and let live;* but is unfortunately when in a war zone. As a form of consumerism, it is also a state of terror that others wish us to live in today that is exploited in Amendment I.

Realistically, although we cannot control anything, we can manage things. With our young, we do have the opportunity as parents to help shape their views.

Part of moral courage that I have taught my children is to live and let live, and help to foster that as a sustained way of life. That is, regardless of their experience as children in 9/11 where their instincts were required.

Live and let live is also a fleeting reality if not regarded highly. To serve the people in our highly complex society our laws must demonstrate this.

Our laws on survival and personal possessions must demonstrate mutual respect and human rights if they are to serve us as in the Bill of Rights.

The New Deal, an Election 2008 Primer
7.3 Belief in God

As a child, I attended protestant churches, and schools, and had some teachings about the Christian Trinity. Then, I had this image that God was this fellow with long white hair and beard, sitting on a throne, and had the Angel Michael , Jesus Christ, and the Holy Ghost in reach, or that they were sent out on some mission. Additionally of course, there was the Devil, who resided in Hell. My oversight was in confusing the idea that man was made in God's image where we actually make God in our image. This seems to be the case in most religions where what they do have in common is God the creator.

In wondering about the Universe, later, I acknowledged that if God did make everything then every thing was actually made in the image of God. I also became impressed when learning that Galileo had attempted to demonstrate to the Church at the time, that we were not at the center of the Universe.

God for me now translates into something shared that I call the *'Gift of Divinity'*. It explains, personally, why God's image is in everything. This includes the Universe and that there is no center needed to have the sense of the divine order. In other words, the *Gift of the Divine* is in all of us when we seek to find it. Consequently, God's image is however we wish, and capable in seeing it.

I find myself praying sometimes, such as when seeing the kids pictures on television that have lost their lives in Iraq. I don't assume that there is a switch board in someplace called Heaven that responds back with "as you will appreciate he receives many millions of prayers a day and it is not possible to personally reply to each". Prayer to me, first before it can actually go anywhere else has to go deep inside of us. In doing so, it can yield wisdom or prudence. It all depends on why and what we are praying about and for, and what are reasonable expectations are about it. I believe that in dealing within ourselves, generally we will hear the answer to our own prayers. In other words, in order to have your prayers heard, 'to thine own self be true'.

As far as Heaven and Hell are concerned, let fear be based on illusion. I'm willing to accept that the wonder that creates life has plans for it and no matter what those plans entail, they possess the same wisdom as the phenomenon of life itself. About Hell, that just seems to me as to what we create for ourselves in this world when we do not regard the wonders of life. Moreover, that's my own beliefs, based on Amendment I. We are entitled to our very own beliefs, and can even be represented by a religious following. Thanks also to Amendment I, they can never be imposed on others which leaves our beliefs to be discovered as part of our personal path in life.

For the Strategic Future of Our Nation

7.4 On Original Sin and Reason to Be

I do believe in Original Sin. It is in how I interpreted the lessons from Genesis and equivalent teachings from religions like Buddhism.

In both cases, Original Sin, I saw as in not exercising our faculties when given the opportunity to do so. Here is what I mean:

In the Book of Genesis, God had intended for Adam and Eve to have *faculties of reason* but then in fact told them not to use it. Instead they were to basically accept blind obedience or be cast out of a perfect land.

We have reason. If we believe in God, then he gave it to us. If God meant for Adam and Eve to have reason , then they would have to leave Eden. Or what good would the *faculty of reason* be for, and therefore, a *'reason to be'*? That is, if not to at least at the onset of creation, the faculties of reason are to serve them and their needs like a farmer knowing his tools.

On the other hand would it not be a *real sin* if Adam and Eve actually remained complacently in Eden. Would the faculties of reason atrophy like any muscle not used?

I would think any creator would not be real if making a universe and then wanted those given the faculties of reason to just tend the creator's flocks and herds in only one little place called Eden. This attitude is more of a human being that creates indentured servants as opposed to one who is capable of creating our universe.

We could also say that my notion of something called 'The Gift of Divinity' is all heresy. But consider just the things we have paid for compared to what we have not. Then which do we value more. As an individual, with reason you are given the opportunity to go beyond simple guide lines fit for crowds, that is, if willing to reason.

You are also required to pay for it. In life we can either be stymied or learn wisdom. If stymied we eventually feel cheated, but with wisdom we can make a further investment in life. There is no stated guarantee as to the pay back of such an investment but there is a guarantee to what happens to your life if stymied. So it pays basically to have spiritual faith.

Then we can ask ourselves - So what is life. Is it a prescribed path, where 'your hormones go off, and then you nest' ?

The New Deal, an Election 2008 Primer

We can say that this is basically life, but is also symbolizes much about the foundations of life, or that 'reason to be'.

If we are made up of the primordial, spiritual and the conscious day to day world, then it is something that is us. It is also something that is greater than us. Hence we can have a relationship with our God. This is shared in every religion.

Reason then allows us to have these qualities as in their harmony as a trinity of feeling, thought and action, provides our 'reason to be'.

So basically for me, Original Sin is in dismissing what life can really afford us and others by choosing to not think about it.

Life is not such a simple item and when not thinking about it, it can pass us by.

In a leadership role of what ever capacities, if we don't think about it, then we have also done a disservice to others.

For the Strategic Future of Our Nation

7.5 The Good and the Evil

To run a scam, promoting fear and evil offers leverage. First and foremost I will not ever promote who or what is good or evil. I am not about to rewrite the Apocalypse of Peter in the name of national security, and do not believe any US president has this right, nor for that matter anyone.

Evil is something I believe is best resolved within ourselves as opposed to accusing others of it. In other words, to contemplate evil is one thing, but to stare in the face of it is another. Irony is, like when looking in a mirror, 'live' spelled backwards spells 'evil'.

I believe this is what we should look closely for when seeing our reflection in the mirror every morning. Who we are is reflected in what we do in our every day.

> We are not good and evil, it is not what we do as good or evil, but it is in the collateral affects of what we do.

An example is the 'Axis of Evil' where G.W. Bush claims and even accuses other nations as 'Biblical Evil Doers'.

Most of these nations represent impoverished people, which can cover the gambit of economics and human rights issues. It positions them as collaborative players to be compromised in the world today. This does not mean that we as the United States are to liberate the world, as this is the job of the UN to tackle.

When at a consulting firm in 1994, I stated to a partner in charge, that the Iron Curtain was destined to come down, as there was no way that the Soviet Union could sustain itself in the burgeoning global economy.

In fact, the 'Wall' I noted was a wall that sealed them in. This is equivalent to a castle in medieval times that would be sealed in from obtaining supplies when under siege by an outside force.

The partner in charge told me that I was 'nuts', that the Soviet Union was a major super power, and that we would never give up our Pershing Missiles. On Reagan's watch in 1989, the wall came down, and the Soviet Union was no longer looked at as evil. It was then viewed has doing something that served the good.

The New Deal, an Election 2008 Primer

If we were to threaten a hungry dog, by instinct it will only become more vicious. I believe it is only over time that the hungry dog learns trust when food is likewise extended.

Human nature is very much the same. Trust, in the name of opportunity, can only occur, 'one step at a time'.

Trust cannot be assumed as the requirement as it cannot also be imposed. It is by example that trust is earned.

North Korea is an impoverished nation that has their nuclear missile when they want to show their teeth like a hungry dog. It is not a trick that one has to teach an old dog when working 'one step at a time'.

The Middle East has great distances to achieve in trusting their fellow neighbors.

In our collateral affects, we can bridge great differences with trust. This starts by looking at our own collateral affects within our communities and how they set standards to reflect our nation's standards.

For the Strategic Future of Our Nation

7.6 Religion and the Separation of Church and State

The first Amendment in the US Constitution of the United States says in clear English:

> "Congress shall make no law respecting an establishment of religion, or prohibiting the free exercise thereof; or abridging the freedom of speech, or the press, or the right of the people to peaceably to assemble, and to petition the Government for a redress of grievances"

Amendment I says that government has no business in telling you what religion to follow, or what religion is. And no religion is to tell you the type of government we are to have.

First, I wish to point out, that if we were to give this right up, does that mean to outlaw religion, or have religion run the government?

So without Amendment I, could we have anarchy. Further, in one case what then is to distinguish our liberty and in the other case what would distinguish the United States for countries like Iran?

Secondly we can consider the question from the standpoint that religion is a man made item as much as the US Constitution is. In general, both religion and government can serve many good purposes and sometimes for some misunderstood purposes.

In the story of Moses from most published bibles, he came off the mountain with the 10 Commandments in hand. As 10 morals, they served as the foundation of some religions in the similar manner that the US Constitution of the United States serves this county.

Where they are similar is that the 10 Commandants were the most fundamental guides for survival of a people who for the first time in their lives were to suppose to have been liberated from the tyranny of slavery. As a newly formed social structure they could regress where Moses brought to them the *word of God* as the authority for their new guidance.

The Constitution serves a similar purpose but I wouldn't wish to infer that one obsoletes, or replaces the other. The Constitution is a working model that provides the necessary structure for the government of our nation and its accountability. As George Washington said, "Let us raise a standard to which the wise and the honest can repair. The event is in the hand of God".

The New Deal, an Election 2008 Primer

As a foundation, the 10 Commandments regardless of the sacred canon have lasted throughout centuries. In a similar manner, writings from other religions have served for the benefit of human kind too. In all cases, the purpose is to prolong human life and provide a path for its tomorrow. Irony is that like in Great Brittan and Ireland, the 40 year civil war in France was over which Christianity was the right one. And then there was 200 years of the crusades, and many other wars based on Christianity.

The Constitution in effect does the same as the 10 Commandments of Moses, but with a structure that provides representation of the people in a civil society and the Bill of Rights.

Thomas Jefferson demonstrated a special wisdom in my opinion in his letter to the *Danbury Baptist Association* about the 'Separation of Church and State'. As man made items, both religion and the Constitution hold great power for the leaders in question. The Danbury Baptist Association by virtue of representing religion is to serve God where the Constitution is to serve the people.

The Constitution through its diversity of bodies is intended to regulate government power in the name of the people. Like religion, under what interpretations in terms of actual day to day practice is also man made and therefore, subject to the abuse of power from human failings.

In the history of religion, persecution of people and wars in its name demonstrate this. Through accountability, the Constitution provides balance in the management of power when subject to the same human failings.

Although the Roman Empire has been viewed in terms of its greatness, and in fact had a Senate, Caesar was viewed as a god. Historically empires do not last where wars have been in the name of 'God'; or in having leaders who claim to be gods, or to have a special relationship with God. Instead such leaders condemn their empires to ruin. In addition to the Nazi empire, we just have to look even at the Crusades, or the Ottoman Empire in their siege of Constantinople. All have been in the name of God besides every war in the Middle East.

Today, we use the same slogans in the use and squandering of life. Osama bin Laden ostensibly has used this reasoning to kill all 'nonbelievers'. In our retaliation in Afghanistan, and in our invasion into Iraq, both had inferences to be in the name of God in killing 'evil doers' *or non believers*.

The Constitution further avoids the opportunity of using plausible deniability of saying that 'God told me to do so'. Instead it requires that we as a nation

For the Strategic Future of Our Nation

take more timely responsibility for our actions. The Constitution also does not allow us the 'exit strategy' of being forgiven for our sins. In this accountability, the United States has the opportunity to not be an empire that will someday fall, but instead have the ability to endure time as a structure of government for its people through the just balance of power between its branches.

'Blessed are the peace makers 'is something that has always impressed me as a statement. Given that the practitioner's of religion regard this, like the 10 Commandments, then they can serve humanity more readily than just praising its creator or advocate war in its name.

When its practitioner's seek peace just in the United States alone where there is no more the notion of the 'red and the blue' or who has real values and who has false ones, or any other form of divisive discrimination practice, is something I believe can offer their congregations a very tangible expression of God's way.

The New Deal, an Election 2008 Primer

7.7 Liberal or Conservative, the Vital Balance

The terms liberal and conservative suit labels only. They have been crafted to describe illusions of some way of life. It's very much like consumerism. Like target marketing, for politicians, it is our attempt to pigeon hole a view, following or position on something. Simple examples:

- Compassionate Conservative = having compassion (something good) and Conservative (values like my own ?)

- Liberal = accepts faults (will accept mine too ?)

I view both of the above as psychological misdemeanors when we want to associate ourselves with something that is supposed to have solid ground. The best way to clarify my position is in terms of when and how we make judgments.

About being Conservative

I would want to think of myself as somewhat conservative in terms of the use of resources and in making judgments. Judgments that we make are most of the time final. We have the responsibility of our judgments. So basically, I advocate to not rush in making judgments till all the facts are in. Part of making a judgment is in determining what purpose the decision really serves and also the time frame that it must be made in.

I view that if we opt to judge without facts, then it is the same as opting out to just pigeon hole for the sake of our own convenience in how we try to put an issue behind us or to serve a very personal agenda. But, on the other hand, we actually are not putting the issue behind us, as again we have to live with the decisions that we make. Mostly, such judgments in history will eventually speak of our personal agendas. An easy example of this is to free Iraq in the name of Weapons of Mass Destruction, then to capture and prosecute Saddam Hussein, then to provide the Iraqi people the right to vote for who we wanted as their government, and then to fight their civil war, and then ultimately to remain in Iraq for so called American oil interests.

What ever the spin, history will identify the true basis for the judgment taken for irresponsible actions. The George Bush junior. administration took us to war in Iraq. In my opinion, history will speak of its distortion of 'manifest destiny' to serve for certain individual's pure profit at an immeasurable cost and harm to many.

For the Strategic Future of Our Nation

About being Liberal

I'm still not sure what a Liberal is, but have heard of something called a 'bleeding heart liberal'. I think this term actually only serves the purposes of the one using it and not the one that is being referred to. We cannot call others out right nasty names these days, so 'liberal' could be the a workable alternative if in fact we also craft its image politically, as in being an irresponsible wet noodle, in using the term.

If I wanted to define the notion of 'liberal' instead, I would want to apply it to an example such as in being open to alternative *'points of view'*. Again, here I am seeking for something that is similar to facts, but not necessarily facts, but also that which could put context in place for the facts.

It is commonly believed that Saddam Hussein would be inclined to use 'weapons of mass destruction' if he had them to use. I accept this as a conclusion based on many facts. From weapons inspectors, we also know that he did not have WMD at the time the administration decided to commit American lives in taking over Iraq in the name of liberation and furthering the Democratic way.

Points of view from both a conservative and liberal standpoint could be, could we have waited until later for invading Iraq ? This is while putting our full focus on rectifying September 11, 2001. In other words, to put our resources into bringing those who we believed are guilty to answer for this. Example, Osama bin Laden, and the Al Qaeda was our original objective; and 'points of view' must be accounted for that believe that we could have caught him and disassembled his following more readily if putting sincere focus on this.

Is rushing to judgment conservative or liberal in view ? The rush to judgment put our kids in harms way in Iraq. This is at the cost of many lives, with no intended exit strategy. This is while Osama bin Laden is probably basking in Sweden. We have just ended up creating a justification for a growing Al Qaeda movement. We further compound this problem by assuming to put some form of government in place for Iraq where our focus is in pumping its oil. This is as opposed to figuring how to have 'Peace with Dignity' in order to get our heroic solders home.

About Saddam Hussein and the threat from Iraq, when considering him to be such a great threat, the question remains, 'How was it so easy to overcome him and his regime ?'. From the military standpoint he was not really any threat; from the accountability standpoint, served as a distraction from 9/11; and where from the political standpoint gives a president a mandate in hand where results can be seemingly tangible when wanting to win a battle in the war on terrorism.

The New Deal, an Election 2008 Primer

7.8 On Pro Life / Pro Choice

As the new version of the *Scarlet A*, abortion can serve as a means to distract the people away from more compelling and immediate issues. This is while splitting the country over moral indignation. In its chaos, those who promote this divisive issue can grab power through mob rule which ultimately persecutes others. Just recall, once *witch burning* was considered morally correct in our own country.

> The president, in order to serve the people cannot be on one side or the other of such an issue, but to address it for what it really is worth !

As president, the bases of this issue has to be more of a question of 'big government vs. personal values'. There are consequences from either standpoint that must also be accounted for in the due diligence of the government and for all involved.

Let us keep in mind that the right to life implies divine life at conception yet the same moral values generally include something called *original sin* upon birth as the ignored dichotomy. Our sin is the disregard for those born unloved.

This dichotomy need not be challenged when we consider that moral values are ultimately personal values; and that the 'right to choose' is then translated to the morality of our choices that we must live with.

'Big government' implies making laws to control what our personal values are. By this definition, an irresponsible pregnancy is simply a moral or personal value which in turn could be outlawed by the same reasoning as the right to life. This does not serve the people.

Exploiting irresponsible pregnancies also makes good business profits. Commercial time for the day time network TV industry comes into demand. They promote DNA testing as an example of 25 men where one might be responsible for fathering a child with a so called innocent young teen age girl; or where there are multiple women/girls that are pregnant by the same male.

Our moral values could be such that illicit pregnancies are outlawed and punishable. But then what do we do with all the night time TV shows on family values that promote illicit sex indirectly such as 7th Heaven, & *Fresh Gilmore Girls*, etc ?

For the Strategic Future of Our Nation

In both cases , what is the government's obligation in terms of the real victim which is the child. Or could we even rationalize, that the TV industry could be victimized if they couldn't have such air time? It could cost them. People could lose jobs in DNA testing labs, and advertising as well as the business opportunity for TV lawyers and court TV. Even Oprah and Dr. Phil who want to 'right your wrongs ' might have to look for alternative employment.

Should our moral values even swing instead to the opposite direction and opt to be more like the Mormons in having multiple wives for one man? This could also solve the moral problem.

Simply, where do we draw the line of reasoning in allowing 'big government' to make these values for each of us where it has the possibility that laws could be weaved that accomplish nothing more than just to suit convenience and fashionably palatable political agendas.

We the People cannot turn a blind eye to what we are dealing with, or what exactly are the "real moral values" ?

Until we regard the unloved, the real question is, what right to life are we actually giving them. Until then, do we have the right to outlaw the pro choice settled law ?

Abortion, like birth is an act that one must live with afterwards. I don't know of any woman alive that does not find both a traumatic experience. This is regardless of whether it is suppressed. In addition to moral values, abortions are against instinct even if personally rationalized to oneself as a necessity.

Saying that it is a women's right to choose, does not imply that the choice is arbitrary and indifferent. Every woman like every family is different. In each circumstance, every abortion has different reasons that must be lived with afterwards as extra moral baggage and self persecution.

How are we to judge moral values when a birth is considered divine in conception but when a child is born, it is statistically ignored more often than not?. Then, in some cases the unfortunate child is even born with Aids.

How are we to judge moral values when a child is born to an impoverished family where the pregnancy and delivery could have been avoided ?

Once I watched a family with 8 children enter a NYC subway car. They were a loving family. This was obvious in how the father cut up an apple to give to the youngest of his children.

The New Deal, an Election 2008 Primer

Unfortunately, the entire family was more than mal nourished as each had their eyes sunk into their heads and lack of the fundamental body fat necessary for proper development.

It is to easy to pass this off in the terms of the *you should of's* in terms of the use of family planning, contraception, abstinence, and the fact that there were 8 innocent victims of mal nutrition, where the parents, no matter how much love they had for their children, could not sustain them.

How are we to judge moral values when self inflicted and back alley abortions were the norm for the poor and desperate prior to abortion's legalization? The result was more often death of the female.

How are we to judge moral values when taking of life of hundreds of thousands of children through our collateral damage that we have caused in our fervor to liberate Iraq ?

How are we to judge moral values when allowing genocide across the globe, as well as abject poverty even in our nation's capital, Washington D.C.?

If we are to wave the flag for the right to life, or for pro choice, then we should not live in glass houses.

I think many serious questions are warranted as a moral responsibility of those who decide on such laws. Or let's just change the term to the 'right to birth' with original sin as ones' inheritance when conceived for the wrong reasons and born unwanted by most.

Let as also change the term pro choice to 'deal with it' when and if we endorse abortion.

We need backbone to embrace the decisions that we make, or our decisions are nothing more than just washing our hands of the issues at other's expense.

For the sake of fairness and sanity in our nation, we owe it to the people to demonstrate the thinking behind workable solutions that account for responsibility for all concerned or we should all wear the *Scarlet A*. This is no matter if we personally believe in pro life or pro choice.

We as people will never have the *absolute* in terms of one view over another, or abolish illegitimate children, and abortion, or have in any way a perfect world that does not assault our personal sensibilities. This is something that each of us must own up to within ourselves.

For the Strategic Future of Our Nation

We could in all fairness accept the faults that are inherent in human nature no matter which way we choose to look at it.

We could even endow our educational systems in not teaching values but in the cost of not having them. This provides temperance, and acceptance of our own faults, and could instill our efforts to improve on our personal standards of life.

Through our own due diligence we can as a nation have less unwanted children, less abortions, less failed marriages, and less fatalities, and persecution of people.

Instead of trying to control something, we can always learn to manage it like our very own personal faults instead. As Christ had said, 'let the first without sin cast the first stone'.

The New Deal, an Election 2008 Primer

7.9 On Same Sex Marriage

Marriage is not an institution. Let's try to put this into perspective when considering the statement made by Presidential Candidate Lewis Cass in 1848 when associating the Institution of Marriage with the right to own slaves:

> "If the relation of Master and servant may be regulated or annihilated, or may the relation of Husband and Wife, or parent and child, and any other conditions which our institutions and the habits of our society recognize"

Our family is our own personal institution. As much as the notion of 'institution' is defined by the era in which we live, marriage itself has not been compromised by abolishing slavery, or other acts of social evolution. In being with my wife Carolyn for over 24 years I can say that marriage is not something that is an institution but instead a commitment of love. Statistically, most heterosexual marriages do not last. In our case, love is through commitment. This is the only real basis for marriage. It is irrelevant to me as to why two of the same sex wish to marry, as first I believe that each of us have to understand what marriage really is for each of us. This is before we can simply apply any ascribed standard that determines who can or cannot marry whom.

I believe that in the Bible, Christ said in so many words, 'let the first without Sin cast the first stone'. This is a question we should ask ourselves every morning in the bathroom mirror when washing our face. Sexuality is also not specifically a choice such as what shirt one chooses to wear on a given morning.

Any geneticist will tell you that there are few perfect XX and XY 's really walking around. Any psychologist would speak their opinion as well on cause and effect of sexual preferences. The environment and our genes are very much a pair to deal with when it comes down to basic discrimination. This demonstrates what our moral values really add up to.

In terms of Amendment I, what is morally right in my opinion is to recognize that although we are all different, that each as adults still need and are entitled to adult companionship; and that it is a personal value as in Amendment III, that we live with in our sense of self, and should never be dictated by other's values on us as intended in Amendment I of the Constitution. Children need mentors in their developing years, and this is by both genders. Let's consider a single mother with a son, or a daughter. Both genders of child need to know what a male is, as much if a single father should have his children know what a female is and a mother. I would hope that this responsibility is accounted for when claiming to love our children no matter what our own sexual disposition is, or opinions about the opposite sex.

Chapter 8

About

Orion Karl Daley

Family

and

Biographies

The New Deal, an Election 2008 Primer

8.1 About Orion Karl Daley some Transparency

VIEW TO DOWNTOWN   NEW YORK CITY

Keeping in mind that the State of the Union Speech in the Constitution is the fundamental job description for the President of the United States, I authored the Promise, for Election 2008 that is in Appendix I in this book.

In 2004, I wrote it in wanting to set a standard, and have it become known as to what any candidate must match or exceed in providing this country a fair deal that is backed by true commitment in his or her leadership when being entrusted and held accountable for, by our nations people, and with respect to the world around us. For me, in this manner, let the best in leadership win the regard of the people in 2008.

I am no icon, have my lovely wife Carolyn and family of 3 children of college age, and like every body else, pay and owe taxes.

I wanted to share the following so you know more about me. I see **true leadership** as in being a straight shooter, and *Transparency* is key to this. You have to be who you say you are, in order for others who have entrusted you to believe in what you say.

For the Strategic Future of Our Nation

I am not a politician, but as a working man see myself as a statesman. In the following, I would like to share some background. It's not intended as some resume, but to help explain where I am coming from, so it will be easier to understand where I want us to go.

I founded Orion Computer Systems in late 1985. I started my career as a self taught electrical engineer in 1978. This evolved into a management consulting practice at Price Waterhouse before forming OCSI (Orion Computer Systems, Inc.) as a bid based systems integration consulting practice. Now I work as a per diem contractor. Since its inception, I have managed successfully many industry based projects, teams and resources for clients. Prior to PW employment included ITT World Comm, Bell Laboratories, Burroughs, and Raytheon.

Undergrad work was pre-med/psychology. Also too early in life had a first marriage at 19 that caused some bumps and hiccups in what could have been a well laid plan in medicine to become a healer. She was a little older, and understandably so, wanted a salesman and not a student. We parted eventually. While attending WVU, med-school was out of the question dollars wise, but I was offered an in state tuition if first abstaining from attending school for a year to earn residency. In the beginning of that year, I got quite interested in what was called Microprocessors, and also needed a way to make a living. Six months later after two interviews, I was offered a career start as an Electrical Engineer at both Raytheon and Burroughs. Peer acceptance took some time when being self taught, but it is only a matter of being who you say you are.

The *dot com boom* occurred right when a client was downsizing much of its NYC operations in 98. I created a company called 'The Trading Systems Network, Inc.' It was a vision for a Fidessa:Bloomberg like hybrid. With little funds, it too had its bumps as a startup. I was honored in the trust afforded by my angel investors, and by clients and friends who contributed computers; and also by the NYSE, NADASQ, and AMEX for my accountability. The Exchanges allowed me to distribute real time market quotations on the Internet from my home. One angel in particular, an Iranian Jew who with his family narrowly escaped as refugees in the 70s's from Iran, had put a significant part of his life savings into the business. We have been friends now for over ten years. Back in 2000, we had finally had gotten the recognition of an investment banking firm. It was located in the WTC. We had started to see my proof of vision about to go places in August 2000. Things looked like they were going to improve. Finally we were to hire some friends with great talent; and setup an office of about 40 people on Broad Street. We never got there of course, as like for all, 911 had changed everything.

The New Deal, an Election 2008 Primer

I had to keep my family going afterwards. There was no real work. For a contractor everything was instead being off shored to India. Even my wife Carolyn had been laid off by her employer, Arthur Andersen a month before the Enron investigation. As the WTC was like the trees in our front yard just up the street on 7th ave in NYC, our 3 kids were our most concern. I wanted to minimize the ripple effect on them and created a family continuity project to keep us busy. We have plenty of computers at home, so we could build anything we wanted for the Internet. It might make money, and might not, but while out of work, I needed to keep busy, and they learned basic skill sets. This cut through the shock that could have hit them as our neighborhood was generally taped off, loaded with rescue vehicles and a lot sirens. We built ModelsUnlimited.net which was in applying some Wall Street business concepts into another industry. Our kids became very proficient in graphic art work. Today they have these skills, if needed to fall back on them another day.

It was a long 3 years before election 2004, and we had stayed real tight together. Our oldest daughter did get side-winded when I could not have her return to college back then. Fortunately today, our two daughters are currently in college, and we are looking forward to our son going in Fall 2007.

I waited patiently for election 2004, and put desperate faiths in the leadership of the Dems, but regardless of any election day issues, their leadership looked like milk toast; and voter belief was expected like blind faith instead of 'Trust but Verify'. Only religions can ask this of you, but not your nation's current or future leadership. I figured that the Dems were hopefully less ignorant and less contrived than the current leadership. But as for the Dems, I saw no real solutions, nor strategic path, and no horizon. The only message that resonated from them was some lip service about how life was unfair, and help get them into the White House. I had an issue with this as in knowing that if we put self serving agendas aside, workable solutions for this nation abound as described in this book.

I am not sure what 'fair' really means these past 6 years by the current administration, or by the 2004 Democrat candidates, but do know very clearly what the 'health, safety, and welfare' of my family means to me. And in a similar manner as the love I have for my family, I do know very clearly that this also applies to our nation as a people.

In 2004, in press releases, I announced the Balanced Party based on 5 very clear principles that our nation as a people, and its government to serve their needs for our strategic future. As I want a future for my family, which goes hand in hand with the future of our nation. Expectedly, I would want to eventually see leaders include in their vocabulary the words: 'Principle', and 'Transparent and Accountable Government, The Dignity of Human Rights, Balanced Trade, Economic Solvency, and to Conduct workable Foreign

For the Strategic Future of Our Nation

Policy'. But to use them, they must be more than sound bites for self serving agendas.

Again let me emphasize, that I hope to set a standard, and have it become known as to what any candidate must match or exceed in providing this country a fair deal that is backed by true commitment in his or her leadership when being entrusted and held accountable for, by our nations people, and with respect to the world around us. For me, in this manner, let the best in leadership win the regard of the people in 2008.

8.2 About Carolyn Sue Daley

I met Orion while I was attending West Virginia University in Morgantown, West Virginia.

After obtaining my bachelor's degree in Speech Pathology and Audiology I was eager to have a job serving my community. I became employed in the public school system of Barbour County, West Virginia where I traveled from school to school in small mining communities providing speech and language therapy to children.

Following a failed young marriage with one child I relocated to NYC in 1984 to reconnect with Orion.

Once in NYC I started out as a gal girl Friday for a small printing company then worked my way up to data entry and ordering in a sports clothing office and showroom. With some office experience and a college degree behind me I was then hired to work for an international insurance company working in a systems and special projects department that reported to the chairman of the company. I was praised for my enthusiasm and efficiency and soon was studying at night at a nearby university to become a business analyst. Orion and I were soon married and immediately decided to have children. While the children were young I chose to work at our home office supporting my husband's consulting business, Orion Computer Systems.

For the Strategic Future of Our Nation

When the youngest of our three children was settled in kindergarten I went back to the international corporate environment, this time working for a consulting firm in their information technology department typing proposals, creating graphics, and organizing recruiting events. Three years later I decided to explore the real estate business by starting in the legal department of a midtown company which was soon bought out by a larger firm at which time I was laid of during the reorganization. It was then I became an employee of an international accounting firm as an administrative assistant in the Financial Markets department. Five years later I was laid off again due to the recession in late 2001 when the company I worked for was downsizing after 9/11. Within a month I found a job working in a legal department of a large national food and tobacco company and later transferred to their Mergers and Acquisitions Department where I am now.

During the 90's I was active in the parents' associations of private Manhattan schools where our children attended – organizing various fund raisers and social events. I also solicited a corporate sponsorship for the American Cancer Society awareness event.

Following 9/11 our two younger children were moved to NYC public schools where I became the secretary of two high school parents' associations and our oldest daughter returned home from college to work to supplement the family's income while the consulting industry was non existent.
In 2005, while the economy was starting to return, the consulting opportunities were sporadic, consequently, I became a part-time cosmetic sales representative in addition to my daytime job. During this time I conducted workshops and donated skin care products, cosmetics, and clothing to homeless women staying at the Grand Central Neighborhood to give them some attention are care and to encourage them to feel confident for job interviewing.

Currently, I am the President of the Parents' Association of our son's high school. It has been exciting being a part of a caring group of parents, scheduling speakers for our meetings and organizing community fund raisers.

Appendix

Appendix I

The Promise

The Promise is the State of The Union Address drafted in 2004. It is seen as what is needed for January 20th, 2009. The New Deal is based on the Promise. Much of the wording is the same less the detail provided in the book.

In not intending to draft a speech that is longer than President William Henry Harrison, it is extensive.

It was drafted from many standpoints. As a working man, my interest is the health safety and welfare of my family. This depends on our communities, which then depends for the same on our nation.

As people, our health, safety and welfare are uniquely distinguishable but inseparable factors that can be regarded in the same way as for our communities and be applied as standards for our nation.

The State of the Union Address is extensive due to addressing these factors uniquely and in their dependence as a nation of people.

The standards proposed for our nation, communities and as individuals is based on the 5 principles:

1- Transparent and Accountable Government to serve the people.

2- The Dignity of Human Rights in our mutual regard

3- Balanced Trade in how we work with foreign importers

4- Economic Solvency in our economy

5- Conduct workable foreign policy

The State of the Union

for January 2009
by
Orion Karl Daley
Draft 1 - 12/18/2004

In order to steward and ensure a more perfect union for the people of the United States, and in its representation to its neighbors, I hereby pledge the following commitments while in office as the president of this great country and as the management of the executive branch of its government.

The Health, Safety, and Welfare of the People of the United States

The health, safety and welfare of the people represents the state of the soundness of this nation. It is in the combination of these uniquely distinguishable, inseparable factors, that provide the purpose of the Government and nothing further, nor less. It is in the *standards of measure* for this soundness, that the state of its people, and thus the Union is served.

People are more empowered to stand on their own two feet when there is an environment conducive for them to do so. The health, safety, and welfare of this nation, as expressed in its people, is the foundation for this.

Health, safety, and welfare all have many unique facets. These facets are regarded here for their importance at a personal level for each of us, at the community level where we live with others, and in terms of federal government in its responsibility to all of us as a nation.

Although the following is lengthy, I ask for your patience in its reading. It addresses much that has been on each of our minds. It is how my administration addresses these issues as responsibilities and how it is to be held transparently accountable for them by you.

For the Strategic Future of Our Nation

1- The Health of Our Nation

The health of the people is the strength of our nation. It is not muscle that has strength, but it is the strength in the heart and the mind that provides strength to muscle. In this manner, the people are the strength of our nation.

The measures of health have to be physical, mental, and spiritual, where they are manifested uniquely in all of us. Combined, they reflect the health of our nation and our government.

1.1- Physical Health: This is key to our sustainability as people, and by default, is entitled by all. It is the objective of my administration to make respectable health care obtainable for all in this nation. This is no matter if one is impoverished, is a worker who normally does not qualify for existing assistance, is an elderly person who should have the respect of those generations that follow, or is an affluent person who has been able to obtain the best health care available.

1.2- Mental Health: Our health is also subject to the quality of foods we consume, and the environment we live in which all in this nation are fully entitled too. Both of these like our *mental health* should not be regarded as minimal , but as a high bar for standards. As we are entitled to quality and the availability in our foods, and a livable environment, our mental health is served best with quality educational systems. It is the commitment of my administration to provide quality and availability in food, and environmental standards that meet our needs, and the availability of education for all US citizens that are able and willing in this nation.

1.3- Spiritual Health: This is measured by the stamina in one's basic spirit for life, and in the level of resilience to its challenges that we uniquely confront. The building blocks to enable spiritual health are the combination of one's physical and mental health. Without this, there is no vessel for spirit, no matter where we deem to be its source.

We can overcome the use of detrimental drugs, and the abuse of those that serve our indulgences when our Spirit is strong. *Simply, need there be a war, if there is no enemy ?* As much as our nation has been afflicted by heroine, cocaine, ephedrines, and other harmful substances, our nation need no longer be starved by being disenfranchised from the sense of self when having a real vessel for our spirit.

It is the commitment of my administration, that no matter however one wishes to fill their vessel, through faith based followings, beliefs or otherwise, that they are entitled to have that vessel of their own to fill and not to be exploited by others.

The New Deal, an Election 2008 Primer

2- Our Nation's Safety:

Our nation's safety is composed of 3 distinguishable, but inseparable areas of scope and focus. These are our personal safety, communities, and the nation's.

2.1 Personal Safety

The Amendments to the Constitution known as the *Bill of Rights* are the basis for the definition of our personal safety. They are intended to "prevent the way to tyranny by the central government". It is these Amendments of personal empowerment that enable our communities, and therefore, is part of the foundation for our nation's safety. Our personal safety is based on our health, and the homes, assets, livelihood, peace of mind, rights to our privacy, and the respect of our beliefs and orientations, being not from ill-gotten gain, nor from the misfortune of others.

Subsequently, the actions and recognition of 1964 Civil Rights Act, the mandates of the ACLU, NAACP and the outright regard for race, creed and color, and work by organizations such as the AFL-CIO shall be regarded for their contributions.

It is my commitment to continually seek the improvement of personal safety on behalf of the people. This is through the cooperation of federal and state governments. Laws and/or the need of, will be regarded that deal with credit practices and the respect of personal assets. They will allow viable means to further instill the ability to maintain and grow one's homes and assets through ethical means; hence, the means for *The American Dream.*

2.1 A- The Right for Livelihood is a given right when exercised in a legal and ethical manner. This right is to be supported without limiting it to the following:

- Through 'Balanced Trade' initiatives, we will pursue the prevention of lost jobs, discounted wages, and unnecessary layoffs.

- Affirmative Action policies and practices will be pursued for compliance by all employers that operate within the United States. All United States based employers will further be required to be in compliance with polices and practices in the hiring and employment of U.S citizens that work, or are employed offshore on behalf the employer. Further, Affirmative Action will be examined for its effectiveness and relevance in protecting jobs for US citizens over and above foreign visitors that have visa sponsored labor offerings at below market salary value.

For the Strategic Future of Our Nation

- Unions like the AFL-CIO will work with non union workers. The need to afford union dues by non-union workers within union places of work where union labor is performed in an equivalent manner, focus and scope in employee performance and responsibilities should be permitted. These union dues on non union workers are to ensure for the non-union worker, the same representation, rights and benefits that are afforded to union workers of the same classification within the same work place of employment.

- In non-Union workplaces, union petition is to be permitted, where its formation is to be only accepted by a 2/3 vote by associated employees within the workplace in question. Voting is to be held in privacy such as in the manner of government elections, and vote counting to be performed by impartial and objective means.

- Living Wage is to be examined based on economics for geographical areas. Wages are to reflect the actual cost of living for the community where the employment, and residence occurs, and subject to the *inflation index* as opposed to the 'take it or lose it' types of today's employment offer. Minimum wage and what is defined as the poverty level must also be treated geographically.

- Fixed Price and Overtime is to apply for every worker. No matter if directly employed, or via third party contract, they must be paid for work done. The professional day as set to eight hours does not obviate the responsibility of the employer to provide monetary compensation for overtime. For direct employment, overtime is to be paid as 'time and one half'. For contractors, time is to be paid by the hour.

- Poverty Level: This must be set based realistically on the cost of living, and the inflation index. Hence, minimum wage must be accounted for in this as being above the poverty level. This can be different for many locations in our country.

2.1 B- The Rights to Our Privacy, I view applicable to all as our personal privacy is held most dear to all of us. As during the authorship of the 'Bill of Rights', the word *privacy* actually did not exist, I view that this right is demonstrated in the notion of allowing each our own sense of 'personal space' with the message of 'live and let live' as is demonstrated in authoring of Amendments III and IV. I do not personally believe that the intention of these Amendments need to be second guessed due to the absence of the word 'privacy'.

The New Deal, an Election 2008 Primer

Public figures as elected officials are public figures where this is considered by me for the need of full transparency and accountability in terms of the work we do as public figures in the name of the people.

For public figures to expect the *right to privacy*, that right must be for all on an even playing field.

Public figures, otherwise have their private lives, and considered as just people that are non-public figures. When it comes to private lives, all must account to themselves and to ones in their personal space.

2.1 C- Respect of our Beliefs

Demonstrated in Amendment I is the clear regard of the Separation of Church and State; the respect for individual rights and for beliefs and religious followings. I remain aligned with Amendment I for its stated purpose and reasoning for right for free expression.

In terms of our educational systems and our children in schools, I would further wish others to consider the value and presence of religion in schools. This is where there is no one religion, but the sincere mutual regard for the religions of the students. Forbidding religion in schools is not out of respect for one's beliefs, but a convenient opt out when they are in stalemate.

School is a place for learning, and in learning about the world of other students, one can learn far more about one's own world.

I would further say, that in contrast to the removal of religion in schools that the students are permitted to practice their religion when necessary in all schools.

The term 'God' basically means something very special no matter what religion one follows.

Hence, all established religions that do not demonstrate mal intent should be respected if we are to expect others to respect our own religious followings.

For the Strategic Future of Our Nation

2.1.D Our Orientations

Our orientations have served as means to polarize. They have also served for others to respect. These orientations are unique for each of us. Being united, includes all orientations of the people.

We are humans. This is no matter if we choose to align ourselves with what is called 'liberal or conservative'; or our opinions, beliefs, and attitudes towards 'pro life and pro choice'; or how we might compare our own views to others on the definition and right of marriage.

Being unified, America is strong, but divided, our country becomes weak. Unity is similar to a team, where all the people from all walks of life in this country make up that team.

Dogmatism, fascism, or any 'isms', or encouraging the '*will*' of the most powerful onto the many can only polarize us into groups.

This polarization ultimately can break our system of productive representation in our country as this in of itself can steward the roots of tyranny and terror.

Respecting each others orientations allows us to be united in how we stand.

The New Deal, an Election 2008 Primer

2.1 E- Not from ill-gotten gain, nor the Misfortune of Other*s*

When opportunity is received by ill-gotten gain, it is typically at the misfortune of others. *Simpler put, where there is money, there are crooks.*

We generally refer to this by the simple term called the *system*. The momentum of this *system* is experienced in our every day lives mostly in an amorphous form.

It can be experienced as just frustration in attempting to accomplish an effort where processes are beyond our control, or deal with to entities that encourage its will on us like drug companies, HMO's, media conglomerates, big banks, and polluting industries. This system can be promoted as basic prejudices, or how our needs are responded to with complacency, negligence or indifference. In some cases, we can even be exploited by others in ruthless, shortsighted self serving ways.

> Sometimes you can hear someone say, "it's the System", or to blame the *System* for some sense of injustice felt done to them.

We see this in our every day life as a permissible behavior. Examples of this are in attempting to communicate our needs to bureaucratic infrastructures with endless call management systems and convoluted policies; or the use the *vale of good accounting principles* from lending entities that can cost us our credit rating; the policies or the attitudes in how sometimes we are treated by employers, and by other corporations and even perceptibly by the Government; to false advertising, and misrepresentation of things that are intended to appeal to us as consumers.

> In our highly complex information saturated capitalist society, this is more common as an ethic in how we conduct business and commerce than not.

> Being mere human beings, we are also encouraged to comply with, and/or to beat the system at the same time. The less stamina that you have to give to the *system*, the more you are encouraged to beat it.

There is no reason for the need to beat the system, *if the system is truly there for you*; as there is no reason for the system, except you.

For the Strategic Future of Our Nation

A lot of this is resolved in looking at who we are as a nation, and some of this in the nature of crime that things can evolve to.

> Most crime is nothing more than a chain reaction of circumstances.

> Petty crime is nothing more than the aftershock of, when taken to task, of more sophisticated techniques in crime and coercion, or at the least , basic unfairness in our standards towards others.

> There is no difference in loan sharking, and predatory lending of a large bank, less that the latter is more legalized in its strategies in basically extorting your money from you.

> Street crime is nothing more than the aftershock of petty crime.

> In business, this is typically known as *screw the other guy first, or get screwed.*

> Civil unrest is nothing more than the reaction of a similar overbearing *will* when one's capacities have become exhausted.

It is my commitment to pursue the further development and compliance of fair commerce practices in a top down manner. Sophisticated business entities like banks, in their compliance, will send a new shock wave of honest and fair commerce practices in terms of the consumers of their services and products.

> The more they value the consumer's good will, the better quality of business will be offered.

It is the additional intent of my administration that small business will get the hint for the same compliance if they choose to survive in our capitalist society. Street crime therefore will have fewer examples to follow.

The New Deal, an Election 2008 Primer

2.2 -Community Safety:

I recognize and respect that *Community Safety* is based on the work of civil servants, police, fire, emergency, and medical services, educational systems and teachers that are made available in our local municipalities within unique states; as well as smaller communities within them.

Communities that are short changed in terms of Homeland Security funding formulas as one example, cannot provide community safety where it meets the needs of the community and *first responders*.

In recognition of this view, I also appreciate the need for federally subsidized programs that demonstrate enough to enhance the viability of the needs at the local level for community safety.

I will endeavor on an ongoing basis to see that there is no hiatus in federal government for the delivery of subsidized funds to states, and that funds, and related programs are not cut; and where signed into law are not shorted; and where states deem the need for more support, that the federal government hears and responds to the stated needs in a timely manner.

The reduction of crime itself, reduces the cost of enforcement for both community and personal safety. It is the expectation of the administration that communities will understand the need for compliance with fair commerce practices. This will enhance the effectiveness of federally subsidized budgets overall.

As much as education is the key to the future for personal development, communities suffer the impact of its absence in its younger generation.

Moreover, communities should be empowered to develop the skills and abilities of its local youth. This can be in after school programs, tutoring where necessary, and other areas of focus that reinforce the sense of self esteem in the youth where attraction to gangs and frustrated groups of kids become less of an issue.

> I also want to see interest from the ACLU, NAACP and AFL-CIO in their involvement in assisting communities in developing such programs, in addition to after school care programs and faith based followings.

For the Strategic Future of Our Nation

When we re-enfranchise our disenfranchised citizens, we build stronger communities.

We are currently missing many needed safety nets in our Communities and in their Social Welfare Policies.

By communities providing support services and safety nets, I am interested in pursuing tax incentives and further subsidized assistance to support this effort.

The New Deal, an Election 2008 Primer

2.3- Nation's Safety

Our nation's safety is viewed in terms of our Homeland Security, our National Security; and the nation's intelligence system.

The **Nation's Safety Program** to be implemented is to provide the Homeland Security budgets that meet the supported expectations of each state, the sharing of information between our first responders and the Homeland Security Department; the furthering of purpose and responsibility of commissions to enhance our position against threats; provide a robust national security platform that is built with strong defense posture and diplomacy with wisdom, and the further refinement of our intelligence systems through a federal information plan.

2.3.A Homeland Security

Homeland Security is viewed as not a witch hunt on our shores for suspicious foreigners, but to be competently developed, and be adequately funded as programs that address our needs It is to have the necessary watchdog committees to remain in place such as the 911 Commission to review and advise ongoing about the effectiveness of the Governments awareness, and competence in terms of these programs; as well as tangential issues that could directly relate or indirectly relate to the quality and usefulness of our Homeland Security in serving the United States.

- Homeland Security Budgets *are not to be slashed*, but to be reinforced with delivery dates that will meet the expectations of the communities of the United States.

- It is further my commitment to steward the proactive participation of commissions in managing, and furthering transparency and accountability and the discovery process for its needs in government, and in the private sector.

- Homeland Security policy will not endorse the incarceration of people without fare representation, and scheduled due process as is described in Amendments IV - XII.

- Moreover, Amendment I of the Bill of Rights will also remain as it is not to be compromised.

For the Strategic Future of Our Nation

2.3 B- National Security

Foreign Policy is not to be an attitude, and defense is not to be weak.

I do not view diplomacy and defense as being exclusive of the other, but are mutually dependent on each other for each one's effectiveness in serving the other. Simply we *walk with two legs*, not one.

The defense system gives d*iplomacy its teeth*, and diplomacy provides *defense its faculty of reason*. It is my view that the two are inseparable when engaging in preemptive and unilateral actions.

Combined, our actions towards others have a more formidable and daunting purpose. This is while enabling a viable conclusion and exit strategy such as for Iraq.

Combined, our foreign policy can also be effective in helping others find their exit strategies such as for nuclear prone nations and the Middle East crisis.

Diplomacy orphaned from defense can only be *'meaningless lip service'*, and defense when orphaned from diplomacy can continue in a *non focused manner*, that is subject to tangential agenda's, or simply *the business of war,* while at the cost of squandering American lives and of the innocent.

If the two halves of a brain cannot work together, then the body cannot function properly. If the two vital components of National Security do not work together, then our National Security does not serve our Nation's Safety.

2.3 C- The Nation's Intelligence System:

This was key in the initial focus of the original 9/11 Commission report. The military must have its real time use of intelligence, as well as Homeland Security.

The further refinement of intelligence of the National Intelligence Systems and its purpose as a bridge between national and Homeland Security will continue to be strengthened as well as the reporting of intelligence events to both the executive staff and to Congress; and the intended oversight commissions.

In this manner, intelligence will have the rapid delivery that is needed to those who need to know with the necessary transparency for those who should also know of its content and use.

The New Deal, an Election 2008 Primer

3- The Welfare of Our Nation

The welfare of our nation is by definition for me, the welfare of the people. For my administration, it is a *Financial Matter*.

The level of economic solvency of the nation is the foundation for the financial welfare of the people. Consequently, there is no way for the people of the nation to assured of their health, safety and welfare unless the nation as a whole is sound financially.

- There is no way to have a safe nation without fiscal soundness.

- You cannot make a fair living, have a vision for your tomorrow, let alone even consider having a job tomorrow without fiscal Soundness in the Nation. There is no way to enact and to back all the federal programs needed with our fiscal soundness. As consequence, our communities, and we suffer; but most importantly, our children do.

- There is no way to further business development in this country if there is not fiscal soundness. There is no way to recover lost jobs without this.

- There is no way for the nation to have independence and autonomy, and standards in its foreign policy if the nation is not sound fiscally.

We must recapture our dwindling economy, and then make fundamental investments in it as a nation and as its people or we will be destined to borrowed time as a great nation.

For the Strategic Future of Our Nation

3.1 Recapturing Our Economy:

It is not a solution to just tax more, although some should be able to pay more. Nor is it a solution to just borrow more foreign money and then hope for the best. It is not a solution to attempt to close tax gaps on those who have outstanding taxes, as in this economy, they simply might not have the ability to pay. It is not a solution to further lose the value of the U.S dollar, or to offshore while telling you in the same breadth to go out and get new education and training in order to replace the job that you lost.

Simply, deficits do matter, and it is the commitment of my administration to achieve fiscal soundness, and in this way to achieve economic solvency. The welfare of our nation is based on our level of economic solvency and the ability to manage trade. Managing trade is viewed by the administration as part of the road to achieving economic solvency, and can further benefit from it, but does not constitute in of itself, the total strategic solution for our economic recovery. This has to be through our economic solvency.

3.1.A- Balanced Trade

Artificial trade tariffs, which are the most we have been able to do is like trying to plug a dike. Tax incentives for not outsourcing is also a long shot when considering that such incentives are overshadowed by manipulating the cost of offshore labor to make up the differences.

The volume of imports is not regulated, and when putting a higher price on foreign goods that are dumped on our shores, just means more compromise of foreign workers rights in order to realize the same profit for the foreign manufacturer.

By limiting import volume into the United States, the price of the import would increase due to level of availability and in order to obtain a reasonable profit margin. This is supply and demand mechanics.

By loosing the offshore incentive, US manufactures would not need a domestic tax incentive. This is while also not needing to lose their workers who are the actual ones who buy manufactured goods.

The same principles of trade volume in manufacturing and textiles, can be applied to agriculture, as well as the outsourcing of technology labor.

It is my commitment to help Congress in forming "**The Trade Committee**". The charter is to set volume levels on imports that are consistent with our export levels of volume.

The New Deal, an Election 2008 Primer

3.1.B An Investment Economy

Tax and Spend or Borrow and Spend does nothing but impoverish our nation, and lead us to compromise in global presence, and as a follower, and not a leader of the free world.

As we devalue our dollar through the use of continued offshore lenders, our tax dollars become of less value, and hence becomes like a chronic drug habit, where the last dose does not provide what is needed to ease the symptoms of the addiction to our need for spending with respect to our levels of debt.

Balanced Trade can help shore up the foundations of our economy in preventing the under tow of debt in having what we stand on from being washed out from under us.

But we must work strategically in order to stabilize our levels of debt, where our tax dollars can create a level of consistent value. A simple lesson from the dollar market speaks to protecting the dollars value by simply purchasing the currencies that will benefit from its slide. It should not be beyond reason for the U.S Government to understand this.

The Currency Link Note (CLN) can address how to stabilize Fix Income investments like foreign debt with a currency hedge. AKA, the Bond Stabilizer, prevents a divergence of the investment from within a risk spectrum. In the CLN, the bond is based on USD, where it has a periodic coupon. Hedged with another currency like the Yen, the blips in the chart are used to offset the difference in the coupon thereby insulating it from the depreciating dollar. This provides a fixed rate of return in the coupon with respect to global markets when the dollar falls. If the dollar rises, then you regard the fixed rate as a base for a variable rate and the Yen as the cushion for when it falls again.

When regulated and structured, investment management can serve our objectives for a path to economic solvency and therefore, serve the people well.

> *If it is better to invest the dollar than to spend it, it is better for the Government to invest its dollars for the People.*

It is the commitment of my Administration to make the US Treasury Department, dollar savvy. One component in the solution is by implementing a structured investment management department in the U.S. Treasury for the purposes of paying down our interest and eventually the outstanding debt from foreign lenders.

For the Strategic Future of Our Nation

3.1.C Efficiency and Effectiveness of Tax Collection is in question when considering the huge tax gaps, questionable schedules, cuts, and the overhead of the Internal Revenue Service in of itself in dealing with their responsibilities. The administration is committed to pursue fare and effective tax collection that is cost effective in aiding our economy.

What incentive does the IRS employee have for the efficiency and effectiveness in doing their job when the processes in place are not efficient or effective ?

What return on cost does the IRS provide in having broken processes to manage with ?

How do you fix broken processes when the tax system achieves nothing further than painting itself into a corner in compounded complexities ?

It is the commitment of my administration to help the Treasury Department and IRS to stream line costs based on the following:

3.1.C.1- Tax Cuts and Questionable Schedules

Tax schedules and cuts can be graduated for 'All' based on the level of solvency vs. debt burden that the Nation has. It is then no longer necessary to say 'read my lips' as just lip service. This policy in its flexibility is to allow for financial planning top down from the Government to the people it serves.

3.1.C.2- Process that lead to no where

Without *fair and remedied schedule of conclusion* tax collection processes do nothing but (a)- cost the IRS's budget, and (b) - compounds the challenge of the tax payer in dealing with their escalating tax burden.

This can even motivate predatory lending practices to exploit the opportunity of the tax payer. This in turn just further burdens the tax payer in paying future taxes. The IRS must serve the people in order to serve the Government cost effectively.

For both the IRS, and the tax payer, it would be best to get the tax paid at close to the original amount than having to deal with irresolvable and unrealistic interests, charges, fees and related costs in the wishful thinking of collecting inflated debt.

The New Deal, an Election 2008 Primer

3.1.C.3- IRS Agents can do their work when information is made available to them. Much of the time, information can already be on file, but not accessible to the agent. The agent under such circumstances will put the onus on the tax payer for reproducing this, as well as other laundry list items of information within a period of time that serves the convenience of the agents work load.

By providing the right information access tools, the agent's work becomes more efficient for the same case load. The tax payer has more bandwidth to meet the agent's time frame for the balance of a requested laundry list. Case tracking can be established for historical audits on case performance closure, as well as case inheritance. Case exceptions and escalation / resolution can be achieved more readily. Cost / benefit analysis can be measured on *Fair Remedy Conclusion*. Effectiveness of the agent for closures can be immediately scored.

The tax payer can get on with their life sooner at less impact on livelihood

3.1.D Government Budgets and Spending: Government entities cannot have budgets where there is latitude in spending focus. The term miscellaneous does not serve the people well when it comes to the use of their money.

It is my commitment to work with budget committees in Congress for their active participation in government departmental audit reviews. This is where such reviews are intended to determine compliance with budget allocation directives from budget committees, and departmental compliance with said directives. Additionally, all vendors will be identified in terms of compliance with the proposed lobbyist disclosure act.

- Committees will have the competence to make reasonable and accurate assessments of said estimates.

- Variances in budgets will be stated by fixed policies.

- Accuracy in spending will be automated such that committee members can review compliance with allocations on an ad hoc basis.

- Department errors are to be reported upfront, or as when discovered, and not after the fact.

- Misappropriations, and misalignment of budgets, or expenditures not accounted for, or signed off by a committee, will have those responsible in managing the budget in reprimand.

For the Strategic Future of Our Nation

3.2 Investments in Our Economy:

An involved government is not to be a 'big government', but one that is to serve the people efficiently and cost effectively.

The notion of 'pork programs' and 'big government' is typically used to convey a government that wastes money, as in 'tax and spend' or 'borrow and spend'.

Those that use the sound bite 'big government' intend to suggest a government that nursemaids some of the people and prevents them from being able to stand on their own two feet at the expense of 'real and honest hard working tax payers'.

Corporate write-offs and tax avoidance are what really costs the tax payer which is not included in the message of the sound bite.

"We the People" are the first three words of the Constitution. Any Government that advocates otherwise is viewed by me as nothing more than a pork government of self serving misrepresentation.

> This lack of leadership example instills the same in our corporations, which then instills the people to be nothing but self-serving for the 'here and now'.

The government that provides economic recovery and solvency is empowered to responsibly provide the environment for All to be able to stand on their own two feet.

Government that advocates otherwise, is one that advocates for you to try to stand on quick sand in a no man's land.

The following outlines investment plans in federal government to enable its cost effective efficiency in operation, investments in our communities where the people of this nation live, and investments in the welfare of the people so that they can be empowered to stand on their own two feet.

The New Deal, an Election 2008 Primer

3.2.1 - Federal Information and Computing Systems

A government that can serve the people responsibly is a cost effective government. A cost effective government is one that manages its information properly.

One of the most important parts of our government is in the management of information. This is not intended to suggest abuse, loss of a citizen's privacy, or that we all have some hidden DNA profile with the government, but that the information systems themselves are fundamentally obsolete and not effective. Without a top down federal information systems plan, there is no way to fix a broken and dysfunctional information system, where the government as a result operates at a much higher cost to the tax payer than is needed.

For example, consider reducing 65% of the cost of administrative over head. In other words, to operate the government costing only 35% of what it use to be just by the improvement of its information management. Further, until an effective information system plan is in place, government employees are limited in the ability to do their jobs which for its stated purpose is to serve the people. We can look at slashing needed programs such as education, health research etc, or we can improve the government's fundamental operation over all.

The sharing of intelligence information, the protection, and privacy of information, the lack of information, and the confusion of what information, its quality and accuracy, rights of use, potential misuse, its purpose in serving efficiency, and effectiveness in managing the Government and protecting the people all have to be based on a top down Federal Information Plan.

It is my commitment to help steward Congress to address the issues at hand, the functional requirements of Government departments, and the criterion of classification, and sharability.

> The outcome of this is to be an Information Bill that is to serve as the guideline for the Federal Information Plan.

3.2.2 The Federal Information Plan must regard needs, rights, security, cost, and effectiveness, and the strategic map for this, and how to properly manage information in government for all levels, over all.

For the Strategic Future of Our Nation

3.3- Community Welfare

The role of the economy for our communities relies on interstate and intrastate commerce. The cost and impact of energy usage and environmental impact must be resolved.

I view that through innovation, energy sources can be of less impact to the environment and can help instill our future economy cost effectively.

Fundamentally, the use of electricity as an energy source must be less than the costs of fossil fuels. The creation of electricity sources in of themselves cannot pollute or to they are have less pollution than fossil fuels. Fossil fuel alternatives for combustion must become more sophisticated to achieve cost effective use.

3.3.A- Emphasis on Transportation and Infrastructure is viewed as paramount in re-instilling the foundation of our economy. Reducing the costs of transportation reduces other costs that transportation is relied upon for.

By improving our delivery systems, the costs of goods and services to reach their markets can be reduced by a magnitude. This means that costs can be reduced to 1/10th.

For railroads, *electric and electromagnetic powered rapid transit* can be achieved to deliver steel from its sources in Ohio and Pennsylvania to our defense manufacturers and construction; and locations points West and East, as well as for export from the coasts.

With the reduction of transportation costs, the cost of steel itself comes down making a more competitive steel industry. Many industries can take advantage of the same benefits in rapid transit.

For roads, the cost and impact of fuel usage and related pollution should be reduced. Less idling of combustion engines obtains more miles to the gallon of even cleaner fuels that would normally be wasted in traffic jams.

Our commuters have a better chance at longevity which lowers the future costs of health care. Fewer accidents occur on the road for over tired and delayed truck drivers. Fresher produce is available due to on time delivery. Over all, the costs of products due to reduced delivery costs enables us to live within reasonable budgets as producers and consumers. This is while providing more impetus for employment of US citizens on US soil; and in being able to reinvigorate industries that we once were losing.

3.3.B- Emphasis on Energy Management will be highly regulated and viewable by the public eye. There are numerous avenues where energy usage can be cost effective, clean, and provide for the strategic future of our nation.

In providing incentives to public utilities companies for the use of cost effective alternative energy sources enables new avenues for entrepreneurs, companies and employment to provide the solutions also to utility companies.

Communities will not be manipulated by Enrons. Simply put, a deal is a deal, and once costs are consummated, providers are to committed to agreed price caps and consumers are to be entitled to reliable energy delivery.

Electricity is regarded as a commodity, and the blackout of Calif. was due to treating it only as a commodity. It must be a regulated commodity where it is made available as needed, and not through its market extortion.

3.3.B.1 Public Utility Assistance: will be emphasized for its importance in providing cleaner, and lower costs fuels and energies.

Although nuclear power appears attractive, my administration will be looking for public utilities to be forward thinking in the use of wind and solar power.

- Where tornado zones exists, it's simply a question of transferring electricity via the 'Grid'.

3.3.B.2 Agricultural Assistance will be furthered for the production of bio energy sources that can be sold as fossil fuel supplements and alternatives; and for providing additional cost effective solutions for public utilities for use in supplying electricity. Environmental management is compromised by the amount of carbon we emit into the air. We can work in building our economy by the further use of crops used to generate heat, electricity or produce liquid fuels.

3.3.B.3 New Energy Research Assistance will be in the form of federal grants and loans for any existing or burgeoning industry. They must demonstrate new avenues of cost effective energy development, delivery, and use. *Supporting industries will also have the opportunity to qualify for such federal assistance.* In addition to agriculture, there are supporting industries that serve it such as producing biodegradable fertilizers and soil enhancers for producing crops. If it can improve our health, and our environment, and can be provided cost effectively, it must be considered.

For the Strategic Future of Our Nation

3.3.C Environmental Cleanup programs are to be emphasized by my administration, as we must clean up our past abuse on the environment in order to live here longer. Environmental impact is compromised by the amount of carbon we emit into the air. The water and ground we have polluted lacks replenishment of the resources that we have taken from our land. I commit to *Proactive Pollution Prevention and Environmental clean up and recovery programs.*

Pollution laws are to be reviewed for their scope and effectiveness, and related remedies. Existing accountability will be reviewed in terms of violations to the laws, and due diligence to be enacted on accordingly. Pollution laws will be revised for effectiveness, and empowered where not empowered.

Program Definition and Scope - The existing pollution laws will be a single component , where remedies in terms of cost of clean up will be financed based on fines and assets of those considered contributors to the pollution problem at hand. In a similar manner, where the land has been compromised, such as forestry and land erosion, remedies for replenishment will be sought by the contributors.

One might own a mountain, or a valley of land, and have sold off the timber in order to build, or the land for others to build developments. In such cases, zoning ordinances will be reviewed for the necessity of the development in its relationship to the impact on the environment. Ordinances that appear to be lopsided at the cost of the environment will be revised by federal statue.

Program deployment will be monitored by the Congress, and the EPA, and other related federal agencies. It is expected by the administration that this deployment due to its scope of effort will be in stages, and in areas of focus with stated milestones of accomplishment. It is expected that deployment in one thread of the program can be in parallel with other threads that are in the definition and scope phase.

Program measurements are viewed by the administration as key to keeping the promise for clean up and recovery, and will be made public via the Federal Information System as deemed in review by Congress.

The New Deal, an Election 2008 Primer

3.3.D Food and Agriculture Quality improvement

Our government needs to *invest in the quality of our foods and agriculture.*
Today raw chicken, or a raw egg can give you Salmonella poisoning, raw beef
can give you E Coli poisoning, and you might want to question where the fish
you eat comes from. Then we have hormones for some other strange reason in
our foods and our vegetables need wax in order to look like vegetables. If we
can live with frozen foods, we also know that the vitamins are generally gone
in them. *We are what we Eat* !

Although there is no linkage documented between cancers, and diseases and
the foods we eat, it is imaginable that if our foods were of better quality, we
could be composed of better quality building blocks too. Quality foods should
be able to improve our health which should cut some of our needed health
costs as we are the food we eat.

The automation of food preparation, from start to finish, over the past few
decades have traded off quality for profits. Our FDA, and other agencies have
standards where these foods supposedly are in compliance.

The argument can be made that better quality foods offer long term profits,
and less quality foods short change the food company's share holders.

When we trade off quality in our industries for higher near term profits,
we have ultimately devalued the industry itself to be invested in.

American corporations must have their ethics continually held accountable to
serve their respective industries, to expect quality in employee loyalty, and to
provide an accurate representation of shareholder value, and not 'perceived
shareholder value'.

Simpler put, poor quality food demonstrates contempt for its consumers
who are the actual investors in the industry.

My administration commits to pursue stewardship of Congress to work with
the FDA and other agencies that manage the quality of standards and laws that
are involved in our food chain to raise the standards.

I view that this is an investment in our health as well as in our economy.

For the Strategic Future of Our Nation

3.4 The Welfare of Our People:

Safety Nets have pragmatic reasons besides humanitarian ones. I dismiss the notion of the bleeding heart liberal as well as compassionate conservatism when advocating the need to care about all the people of this nation.

Pragmatically, the disenfranchised are not active participants in our nation. They are not able to contribute as tax payers or voters. They cannot be of benefit to themselves or others. For this reason, they must be re enfranchised.

Safety Nets have to serve pragmatically as part of the road to becoming re enfranchised. They must also prevent people form becoming disenfranchised or the Nets simply have holes in them that are too large to be of productive use.

We also have to face the fact that some cannot stand on their own two feet, as they can be to severely wounded as veterans, or handicapped in ways that prevent them from doing so. But they too have a voice when it comes to deserving the quality of life that is entitled to by all US citizens.

3.4.1 Assistance Programs: Through the path for economic solvency, the House and the Senate should be able to reach across, or even share the isle in terms of the programs that they and the executive branch advocates.

> Employment, veteran, Social Security, welfare benefits, health and human services, and education are just a few of the many programs that must be reinforced for the effectiveness in serving the people.

I further commit to not sign on any program without the money accounted for it.

> This money will be sought from both our Path for Economic Solvency, and from *Fine Sources from Corporate Reform* initiatives and from case action suits that are sponsored by the government on behalf of the people from.

The Disenfranchised covers many categories of situations and walks in life , that include the impoverished, unemployed, veterans, the homeless, the aged, and others that find themselves without a way of life that is conducive to the basic needs of their health safety, and welfare, as well as conducive for others.

The New Deal, an Election 2008 Primer

People affected can be from, and live, anywhere in our nation from our most rural areas to our urban centers. These people are also potential tax payers when given the opportunity to be re-enfranchised.

It is my commitment to review the effectiveness of these programs in terms of the intended merit and design and methods of accomplishment for the purposes of affective funding.

Duplication of effort in different programs will be resolved and normalized for cost effectiveness. New agenda's for existing and new programs will be reviewed

3.4.1.1 - Addressing Unemployment

To be unemployed is to be disenfranchised in our capitalistic system. We can blame corporations for wanting to save costs by off shoring or locally to nickel and dimming employment offerings with preferences for visitors with green cards, migrant farm or factory workers; but moreover must achieve balance in our industries and government for the employment of qualified US citizens.

> We could argue that unemployment benefits cost the tax payer, but a better argument is that employed people are tax payers.

As a responsible government we must address unemployment at a minimum in the following proactive manner.

Unemployment benefits, must be extended - with the proviso that <u>when offered a job</u> it is compulsory <u>to accept that job</u>, being in that it is a sound employment, and meets the same , at a minimum of the unemployment payments made to the unemployed. It is the responsibility of the unemployed to improve themselves from this starting point, or to forgo unemployment assistance from that point on. When given a starting point, it is self esteem that is to carry us forward.

This does not intend for employers to provide employment opportunities at below market rate, but does intend that employers will make an offer at market rate for an employment position that could even be currently filled by a foreigner with an active visa or green card that is currently filling the same position on US soil.

Proactive marketing of the unemployed is to be enacted. Through the Federal Information System, employment / vacancy opportunities are to be reported for federal, state, city and private sectors.

For the Strategic Future of Our Nation

Vocational training assistance and programs must be made available such that people can have a starting point for a career or new one, as opposed to just a job if desired, or needed.

Rights to work for a fair wage must take precedence of green card and visa based workers. Employment opportunities are defined as both vacancies, as well as employment positions, whether temporary, by contract or permanent that are currently occupied by foreigners on U.S soil.

U.S citizens must come first if we are to expect U.S. citizens to stand on their own two feet and make a contribution in our economy.

It is not the interest of my administration to disenfranchise a foreigner in the United States, but it is the intention to empower the U.S citizen.

Foreigners with legitimate visas and green cards are welcomed to work on U.S soil where it can be proved that there is not an equally qualified U.S citizen available for it within the geographic region of the job.

Foreign corporations, institutions and enterprises that operate on U.S. soil are not to be exempt from this rule.

Foreigners who wish to immigrate need to get a fair deal in being able to immigrate, if in fact they plan on becoming U.S citizens

3.4.1.2 Social Security: By commitment we are to achieve *Social Security Solvency* as a parallel in rate to the nation's rate of economic solvency.

We are not going to offload debt on the future taxpayers of our nation, nor use the Social Security system as a catch all piggy bank to be borrowed from time to time.

We will not privatize Social Security such that we toss people into their own little rowboats in rough seas as the expedient answer to previous Social Security fund abuse.

Social Security was conceived as a guaranteed annuity, and will remain that way. The Social Security system will be replenished based on the progress of and further reinforced by the investment economy.

3.4.1.3 Education Assistance is a vital need in serving the needs of the people, as they are the body of this nation. Education ranges from the very young to the aged. Funding priorities are in the order of state assistance programs, grants and loans. Focus is to be in the following top down priorities for US citizens:

- No Child Left Behind

- Higher Education, and Vocational Grant Assistance Programs

- Ongoing Education Programs

- Optional Education Programs

3.4.1.4 Veterans Services: VA services will be further augmented in scope for medical benefits, financial assistance, veteran family assistance, vocational training, and to provide a support net into state/community level support programs.

Veteran's hospitals are to be further funded to adequately provide assistance in case load. Veteran's hospitals will not be short on supplies nor required staff to serve our veterans.

Vets will not have to wait until sometime in the future for assistance but will get the assistance programs that they need.

There will be **NO deductibles** for Vets of any category. Medical, psychological, and sociological assistance are to be readily available.

A vet wounded is a vet who is wounded. There is no discrimination to be permitted in terms of combat, or non combat related injuries to the self when in active military service.

Grants and loans will be made available for Vets who seek financial assistance and demonstrate use in the vocational training and community support net level programs. Such loans will be below normal bank interest rates for equivalent loans.

Veteran Family Assistance is to be provided in scope, but not be limited to grants for family assistance. Further, the head of household is to assume veteran benefits when loosing an immediate family member in active military service.

For the Strategic Future of Our Nation

3.4.1.5 - Competitive Health Care: programs are to serve the people or the program(s) in question are viewed as non-competitive and should be realigned.

The scope of health care is typically limited, and sometimes filled in by insurance programs that do not serve their stated purpose of service, or have several penalties in providing stated coverage; or coverage is variable based on market price and demand.

- What is required is a means to afford fixed health care infrastructure costs, make services available when needed by any U.S citizen, and cover most health treatments and remedies adequately up to 100%.

  In Business, the imposition of government regulations generally is responded to by innovation in the private sector.

* The Federal Care program is required to afford fixed health care infrastructure costs, make services available when needed by any U.S citizen, and cover health treatments and remedies adequately up to 100%. This is to include but not be limited to chronic care, emergencies, restorative health, post operative recovery treatments, and generic prescription programs.

* 'For the Good' community based offerings are to address the economically disadvantaged where health issues can be circumvented before becoming of significance. Practitioners may take tax benefits based on quota and level of service.

* The Private Sector is welcomed to operate honestly by offering competitive alternatives for such things as elective surgery and post operative care.

This is my commitment to our Nation

Orion Karl Daley
State of the Union Address for 2008

Appendix II

In lieu of debates

some

Commentaries

about

Other Candidates

For the Strategic Future of Our Nation

Summary

I formulated *The Balanced Party* ' http://unity2008.org ' in 2004 and intend to achieve compelling representation by 2008. I figured if Abraham Lincoln could represent the foundation of the original Republican Party, then this is not unusual for good leadership.

Debates are essential in any campaign. Third party and independent candidates will not have this opportunity to debate what can be called the more well known fan fare candidates.

This section provides commentaries. This is mostly about the platforms, comments and outlooks of the election 2008 fan fare candidates. On line, as commentaries are completed, they will be added.

> As humans, we are fallible. For me this goes for all of us across the board. My interest in commentary about the other candidates is not about whom they slept with, their marital problems, or abandonment of their families; or why they are an icon or not. This is something that they have to deal with in their own lives.

When it comes to the leadership of this nation, my questions, in leveling the playing field are in terms of what does 'being qualified and fit for Presidential office' really mean ?

Based on this book and its content, inquires about my qualifications are welcomed.

The commentaries are therefore intended to be pragmatic and provoke thought. They are based on questions or issues I have about these candidates. This goes for all who wish to seek the office of the President of the United States where at the time of this books edition, is mostly about some of the Republicans. The Democrats on the other hand seem to be just as slippery as wet soap, and there is actually very little to say about them.

The Democrats as a group, I see as a packaging strategy that is very much akin to consumerism only. They actually have nothing really to say much about anything. As examples, they 'suggest messages' through sound bites, but have nothing more than this.

When I hear Barack Obama speak, it adds up to nothing more than saying the words 'clarity, wisdom, and hope', and that health care is unfair, and it is up to you, the voter to turn the page'. I gather that this is to imply that Barack has clarity in something since he knows the word. He can speak of wisdom as this requires even less explanation, and that *hope* is a commodity that we all seek and can be prayed upon for. Does Barack Obama represent leadership since he uses these words. Can we put him into office because we can *turn the page* every 4 years in the name of hope ?

When it comes to Hillary Clinton, the only message I have really heard is the 'we have to take back the White House'. I know that she liked living there, but to confuse the issue in using the term 'we' is misleading as the rest of us are not invited even to visit her there. It is also easy for her or any other candidate to say 'when I am president I will end the war in Iraq'. Hopefully any president in their right mind would do this, but again you have to be in your right mind. What is even more important is how to conclude the war in Iraq which none of the Democrat candidates, like on Immigration, care to really speak about.

It might be acceptable just to ask all to have trust in how we make our decisions, but for me personally it is also a moral issue in how this is done.

We cannot just claim that the previous president was wrong in going to Iraq, and then just exit in leaving it in a state of turmoil and decay. As a child I learned to clean up the mess I made in my bedroom, and my wife Carolyn and I have taught our children the same. In Iraq, it is human life that we have put at risk including our own military. without a peace with dignity, all we have done is to serve bin Laden's agendas in weakening our military while turning the world against us. As discussed earlier in chapter 6 on Foreign Policy, we can have a 'Peace with Dignity' , correct many of the ills that we have become part of in the Middle East, and also further American Interest through our good will. There are other ways to steward our 'manifest destiny' than through dominance and being perceived as some form of self righteous imperialist by the rest of the world.

The fact that the Democrats can't even fathom this in their 'phased withdrawal' when the 'time is someday supposed to be right' is alarming. It is as dangerous and as irresponsible as the Republicans in wanting to stay indefinitely in Iraq with sights on Iran.

I am going to skip John Edwards, as regardless of his claim for a universal health care plan, I believe that it must still be on the drawing board. He is a likable fellow but that's really about as much as I see, where a smile should not be the only basis of an election.

For the Strategic Future of Our Nation

About the Republicans, because each is trying to conjure up their own image of what was Reagan as their great mentor, each of the candidates have actually put out some really dumb statements. This is especially about their common sense and not about Reagan.

For Mitt Romney, he appears to be relying on the Bush legacy, while adding the new twist that he is the ultimate conservative. I find that he actually speaks in an uninformed way or is knowingly lying through his teeth. For example, he speaks about a great economy. He does not therefore need to tend to issues here ? Additionally, I find him like the other Republicans in being divisive about other issues such as abortion and same sex marriage which the Democrats prefer to play middle of a red and blue road.

Presidential candidates cannot serve a leadership role as dividers, or as wall paper. As dividers, what distinguishes them from dictators that promote segregation. As wall paper, what prevents this too ? In other words, platforms like *you are either with us* or *against us* are just as unproductive as being united in how we stand on common ground that is like quick sand. As Americans, no matter what our origins, the languages that we were raised to speak and think in, ethnicities, race, creeds and religion should be considered something.

New Gingrich is a great divider in his own little way. He casts himself as some prodigy of Reagan, claims that the 'system is broken' but does not really say how to fix it. Instead he distracts with divisive issues to imply the cause. This is addressed at length in the commentaries. His offering in division is to proclaim that government should have more religion although on our dollars it says 'in God we Trust'; that the government's official language should be English, which it already is; and his answer to health care is in promoting more business choices for your dollars just like cell phone contracts, as opposed to stating what a health care plan should do for you. In foreign policy like Barach Obama the Democrat, he wants to bomb Iran for some reason.

For Rudolf Guillani, although touted as the 9/11 hero of New York City, in living in ground zero neighborhood, I have posed a few questions at a minimum that he should answer. The basis of the questions leads me to believe that although he has a great 'leave it to beaver' smile, he is also one I would only trust to mislead and misrepresent his purpose in leadership.

In terms of the Libertarians, as in being able to have a dialog with them, and in being accused of many 'isms' by one of them, I wrote a detailed response commentary.

The New Deal, an Election 2008 Primer

I begin this section of commentaries with an open letter to one of many from HumanEvents.com. As I find them the most vicious in campaign promotion, wanted to make it clear that they act like political message mules for no other than the Newt Gingrich agenda.

Newt's true agenda I figure is to build the Republican image, where he can either eventually run or obtain an appointment by serving the Republican campaign agenda.

For the Strategic Future of Our Nation

An Open Letter to Tom Winter HumanEventsOnline.com

Apr 25, 2007
Subject: I don't think the sky is falling, and I'm not chicken little !

Dear Tom Winter:

Please know that this is an open letter. I'm writing because in the past two days you sent an email from HumanEvents@HumanEventsOnline.com about 'immigrants threatening our national security', and then today that the world is no longer what it used to be due to 'Muslims'. I don't think the sky is falling, and I'm not chicken little !

Tom, can you really say that in trying to ratchet up the paranoia factor is serving our country ? I am a street wise New Yorker, and had guns to my head, and was close enough to ground zero on 9/11 to get the dust. Your email is like a dud !

I'm sure you are educated enough to know that FDR said "the only thing we need to Fear is Fear itself". There are a lot of Americans that know this too, so you don't want to play them as fools too. I am sure you don't want to be seen as a pyromaniac that wants to keep yelling fire do you ?

Being a mule in carrying the 'Fear Factor message' for someone else's agenda also does not say much about you, and this is why I offer you the opportunity to actually be someone that others can admire. Learn all about how to put out these self serving fires that have done our country wrong at http://unity2008.org !

I see a strategic future for our nation. Any time someone tries to light a match of fear, at http://unity2008.org there are tidal waves of solutions to put it out. Tom we got to instead work on solutions for the strategic future of our nation. So if you are really a patriot, I ask you to join me in this effort. Be a real American patriot. You know, deep down inside I know that you probably are. It's a matter of just believing in yourself, and I think that's what FDR meant !

The New Deal, an Election 2008 Primer
Richard C. Randall's letter to Orion Karl Daley

Apr 20, 2007

Mr. Daley,

While there are certainly some areas where you share common ground with Libertarians, these are at rather high "sound bite" levels. However, your "Balanced Party" solutions share little, if any, common ground with Libertarian solutions.

Upon examining your positions, you appear to be philosophically better aligned with the Democrats - or perhaps the American Socialist Party. As you are, philosophically, a socialist. Many Libertarians consider FDR, who you praise in discussing Health Care and Education, to have been the Father of American Socialism.

You propose expanding the role of government in education "significantly by way of tax exempt Education Bonds". Libertarians would argue that education is not a legitimate role of government - but rather a responsibility of parents..

You do not appear to take a position on Social Security, but rather describe the current situation. Libertarians would argue that individual retirement planning is not a proper function of government in a free society.

You consider paying personal income taxes a "patriotic duty"! And you embrace a progressive tax (promoted by the "Communist Manifesto" . Personal income tax didn't exist in this country until the federal government began to expand through adopting various social (socialist) programs. As these socialist programs have expanded, so has the need to pay for the bureaucracy necessary to support them. Recognize the difference between a progressive income tax (which is essentially modern slavery) vs. excise taxes and user fees (which currently provide more than enough revenue for our federal government to operate within the confines of the U.S. Constitution and maintain our current excessive level of defense spending).

Your solutions to corporatism (which you address as Corporate Reform), fail to address the root cause of corporatism (the influence of corporations over our government officials in America. Ironically, many of your solutions, such as your proposed "3 Step Workable Peoples Health Care Plan", is purely socialist. And would actually further embrace corporatism within America. Leaving me wondering whether you fully understand corporatism and what is necessary for Corporate Reform.

For the Strategic Future of Our Nation

I encourage you to learn about Libertarian philosophy - as it is grounded in the philosophy of this nation's founders. Consider the PROPER role of government, and why the Founding Fathers placed so much emphasis on restricting it within the confines of the U.S. Constitution. Consider what defines human rights. And indeed, what a "right" is - vs. a privilege. Libertarians base every position upon these concepts.

Richard C. Randall
Legislative Director
Libertarian Party of Colorado
LegislativeDirector@lpcolorado.org

From Orion Karl Daley in response to Richard C. Randall's letter

Apr 20, 2007

Dear Mr. Randall:

I appreciate you taking the time for making your comments. I don't recall sound bites, but substance and would be pleased to discuss, as other. In fact, I have contempt for misrepresentation, and if something sounds like a sound-bite that is not backed up in my platform, I welcome you to point it out.

I more than agree that our Government is dysfunctional, and as noted at http://unity2008.org , figure that we could cut about 65% of its over head while providing even better services for the people. Ok, you can label this as you see fit, but I do know how to cut this overhead to extend external services to our people. Further, I see no other purpose in government. It is to manage, not control. For me this is John Locke before anything else.

FDR could be for some, a socialist, and frankly I do my best to avoid labels. He gave a damned after Hoover had really screwed us, and that impressed me. I call that doing the job of serving the people. In absence of such leadership I ask your opinion on how we could have recovered a life of food lines ? I also ask you about today's over inflated stock market and your opinion of it considering the amount of debt we have to the USD.

About Corporate Reform, there is actually much more than on the New Deal Page , and thought I had put a link to it. I have spent about 30 years in corporations, so am familiar with them to some degree. I am a believer in capitalism', but not at its worst in exploiting what it is to profit from. I see that 'binding arbitration agreements' should be outlawed. You are not allowed to give up other constitutional rights or obligations; and as far as the Democrats investigation on predatory lending practices, they forgot to order these creditors to give the money back !

The New Deal, an Election 2008 Primer

About Education, I can only applaud parents who do care to help educate their children. I know we have invested much time in our 3 children where the youngest is now joining the other two in college this Fall. I hope you got to read the paper on Education itself.

As taxes are hard to pay by some, regardless of any one's philosophy, it is a rather patriotic duty as it does require sacrifice. I am not saying that we should like it, and believe that it is handled unfairly. I am also quite familiar as to why taxes in this country came about, and envision an evolution of an investment based economy over a period of years. I can't see any other way out of the debt we have incurred over the past 6 years. Perhaps you have a suggestion ? For Social Security, for me it is something the Government does owe each of us, and I also propose a $10 savings bond to be donated for every child born. And are you suggesting that Libertarians that qualify for benefits now are actually returning these back to the Government ? I like the idea when people reach a certain age that they do not become disenfranchised thanks to circumstances that are beyond their ability to manage. I figure this can be labeled by many 'isms' , but in any case, if sincere, they have merit in my book.

About health care, by default all deserve this, as each is part of the health of this nation. If we are just out for ourselves, then there is no point in seeing the wisdom of John Locke who designed our 3 branches of government.

Assuming that you are a very busy person, I am pleased that you took the time to look at what was sent, and wrote back. For the "ism's and ists", I am my own man, who does stand on his own foundation. I fully believe that we need very real solutions for the state of our nation, and not sound bites. This is why I have worked on this since 2004.

We live up the block from Ground Zero, and as people of this nation, my concern is the health , safety and welfare of my family. This cannot be assured if for the rest of our nation it is not. I wish to think of myself as a statesman , and not a politician. In fact, would like to get back to working on my book on Field Theory when we do have a strategic future. I would not give credibility to the Democrats, nor the Republicans as they only provide sound bites, and in December 2004 decided to do something about it. Hence, this Campaign.

My biggest personal problem are typos in the many documents authored. This I am working on improving . Please write if you wish to explore dialogue further,

Grateful for your reply,

Orion Karl Daley

For the Strategic Future of Our Nation

Mitt Romney is no Conservative

It is always good to listen with an open ear when hearing an Election 2008 candidate speak. I listened to Mitt Romney at CPAC via C-Span. I continued to listen with a third ear. In other words, what is he saying besides in getting to exercise his presentation skills of *Shock and Awe*?

He left me with many outstanding questions, and in particular, ' What is True Conservatism'?

Mitt spoke about having a *Strong Defense, Strong Economy*, and about some of his personal beliefs on gay marriages and pro life. It appeared that for him, this was the position of the true conservative !

In fairness, I continued to listen as wanting to understand what he meant by a *strong defense, and strong economy* firstly. I waited to hear something more about this, but did not hear any thing – So were these just 'touch points' of some sort where he would provide some detail sometime later?

About 'A Strong Defense': So what did Mitt mean by this, as you don't have to be a galvanized conservative to want this; and matter of fact could the better question be ' who would not want it?'

Duncan L. Hunter on the floor of Congress, another Election 2008 Candidate' said that we already have a Strong Defense' – Duncan is also a conservative too !

So what exactly did Mitt mean ? Others though have noticed that our military is over stretched, where some of our brave military are even returning to Iraq for a 4th time. And meantime the equipment is reported to be worn out. So is Mitt willing to actually speak his soul about this ?

Perhaps Mitt also should speak about what he plans on doing with this Strong Defense'. And further, what is a strong defense, compared to a strong offense; or are they considered as one and the same ?

If he was president today, where would his priorities be, and when elected president in 2008. In other words, does he view the War on Terror as a non-ending fight of the '*right*' against the '*wrong*'; or does he have finite military objectives; and in which countries would he commit our troops . Is he actually intending a strong military presence in different perpetual theaters across the globe ?

The New Deal, an Election 2008 Primer

And about financing this *strong defense*, is Mitt willing to figure out how to repair a military that could be fatigued; or if we do in fact have a strong one already instead miraculously after 5 years of war, then does Mitt have some idea on how to continue to finance it ?

And then, what about our veterans, as this was never mentioned by Mitt, or maybe it was, but I simply don't remember this as one of his touch points !

Ah ha ! - Perhaps a strong defense is through having a Strong Economy, which is another touch point that he mentioned ?

About 'A Strong Economy' – Does this mean putting people back to work again? I listened, but did not hear about this; in other words, what about you and me ? What I heard was a 'strong economy'.

If Mitt agrees with Bush that we do have a Strong Economy, then does he agree with Cheny, that deficits do not matter ? So what does this actually mean in terms of our future tax commitments to pay for all this.

Recall, Bush got the green light hands over from congress on 9/12/2001 to deficit spend for defense in order to go after bin Laden. Lockheed also made out well that October in getting a great defense contract over Boeing. But again, this is based on monies that we don't have, and need to borrow, and have significantly since.

The bottom line is that we are really loaned out, but where if you invest in defense stocks, you might make out alright. Any economy is based on a debt/equity cycle where this has not been observed since year 2000. Normally it is an annual thing. So really what is the stock worth if the US dollar keeps loosing value? One solution is that before the bubble pops, just sell out and buy Yen !

And then again what about the rest of us which have to pay for this debt ? We already work from 2 to 3 days out of every 5 in order to afford our government's spending, and we need jobs in order to do this in the first place. I listened, but there was no mention of this.

Gay Marriage and Abortion: The main question I have here is why any president would concern them selves with such divisive issues when considering the separation of Church and State. Is such a candidate questioning the First Amendment in the Constitution?

When it comes to our personal beliefs, as Jefferson had demonstrated, it is between us and our God. Further, what ever our belief in God is, is likewise our own. This is Amendment I of the Bill of Rights.

For the Strategic Future of Our Nation

There are many countries where religion and government go hand and hand. Iran is one of them. More than likely they would have disdain over gay couples, and women who have had abortions. Further consider one of our most hated enemies, Osama bin Laden, and what he has done in the name, and beliefs of his religious followings.

So then what really differentiates the United States Government in terms of moral fibers. Should we just say that we do not approve, or is it against the law to be gay, or are we willing to face the fact that before legal abortions, that there were coat hanger abortions that were also lethal to the mother.

These are truly difficult questions to embrace as there are rights to the wrongs, and wrongs to the rights. But of course they can be answered easily by being either pro or con. In either case, of being pro or con, what is the difference in saying –"you are either with us or against us" which can lay waste to a nation through intolerance.

So I would have to ask Mitt, really what does this have to do with being President, for if you were either pro or con, a devout Christian, or of some following, would this be the way you would actually want to lead a nation when in retrospect, 'united we stand, and divided we fall'. Hence this goes full circle with the previous questions, of 'what is a strong defense if divided, and what is a strong economy if we were to fall '? Then frankly, the final question is, what is True Conservatism?'

The New Deal, an Election 2008 Primer

In response to Ron Pauls statement about Immigrants on CSPAN on March 12, 2007

Although I like Ron Paul for many of his positions, in watching him on CSPAN on March 12, 2007 I recoiled when he made a statement about immigrants arriving here just to go on Welfare due to having a child born in the USA.

Immigration today is a far more complex and challenging problem that we have than this.

What's more, implying that any race of people are like this, I find is consistent with the attitude during WWII when our forces were segregated. For example, Afro Americans were considered lazy and worthless, yet they were the Tuscany fliers who protected our day light bombers, and those who worked hard on building the Alaskan Highway.

Given the opportunity anyone would rise to the occasion of dignity. Racism comes in all forms and immigration should not be regarded in such a trite manner. Perhaps he should explain his position more on this!

There are over an estimated 12 million immigrants in the U.S.A. While staying under the radar, most of them work and pay taxes. 65% of US citizens prefer some form of patriation of illegal immigrants. It costs an estimated $6,000 dollars to obtain a citizenship. Given these parameters, many strategies can come to mind. For example of one is to enable immigrants to have long term structured loans from the government for this excessive amount for buying one's US citizenship.

Additionally, why not have a government driven basic English class which is not some form of immersion. Given that the government corrects the economy, there should be no problem of employment availability for any American.

For the Strategic Future of Our Nation

Rudolf Guillani and Remembrance of things past

In any election, candidates hip shoot, and take like shots during campaigns. In terms of Rudolf Guillani, I assume that he will have his share where there is no need to launch or field any from here.

But as a resident in lower Manhattan for the past 24 years, I do have a number of questions for Rudolf Guillani, the NYC Mayor of 2001. For me they have gone unanswered; or where questions and answers even more recently mix like oil and water.

Leadership and Judgment Calls: I remiss about 9/11 as having questions for our NYC local leaders. In particular Rudolf Guillani did not adequately answer a few for me. When directly witnessing the tragedy of the WTC Towers down the street from our apartment, my thoughts were that we were being invaded, and that it was a bigger than at Pearl Harbor in 1941. I thought about FDR's speech to congress that morning as the WTC1 followed WTC2 in collapsing:

> FDR to Congress: 'Yesterday, December 7, 1941 -- a date which will live in infamy -- the United States of America was suddenly and deliberately attacked by naval and air forces of the Empire of Japan'.

The shock wave reverberated the message that it was war and we were under attack. Our neighborhood in lower Manhattan was totally dusted. I further questioned if any parked vehicles could have hidden bombs. The police started checking all of them. I was desperately concerned about my family's 'health, safety and welfare'; and even if our children should be on the street, or attend school. Some could say that my wife and I, at the time, were overly cautious about our children. On the news it was either Rudolf Guillani or continuous replays of the tragedies. This went on day after day for months while the fires smoldered; and the smell of tragedy pervaded all of New York. It became an imprint, that even years later, when at night, to sleep in closing your eyes didn't help.

In terms of being under attack, consider that Halloween is celebrated in NYC as an annual parade every October. Up to a million people attend. In the parade, people are in costumes and on floats. Its like a marti gras parade every year; but takes place at night. I assumed in October 2001, that it would be suspended since 9/11, just a month before with its fires still smoldering less than a mile away, was considered a more a day of 'Infamy' than December 7th, 1941. Two of many questions I have wanted to ask Rudolf Guillani back then, and even now due to his recent CPAC speech where he pointed out that we were not waging a War on Terror, but defending the War of Terror that has been waged on us in 2001, are:

The New Deal, an Election 2008 Primer

Why would we have such a public event in October 2001 when having a war waged on us, and which occurs less than a mile from 'Ground Zero' that at the time was still smoldering ? Even a participant dressed as Abe Lincoln could have been laced with hidden dynamite. It is as well during every Halloween parade since 2001, an opportune time for taking out upwards of a million participants. In other words, would FDR have done this a month after the 'Day of Infamy' in 1941 as well from less than a mile away Pearl Harbor?

Where was his Due Diligence with the Environmental Protection Agency (EPA) which claimed that the air was all right when considering the amount of microscopic particulate matter that covered the area of New York for months where to this day, although the jury seems to still be out, people have suffered respiratory problems due to it. Then there are other questions that the former Mayor Rudy Guillani about 9/11 Human Remains which he should address.

For the Strategic Future of Our Nation

Life According to Newt Gingrich

Newt Gingrich was the architect of the 1994 conservative party platform that took over the Senate to just later abruptly exit as its speaker due to his personal scandals. Newt is currently the architect of 'American Solutions' as a 'non-partisan' media based organization that is promising to eventually reveal their plan for the nation.

To this end, Newt Gingrich has had two media presentations where the first was with Governor Mario Cuomo on February 28, 2007, at Cooper Union in NYC; and the second at (Conservative Political Action Conference) CPAC without Governor Cuomo. Both were filmed for web casts by American Solutions' and viewable at http://AmericanSolutions.com .

At Cooper Union, Newt spoke for 30 minutes, and then Mario. Tim Russert was considered the moderator, and Mario also ended up suggesting to Newt that he should run on the Republican ticket.

Newt Gingrich touched on health care, his foreign policy, domestic policy, how every one should speak English, and that every one wants 'one nation under god'.

What was not touched on was the economy, such as jobs for you and me, addressing the escalating and insurmountable national debt; returning credit card over charges to the consumer, the current and future state of education, or the actual health safety and welfare of this nation from the standpoint of the individual and communities; nor of the nation's, except speaking about it as a broken system. In touching on health care superficially, and not really going after the other real issues, and not going near Stem Cell Research, pro life/Abortion, and Gay Marriage the question is what is Newt Gingrich doing if not just tossing us a bone. Are we dogs ?

In attending the Cooper Union event, I met with both afterwards, and in introducing myself, had asked if other presidential candidates could be invited to debate. Perhaps that was just too out of the box to ask , but thought it a fair question, as was sincerely intended. I want to debate Newt Gingrich.

In a separate recent CPAC speech covered by American Solutions, his non-partisan organization, Newt Gingrich promoted himself as the conservative political compass and nation's visionary. He finally admitted that he plans for running in election 2008 if given the ticket to do so. I guess he plans to run as a non-partisan, or is it as a republican ?

The New Deal, an Election 2008 Primer

My take is that Newt Gingrich wants to debate Barach Obama or Hillary, or which ever is the democrat candidate. This of course would be on Newt Gingrich's territory, where it is without news coverage except by American Solutions which he is the Chairmen of, and without any ground rules from moderators. In other words, 'Mono (Newt) e mono (Democrat)' ?

Consider if the Democrats offered him the same opportunity. Question is, would the bold new and improved Newt Gingrich step up to the plate, or call it partisan politics.

The following is a more detailed review of Newt Gingrich's burgeoning platform where he wishes is to fashion himself as 'The conservative' , and some questions regarding his statements, and commentary on what some could agree are more workable alternatives.

1- Newt on Domestic Issues:

A- In God we Trust:

Newt Gingrich tried to make some point about one nation under God. He claimed that 91% of the American people prefer "one nation under god".

My only response is, so what's so unusual about this. So what exactly did he mean. Was he advocating his personal beliefs over yours or mine, or was he just wanting to tell the Christian Right that they matter to him, but no one else? If this is what he is talking about, then it is unconstitutional, and can by some be considered unconscionable.

If he is to advocate *the right to choose* when it comes to consumerism, then surely he would be expected to respect others religions of other Americans.

For example, suppose one nation under God is supposed to mean for Methodists only? Then the Baptists or other faithful following would not be considered patriotic. Thank god that we do have separation of Church and State where government can't mess with religion.

As our country represents diversity, in addition to Methodists, and the Baptists, Christianity in our country also includes Catholics, Lutherans, Anglicans, Fundamentalists, Pietism, Evangelism, Pentecostalism, Protestants, and the Holiness movement.

Additionally, others believe in God such as Muslims who also make up the citizenship of the United States.. Respecting each others orientations allows us to be 'united in how we stand'.

For the Strategic Future of Our Nation

B- We Speak English only:

Newt Gingrich stated that 85 % of the American People prefer English as the official language of the government, where you have to pass a history test, and speak English to become a citizen. He wants to establish adequate classes in immersion for others who don't speak English and know all our US history and for prospective immigrants.

Agreed he might have a point, but firstly, English is the official language of the government. It would be more genuine if Newt was straight about what he really meant, in that there would be no other language used for immigrants, et al by the government except English ? Besides, many Americans do not know US History.

Now consider what 85% really means. Who was asked in this survey, was it even a sampling of 8 out of 10, and in what language ? We are a nation of diversity, and responsibly must account for other languages.

Comparatively, imagine yourself in a foreign land, and needed to ask for directions to the US embassy.

Immersion programs are what Mao's China conducted on its people; it is also what North Vietnam did to South Vietnam. We can sugarcoat what we are saying, but it is basically the same old thing. So what about the Dignity of human rights anyway ?

What limits do we actually put on this grand plan for one *size fist all*, where you are actually not in control of your decisions ? On the East coast alone every state has a different accent, or even accents for spoken English. Some of us are from Alabama, some from Brooklyn New York, and then there are Bostonian- and then others from Maine.

The New Deal, an Election 2008 Primer

If individuals from each of these selected states were put in the same room, and tried to speak to each other, it would take some time to understand each other. In the meantime, the event would be like out of the Tower of Babel from the Bible. In other words one would sound like babble to another. The United States is made up additionally of many cultures where in this case united does not mean 'one size fits all'.

Something more significant that Newt could throw out on his speeches is about the need for better education. Here language is no longer a barrier as we even learn to extend our vocabularies. Some might say that they do not need to learn those 50 cent words. But just imagine if we do and where it can get us in our personal job and career advancement, understanding consumer contracts from cell phone can credit card companies as well as other scams that prey on the unknowing.

C- Health Care and The Right to Choose:

One of Newt Gingrich's talking points was in fact on Health Care. He had pointed out that offerings today for the elderly were limited in terms of choices 3 choices. He spoke about having 'real control' over your decisions. I assume he is suggesting having unlimited health care choices as a consumer.

It's a good point, but as a health care plan seems rather casual: i.e. *defer, and let free enterprise have it ?* Cell phones are offered with a slew of choices in a similar manner. They also include extensive fees that show up unexpectedly on your bill. Credit card companies fee you too. Then of course, if you did want to switch contracts there is also a significant penalty so as to encourage you not to.

In retrospect: The alternative offered in the Promise is a Government managed health care plan that is a nationalized plan ,and which in addition sets a standard for the private sector to innovate through more competitive offerings. As much as Wall Street demonstrates innovation in dealing with any new SEC regulation, why can't the health care industry do the same, but with some regulation as not to extort the public ? In other words, to compel the health care industry to lower costs, while competing against a universal health care plan that can serve all by the Government. Additionally, in the way that our schools require community services from students, I also see no reason as to why private practitioners, given guidelines, cannot write off a percent of their services against their normal taxed income that are afforded to the economically disadvantaged.

D- On Broken Systems:

During his time at the Cooper Union podium, Newt Gingrich had commented many times over that the Government was a 'broken system'. It made me wonder if he recently had realized this, or actually believed that he was the visionary of a new realization to an out of touch audience ?

Typically bureaucracy is the term used when referring to a broken system. But what Newt Gingrich had left out of his statements is that its sole purpose is to serve the people. I listened for Newt Gingrich's ideas about this, or in fact what he really meant by it; and then what solution or plan did he have at hand. There were not actual ideas presented. He seemed to only be seeking an agreement that it was a broken system, and to suggest perhaps that in his realization of it, that he was a fresh alternative for election 2008 ?

In retrospect: one the most important parts of the our government is in the management of information. This is not intended to suggest abuse, loss of a citizens privacy, or that we all have some hidden DNA profile with the government, but that the information systems themselves are fundamentally obsolete and not effective.

without a top down federal information systems plan, there is no way to fix a broken and dysfunctional information system, where the government as a result operates at a much higher cost to the tax payer than is needed. Example, consider reducing 65% of the cost of administrative over head; in other words, to operate the government costing only 35% of what it use to be just by the improvement of its information management.

Further, until an affective information system plan is in place, government employees are limited in the ability to do their jobs which for its stated purpose is to serve the people. We can look at slashing needed programs such as education, health research etc, or improve the governments fundamental operation over all.

1I- Newt on Foreign Policy

A- Foreign Policy Lesson 1:

Later in a sit down between the three on stage, Newt had demonstrated his competence in foreign policy. He used Iraq and N. Korea as examples. He first noted that the President is the commander and chief, and this is what our forefathers had intended with General George Washington when he was in the field. Newt suggested, that more currently that the President should at least have a direct report to him about matters in the field.

In retrospect: I thought that this was a good idea at a minimum, as opposed to a president sitting in the dark, but believe that the 'Commander and Chief' , if having a laptop computer, and aided by a working Federal Information

<u>System</u>, can get timely status directly from the 'boots on the ground' generals without the information sanitizing that would go up the rank and file.

This also obsoletes the 'plausible deniabilty factor' such as suggesting that the president can declare victory, where in reality would be throwing a nation into a civil war with our boots on the ground as one of its victims.

B- Foreign Policy Lesson 2:

Newt Gingrich had suggested his fix for a war with Iran. Actually I didn't know that we were planning on having one. He explained that if we were to bomb their one and only gas refinery, that in effect, they would run out of gas ! Possibility theory says that Newt Gingrich could be right about this.

In retrospect: this could sound like a quick fix, where they would run out of gas. But then I considered the question 'what if some foreign power tried that with us ? ' National Pride' is a given for any nation. The recent movie '300' in its manner documents national pride in the event of 300 Spartans holding their ground against the overwhelming hordes of the Persian army. Also in history is Admiral Yi Sun Shin in the 16th century that led his tiny little navy to victory against the hordes of the Japanese navy due to national pride. Although Newt was a history teacher, we don't need a lesson more than the American Revolution to demonstrate that even today, that our own national pride would call upon us if under the same circumstances.

Then the question for a Commander and Chief Newt Gingrich would be 'why to assume that the Iranian's in such a scenario, would be meek, and especially when they can shoot at one of our close allies in the Middle East, and then at our navy in the Persian Gulf with recently acquired Russian missiles'. Whats more, did Newt Gingrich figure in China's fond friendship with Iran: and also the fact that they our one of our largest lenders in funding our war in Iraq ?

It would have been helpful to understand what Newt Gingrich really had intended in his remarks, and if in fact he had actually thought his quick fix all the way through in a way that a good commander and chief might.

The President in addition to being a Commander and chief is also to be the Icon of world diplomacy. So then the question is why have a war with Iraq in the first place, if in fact a solution could be worked out that provides a strategic friendship between Iran's and the US ?

For the Strategic Future of Our Nation

Consider, The Defense System gives Diplomacy its Teeth, and Diplomacy provides Defense its Faculty of Reason. It is my view that the two are inseparable when engaging, or preventing needless wars, or in preemptive and Unilateral Actions .

In the 21st century, strategically, we have to have economic solutions for world peace, but which have to first be built on mutual respect. This can only come from respecting others as we do ourselves. Iran in addition to national pride is a culture and like the US is a civilization. All civilizations are entitled to live in peace with each other.

Newt Gingrich had noted, that Iran does have one gas refinery. This can be leveraged as one of many strategic solutions for that part of the middle east that can have collateral benefits in other parts as well.

Consider that in the outskirts of a neighboring country, say just north of Iran we were to invest in building one to two more refineries. Then we could go to Iran and make the offer of refining their oil so they do not have such a cost in producing their own gasoline. Meantime the deal is that we get a discount on their oil -

There are many solutions for the Middle East, such as even for Israel and Palestine, and for Iraq that should be considered as opposed to just dismissing. In fact it would be of strategic help to our nation in general, if the Commander and Chief, and the Senate and House worked collaboratively for the strategic needs of our nation as opposed to tossing a medicine ball of obstinance between the administrative and legislative branches of our government.

C- Foreign Policy Lesson 3:

North Korea for Newt Gingrich is led by an 'Evil' Doer. Newt really did not elaborate on this, but to remiss that the Bush administration is talking currently with them.

In Retrospect: I find it amazing when one points to the other in accusing them of being the evil one. Fundamentally, we are not Good and Evil, as it is not what we do as Good nor Evil, but it is in the collateral affects of what we do.

Example: here Newt Gingrich has an opportunity to explore further economic solutions for the strategic future of that part of the globe and instead he would rather quote the Bible, and then wage war ? I would hope that he would want to offer our young people more than a limited future as being canon fodder in the name of 'on ward Christian solders'.

The New Deal, an Election 2008 Primer

Consider what a visionary could really offer. South Korea is an up and coming economy, where to invest in it, you can easily start by going to its stock exchange that is located on the Internet at http://sm.krx.co.kr .

Since the US has borrowed a fortune from China, it is obvious that China likes making investments with their money. A shrewed visionary of a US President could encourage China to consider their economic interest in the area. As there is now the Euro, the Chinese Won is due to become an Asian equivalent. Moreover South Korea owes us this consideration, and besides their banks and stock exchange would probably love it too !

This can be transparently offered to both China and South Korea. It is in both of their best interests. What does not even need to be discussed with them is that business is simply business. In other words, North Korea, the proud little state becomes a cost to China where South Korea is an investment for them.

Good business practices could offer encouragement to North Korea to also become an investment. Case in point, with a little encouragement from their big brother, North Korea can save face, retain its autonomy, feed its hungry, eventually offer its people their dignity, and then join the world a few years later. Thats without having to have a McDonald's there the way they do in China. In other words, North Korea can certainly follow China's economic model that started in 1980 which has made it into the economic super power that it is today.

For the Strategic Future of Our Nation